EMPIRE OF OBJECTS

EMPIRE OF OBJECTS

*Iurii Trifonov and the
Material World of Soviet Culture*

Benjamin Massey Sutcliffe

THE UNIVERSITY OF WISCONSIN PRESS

The University of Wisconsin Press
728 State Street, Suite 443
Madison, Wisconsin 53706
uwpress.wisc.edu

Gray's Inn House, 127 Clerkenwell Road
London EC1R 5DB, United Kingdom
eurospanbookstore.com

Copyright © 2023
The Board of Regents of the University of Wisconsin System
All rights reserved. Except in the case of brief quotations embedded in critical
articles and reviews, no part of this publication may be reproduced, stored in a
retrieval system, transmitted in any format or by any means—digital, electronic,
mechanical, photocopying, recording, or otherwise—or conveyed via the Internet
or a website without written permission of the University of Wisconsin Press.
Rights inquiries should be directed to rights@uwpress.wisc.edu.

Printed in the United States of America
This book may be available in a digital edition.

Library of Congress Cataloging-in-Publication Data

Names: Sutcliffe, Benjamin M., author.
Title: Empire of objects : Iurii Trifonov and the material world of Soviet culture /
Benjamin M. Sutcliffe.
Description: Madison, Wisconsin : The University of Wisconsin Press, 2023. |
Includes bibliographical references and index.
Identifiers: LCCN 2023006239 | ISBN 9780299344009 (hardcover)
Subjects: LCSH: Trifonov, I͡Uriĭ, 1925–1981—Criticism and interpretation.
Classification: LCC PG3489.R5 Z885 2023 | DDC 891.73/44—dc23/eng/20230713
LC record available at https://lccn.loc.gov/2023006239

For Kathy

CONTENTS

	Acknowledgments	ix
	Introduction: The Unknown Trifonov	3
1	A Radiant Future of Things: Trifonov's Stalin-Era Prose	23
2	Enthusiasm and Ambivalence: Trifonov and the Thaw	41
3	Empire of Objects: Sincerity and Consumption in the 1970s	61
4	Utopia Lost: Sincerity and the Past in Trifonov's Final Works	81
	Conclusion: Echoes of Trifonov and Soviet Culture	100
	Notes	107
	Bibliography	135
	Index	149

ACKNOWLEDGMENTS

This project was completed in the shadow of Russia's horrific war in Ukraine, a tragedy that represents many of Iurii Trifonov's worst fears about his culture. Like many Slavists in the United States, I first read Trifonov at the college level (understanding very little) and then in graduate school at the University of Pittsburgh, where Nancy Condee, Helena Goscilo, and the late Vladimir Padunov provided new ways of looking at his works. At the time I did not suspect I would devote a book to one of the *shestidesiatniki*. In 2012 I decided to write a monograph about Trifonov, a choice motivated by the deep, compact prose of his later works. Very soon, however, I realized that this task was far more complex than expected.

A few frantic weeks in the Russian State Library in 2015 yielded a trove of articles thanks to their helpful staff. While I was in Moscow, Natal'ia Ivanova and Marina Selemeneva were kind enough to let me interview them, as was Ol'ga Trifonova-Miroshnichenko. I am especially grateful to Ol'ga Romanovna for the unique and invaluable perspective she provided on her late husband's life and worldview.

In 2017 I spent a cold but enjoyable spring in Warsaw, where the staff at the Polish National Library helped me locate a surprisingly varied range of sources on Trifonov. I am grateful for their assistance; at Miami University's King Library, Masha Stepanova and Sheila Sparks worked wonders as they obtained books, dissertations, and all manner of obscure sources about Soviet culture. During the pandemic they went above and beyond to keep faculty researching. Thanks are also due to the University of Illinois Slavic Reference Service for unearthing articles and locating bibliographic information.

x   Acknowledgments

Panels at the Association for Slavic, Eastern Europe, and Eurasian Studies (including its Zagreb summer conference), the Association for the Study of Nationalities, and the American Association of Teachers of Slavic and East European Languages helped me formulate some sections of the monograph. I am particularly grateful to Clemens Günther and Matthias Schwartz for letting me participate in the conference "Firsthand Time: Documentary Aesthetics in the Long 1960s" (Leibniz Center, 2020). Ol'ga Gurova, Birgitte Beck Pristed, and Yulia Karpova likewise organized a stimulating discussion in Aarhus at the 2018 conference, "The Body of Things: Gender, Material Culture and Design in (Post) Soviet Russia." I would also like to thank Adam Bednarczyk, Magdalena Kubarek, and Maciej Szatkowski for selecting my paper for the conference "Orient in Literature, Literature of the Orient: Borders and Borderlands," held in Toruń (2017). Colleagues at the Havighurst Center for Russian and Post-Soviet Studies were kind enough to let me participate in the Statehood and its Discontents conference (Vilnius University, 2016), where attendees provided a number of interesting insights.

Many people have read (and reread) various portions of the manuscript. Colleen Lucey (University of Arizona) was an astute first reader of a chapter, as was Elizabeth Skomp (Stetson University). Oksana Husieva (Defense Language Institute) helped with sources in Ukrainian. At Miami I have benefited from supportive present and former colleagues. Margaret Ziolkowski, Vitaly Chernetsky, Nicole Thesz, and Brendan Mooney (Department of German, Russian, Asian, Middle Eastern Languages and Cultures) read drafts of various chapters. Lolita Holmes, Juanita Schrodt and their student assistants patiently photocopied, scanned, and sorted materials. The Havighurst Center's works-in-progress series was a wellspring of ideas from a wide range of fields—I am indebted to Rad Borislavov, Irina Anisimova, Dan Scarborough, Brigid O'Keffe, Emily Channell-Justice, Francesca Silano, Hannah Chapman, Gulnaz Sharafutdinova, Neringa Klumbytė, Venelin Ganev, Dan Prior, Scott Kenworthy, Zara Torlone. Steve Norris, Director of the Havighurst Center, has been an ardent advocate of all things Trifonov. Like all of us at Miami, I miss the intellect and humanity of Karen Dawisha.

Some portions of this book first appeared in various journals and edited volumes; I am grateful for the ability to include this material. Anonymous reviewers at Northwestern University Press provided useful feedback on an earlier version of this project. At the University of Wisconsin Press I have gained much from working with Gwen Walker and Nathan MacBrien, who contributed advice and solicited thoughtful reviewers for the manuscript.

In this regard Polly Jones warrants special commendation. Without the persistence of Amber Rose Cederström, this manuscript would not have appeared. Holly McArthur and Sheila McMahon made the final steps easy, while Jane Curran and Desi Allevato helped by copyediting and creating the index.

In Oxford, Deborah Lyons, Cathie Grimm, Mila Ganeva, Kelly Tuttle, and Emily Rush listened to tales connected with the research, writing, revision, and publication of this work. The Sutcliffe-Hatcher-Dufrayer ohana, stretching from Big Island to Geneva, has provided love, support, and distraction. In the first year of the Trifonov project the family welcomed Theodore Hatcher Sutcliffe, its youngest member (and most gifted soccer player). Kas Batchelor has contributed her wit and interest in the strange customs of the vanished Soviet empire.

This book is dedicated to Katherine Batchelor, who has believed in its success from the first moment I told her my plans. Our years together in Ohio, Poland, and Luxembourg have been a rich repository of travels, adventures, quiet evenings, and love.

EMPIRE OF OBJECTS

Introduction

The Unknown Trifonov

One day in the early 1950s, Iurii Valentinovich Trifonov entered his family's small Moscow apartment with an enormous lacquered box. The young author bought this gift for his mother, a survivor of Stalin's labor camps. Walking into the kitchen, ready to joke about his purchase, he saw her and his sister in their worn slippers, eating fried potatoes from a pan. His tired relatives were clearly in no mood for humor. "What an idiot I was," he would later confess to his wife.[1] The roots of this scene stem from the way Trifonov's life paralleled Soviet culture, where potatoes and *tapochki* were the essence of everyday existence. The money for the box, however, came from the Stalin Prize that Trifonov received for his first novel, which praised the tyrant who had imprisoned his mother and executed his father. The item itself, a lavish luxury out of place in the humble apartment, symbolized the writer's fascinated unease with the world of things. Trifonov is a central figure in Russian letters whose life (1925–81) spanned most of the Soviet era; he helped define images of everyday life (*byt*) as well as the Moscow intelligentsia and was considered for the 1979 Nobel Prize for Literature. The author inspired several generations yet much of his prose has been ignored because it contradicts critics' assumptions about Soviet culture. Trifonov's significance extends beyond the written page: his prose envisions the USSR's doomed effort to subordinate bodies and objects to ideas.[2]

Almost all of Trifonov's surprisingly varied oeuvre was published in the USSR during his lifetime, albeit sometimes with cuts or delays. He depicted the far-flung peripheries of the Soviet empire as well as its capital. While best known for his writing in the late 1960s–early 1980s, almost half of his literary work predated those years. Despite being worried by totalitarianism, he wrote a novel justifying the murder of Tsar Alexander II by terrorists who inspired Lenin and Stalin. Deeply committed to remembering the past, Trifonov became increasingly frightened by technology's impact on the present and future. His works reflected the battle between memory and forgetting as the country alternately tried to address or ignore the trauma of Stalinism. Trifonov's prose explored the gap between ideals and reality in Soviet culture. I link this troubling difference to three factors that guide my study; for many years Trifonov could not recognize their connection. His later writings deliberately wove them together, forging the works that garnered international acclaim.

The first of these is the USSR's fixation on portraying the body (*telesnost'*, corporeality): characters' physiques represented the desires and worries of a country trying to remake human interactions. As Elizabeth Grosz argues in her seminal study, bodies are just as capable as the psyche to explain human experience. Trifonov's Soviet contemporaries inherited hope and fears surrounding *telesnost'* from culture before 1917. Lev Tolstoy's Ivan Ilych showed how illness indicated an ailing, materialistic society, while folklore both praised and mocked assumptions of male prowess and feminine virginity. After the October revolution the body was an opportunity to transform the person and a source of frustration when this effort went awry: in Trifonov's prose sexuality, aging, and infirmity challenged Soviet ideas about perfecting the human form as well as behavior.[3]

The second component is consumption, which historians Paulina Bren and Mary Neuberger pair with "the appraisal, procurement, distribution, and even production of goods and services—whether ingested (literally consumed), used, or experienced." Investigating this arena of Soviet life leads us "beyond the one-dimensional images of long shopping lines, shabby apartment blocks, bare shelves, and outdated fashions" that allowed Western scholars to dismiss socialist consumption and, by extension, socialism itself. As Pierre Bourdieu concludes, consumption is a way of making sense of objects even as the objects manipulate those who possess and classify them. Things are far from inert—they undergird everyday life and guide our ideas about ordinary existence.[4]

Consumption in the USSR came with a complex, shifting set of anxieties. Both the Soviet state and intelligentsia villainized *meshchanstvo*, a love of objects that becomes the crass materiality of philistinism (*poshlost'*).[5] The government attacked *meshchanstvo* but supported consumer behavior (*potrebitel'skie otnosheniia*) that fit policies promoting a "modern" lifestyle;

Serguei Oushakine notes that the state attempted to find a rational balance between supply and demand. This effort not only failed but contributed to the collapse of the USSR as a whole.[6]

Literature, which was dominated by *intelligenty*, mistrusted the material world. Trifonov followed otherwise dissimilar authors such as Fyodor Dostoevsky and Vladimir Mayakovsky in fretting over the possessions characters accrued. The lowly objects of *byt* (such as the fried potatoes and slippers in the Trifonovs' apartment) were not the issue. The problem was desiring what one lacked and then sacrificing morality to obtain it. Pursuit of material well-being inculcated greed, mendacity, and exploitation. What art historian Susan Reid terms the "consumptive pleasure" derived from a purchase was, for Trifonov, something suspect if not immoral. The way people relate to objects is a key concern for his prose and Soviet culture. Consumption gives form to daily life and defines the response to crises such as the Great Patriotic War (1941–45) and Stalinist repression. As Sheila Fitzpatrick summarizes, the struggle to feed and clothe children shaped how people tried to live ordinary lives in extraordinary times.[7] Historian Alexey Golubev denotes Soviet everyday life as "object-centered": the state and ordinary citizens tried to control the material world and navigate its difficulties. The Moscow inhabited by Trifonov's intelligentsia characters was a privileged exception; for instance, in smaller cities rationing was reintroduced in the late 1960s but not in the capital. Worries about *meshchanstvo* and greed obscured the shortages plaguing the country during the author's life.[8] Recent scholarship has explored the ways consumption was a specific worldview and manner of interacting with others. Outlasting the Soviet Union, this perspective helps us understand the nostalgia for the USSR in Russian culture since the early 1990s.[9]

In Trifonov's prose, bodies and consumption implicate sincerity, the third key concept underlying my study. Lionel Trilling praised this virtue as "congruence between avowal and actual feeling." Ellen Rutten summarizes *iskrennost'*, sincerity's Russian incarnation, as genuineness and truthfulness. These values were prized by the intelligentsia, a group that believed it combined education and morality. Rutten notes how *intelligenty* pair sincerity with personal and national memory. The group saw *iskrennost'* as an antidote to the lies and silences of Soviet history.[10] For Trifonov sincerity was an intangible deficit good, far less common than falsehoods the state proclaimed (and much of the intelligentsia believed). Ol'ga Trifonova identifies sincerity as the heart of her late husband's worldview; *iskrennost'* meant being

6   Introduction

honest with oneself and others. In an interview Trifonov argued that *iskrennost'* defines a good work of literature. Drawing on longstanding assumptions that talented writing is honest writing, he contended that sincerity has esthetic as well as ethical benefits. His oeuvre continued the ties between verisimilitude, realism, and social commentary in the prose of authors such as Tolstoy and Ivan Turgenev.[11] For Trifonov being truthful was only the surface of sincerity—the core of *iskrennost'* is kindness, an everyday humanity stemming from the intelligentsia's belief in helping others.[12]

His writing, at first unwittingly and then with carefully crafted intention, underscored how bodies and consumption created and reflected problems with sincerity. This in turn challenged the ways Soviet culture conceived of past, present, and future as a progression dictated by the Marxist-Leninist conception of history. Following in the traditions of Russian writing, Trifonov's prose reflected collective hopes and concerns but also hinted at issues that could not be openly discussed. He portrays bodies, consumption, and *iskrennost'* to reveal how the quotidian connects different eras within the USSR's society. Poet Andrei Voznesenskii lauded the author as the chronicler of memory. Trifonov's vision of unsettled personal and national histories challenged the optimism in tomorrow that guided the Soviet sense of time. My introductory chapter explores Trifonov's biography and writing in the context of its culture, paying special attention to how bodies, consumption, and sincerity influenced society. Trifonov linked these issues to three more concepts: memory, trauma, and history. I then address critics' responses to his prose, tying this to larger problems in the USSR.[13]

BODIES, THINGS, AND MORALS IN LATE STALINISM

Born in 1925 to Cossack Valentin Trifonov and Jewish intellectual Evgeniia Lur'e, Trifonov had a childhood that was happy amid the paradoxical privilege of the elites that were creating a classless society. There were, however, hidden tensions in the family: Valentin had been the common-law husband of the revolutionary Tat'iana Slovatinskaia, the future author's maternal grandmother. Much later, Valentin married Slovatinskaia's daughter, Evgeniia, the child of her union with Abram Lur'e. I do not read Trifonov's prose as psychological drama, yet his works' interest in the problems of kinship has a strong autobiographical basis. In 1937 Valentin was arrested and subsequently shot (his brother Evgenii died of a heart attack before being detained). The family was evicted from Moscow's famous House on the Embankment, the home for many of the politically powerful. Trifonov's

Introduction 7

mother was imprisoned and Slovatinskaia took in the future author and his sister.[14]

During the Great Patriotic War, Trifonov was evacuated to Tashkent; returning to Moscow, he helped destroy German incendiary bombs and then made radiators for the air force. Factory work coincided with studies at the Gorky Literary Institute, where Trifonov published his senior thesis, *Students* (*Studenty*, 1949), a novel extoling those who oust a suspect professor. Trifonova claims the work was a success, despite its "tribute to the times," an opaque assessment that says little about *Students* but much about attempts to marginalize this narrative. Later Soviet critics and their Western counterparts ignored the novel, focusing instead on Trifonov's works from the mid-1960s onward. Poet and editor Aleksandr Tvardovskii, who had published *Students* in *Novyi mir*, was impressed by descriptions of the capital and asked Trifonov if his parents were Muscovites. The author averred but omitted that they had been arrested. At the time Trifonov desperately wanted to believe in the Stalinist system that had destroyed his father yet seemed wiser than any relative. *Students* was awarded the Stalin Prize in 1950, a stunning start for the son of a purge victim. Evgeny Dobrenko contends that the era's anti-Western policies, focus on enemies, distortion of history, and cult of the military would define the Putin years as well; the 2022 invasion of Ukraine and quick dismantling of civil society show the scholar is correct. In this sense *Students* both portrays Stalinism and, despite Trifonov's intent at the time, indicates enduring problems.[15]

The novel's success with readers was not due to its political orthodoxy, however. What they loved was how *Students* substituted an optimistic vision of healthy bodies and material abundance for the reality of poverty, hunger, and wounded veterans. Lilya Kaganovsky investigates the "traumatized skeleton" that underlay the era; at the time Soviet culture deemphasized or ignored reminders of the recent war.[16] Grosz worries that the body can be reduced to merely revealing what is private—Trifonov's first novel justified such fears by using corporeality to signal subservience. Binding physique to ideological fitness, *Students* made an argument familiar to those in repressive societies: the flesh must serve the state. Keith Livers notes that even the era's massive construction sites were metaphors for Stalinism's attempt to improve the human body and body politic. After the victory over Hitler this meant rebuilding and expanding, which Trifonov praised in *Students*.[17]

Yet, as Polly Jones argues, the novel heightened the disconnect between the endemic privations of *byt* and an imaginary realm of plenty. After Germany's defeat, the state pledged to reward the sacrifices made during the previous fifteen years. Historian Anna Alekseyeva explains how postwar Soviet society believed technology could help secure a more egalitarian future. Late Stalinism also cultivated the certainty of future prosperity, an illusion Trifonov's novel supported by depicting opulent apartments and modern infrastructure. In *Students*, however, political reliability differentiated positive from negative consumption; loyalty to Stalinism determined whether characters deserved a better standard of living.[18]

Students focuses on the intelligentsia as it follows the students and teachers at a Moscow pedagogical institute. Stalinism starkly changed the nature of being an *intelligent*. My analysis considers how Trifonov portrays the intelligentsia (as opposed to the reality of subservience and cooptation); the author at the time believed that intellectuals were central to Soviet society and should actively participate in it. The postwar epoch was one of hidden identities and unmasking enemies, but in Stalinism's final years Trifonov became entranced by sincerity. He praised an *iskrennost'* defined by a state demanding that one's inner thoughts mirror external loyalty. Ironically, after he received the Stalin Prize authorities uncovered the identity of Trifonov's father and the young writer was almost expelled from the Komsomol for not disclosing the arrest. He had failed to conform to the unity between appearance and essence that his own novel demanded.[19]

Hope for the Future, Fear of the Past: The Thaw and Memory

In the first years after Stalin's death Trifonov devoted himself to two projects that mirrored the unsettling ambivalence of the Thaw era. The author's initial effort was a sequel to *Students*; he quickly (and wisely) abandoned this undertaking. The second eventually became *The Disappearance* (*Ischeznovenie*, 1987).[20] This unfinished novel with autobiographical overtones focused on an Old Bolshevik family in the House on the Embankment during the Great Terror. In 1951 Trifonov had married Nina Nelina, a soloist from the Bolshoi Theatre, with whom he had a daughter. Despite being a new father, Trifonov made the first of eight trips to Turkmenia, a region that significantly shaped the author's development. In his early visits Trifonov, in the words of his widow, felt like a "literary servant" as he struggled to write *Under the Sun* (*Pod solntsem*, 1959), a cycle of stories about modernizing the Soviet republic. Much of the collection's material later appeared in *Slaking the Thirst* (*Utolenie zhazhdy*, 1962). This unwieldly but important novel glorified the

Introduction 9

Karakum Canal while mourning Stalin's victims; it exemplifies the Khrushchev era's attempt to combine sorrow over the past with enthusiasm for the future.[21]

Critics at the time read Trifonov through their own contradictory missions for literature and culture. In early 1953 the Pole Tadeusz Drewnowski, for instance, praised *Students* for unmasking enemies of Stalinism. Ten years later L. Aleksandrov lauded *Slaking the Thirst* for condemning the persecutions Drewnowski supported. Yet Trifonov's works during the 1940s–1960s had much in common: bodies, objects, and *iskrennost'* distinguished positive and negative characters, despite the nature of sincerity dramatically changing as society rejected the recent past.[22]

The Thaw's conception of the body alternated between cliché and innovation. Trifonov's *Slaking the Thirst* contains grizzled tractor drivers and buxom women, images recalling late Stalinist prose. However, he also portrayed those whose weakness, self-doubt, and death evince how the purges and war haunted survivors. Decisiveness was no longer the dominant attitude in the author's prose. Igor' Dedkov, one of the most talented Soviet critics of Trifonov, states that the writer used ambivalent male characters to counterbalance enthusiasm for Soviet society. This shift reflected other issues as well. Historian Marko Dumančić notes that Soviet culture began to fear that men were in a state of crisis, a worry that would grow stronger under Brezhnev. One reason was the assumption that fatherlessness (or parents who had participated in repression) created a generation without viable male role models.[23]

The era had a fraught relationship with the material world. Consumption was a troubling topic and one that Trifonov did not fully grasp in his Thaw prose. Historians Denis Kozlov and Eleonory Gilburd discuss how Khrushchev extended Cold War competition to consumer goods; in 1959 the USSR's General Secretary and Vice President Nixon verbally sparred next to a model kitchen transported to Moscow for the American National Exhibition. Bren and Neuberger note that appeasing consumers was inextricable from efforts to discredit Stalinism: the state now needed less violent ways to legitimate power.[24] With the hardships of Stalinism and the war behind, the USSR vowed to outpace the US's rising standard of living but also hoped to eradicate *meshchanstvo*. Fashion was one example; as Larissa Zakharova explores, the industry tried to provide an abundance of goods while regulating consumer demand. Some in the state wanted new technology such as television to "privatize" leisure, creating alternatives to the reading *intelligenty* prized. Reid outlines how the intelligentsia for its part was dismayed by emerging consumer culture, which clashed with the thrift and selflessness that the group claimed as values. Soviet films and satirical cartoons implied that technological advances were harming masculinity. At the end of the 1960s L. N. Zhilina and N. T. Frolova equivocated that useful household goods were necessary, yet people should be their owners and not their slaves. Such proclamations insinuated that technology was deforming its masters.[25]

Trifonov's Thaw writing supported the scientific-technical revolution (*nauchno-tekhnicheskaia revoliutsiia*, NTR), which had begun with the arms race after 1945. As in the West, such innovation was both welcomed and feared due to transforming everyday life. Golubev maintains that after 1953 technology replaced Stalin and even the Party itself as the "essence of socialist progress." One Soviet critic endorsed the NTR but cautioned against the calculating, "businesslike" behavior (*delovitost'*) it produced. Trifonov's *Slaking the Thirst* paired the NTR with sincerity: characters believed that technology would hasten the communist utopia they were earnestly building.[26] His prose emulated the era's apotheosis of *iskrennost'*, which now denoted an "honest" but tentative discussion of Stalin's crimes. As Rutten outlines, even before 1917 *intelligenty* had worried that sincerity was central yet alien to Russian culture. Émigré scholars Pyotr Vail and Alexander Genis observe that in the 1960s the intelligentsia regarded sincerity, moral decency (*poriadochnost'*), and honesty as synonyms—these values, inherited from the totalitarian culture of the 1930s–1940s, were now directed against that same era.[27]

In the 1950s, Svetlana Boym asserts, sincerity meant scorning Stalinism's love of cozy interiors and elaborate architecture. The era demanded *iskrennost'* in design as well as politics and science.[28] Yet even Yury Gagarin, a national symbol of hope and progress, combined sincerity with deception as he inspired interest in the cosmos while hiding the details of Soviet space exploration. After 1953 Trifonov's writing most frequently illustrated *iskrennost'* by portraying its opposite: a deceitful avarice that included whitewashing the crimes of Stalinism.[29]

In the Thaw's most famous literary manifesto, "On Sincerity" ("Ob iskrennosti," 1953), Vladimir Pomerantsev opposed this virtue to the ersatz idealization that had distorted literature under Stalin. While in the 1930s–1940s authors described a world that Soviet policies were supposedly improving, Pomerantsev argued for a more candid literature. He asserted that sincerity called for artistic skill as well as good morals: *iskrennost'* distinguished an "author" from a mere "compiler," who describes a jumble of objects without

Introduction

transforming them into a literary work. Trifonov concurred, arguing that literature must combine artistry with a "sense of truthfulness." Sincerity and memory worked together in his prose after 1953 as both described the recent horrors of Stalinism.[30] This connection was essential to *The Bonfire's Glow* (*Otblesk kostra*, 1965), a documentary novella about Trifonov's father commanding Red forces in the Civil War. The narrative foregrounded Thaw worries about how to combine memory and history. As Jones argues, after Stalin's death the past could be criticized to a degree but many feared the destabilizing results of "deep retrospection and repentance," the very attributes of *iskrennost'* that Trifonov's writing found so important.[31]

Trifonov's characters show that recollection is selective. The ways they view history resemble writing fiction: the objects being described are the stimulus for memory but can also hamper understanding of the past. Creating a narrative and interpreting history (whether personal or collective) are subjective processes; both weaken the Marxist-Leninist claims to absolute truth that the USSR used to unite its vision of past, present, and future. Andrew Wachtel remarks that Russian literature believes history cannot be portrayed by a single voice: "Instead, whatever truth can be achieved emerges from the uneasy existence of seeing and narrating the past" through multiple viewpoints.[32] *The Bonfire's Glow* and Trifonov's stories from the 1960s shifted from the optimistic present and future in *Students* and *Slaking the Thirst* to a past that characters could neither regain nor understand. Roi Medvedev notes that, shortly after writing *The Bonfire's Glow*, Trifonov signed Aleksandr Solzhenitsyn's 1967 letter attacking censorship and protested conservatives' takeover of *Novyi mir*. Like many of his contemporaries in the USSR and the West, Trifonov was dismayed that the end of the sixties had destroyed the decade's dream of righting past injustice.[33]

THE BREZHNEV ERA:
EVERYDAY LIFE AND EMBATTLED SINCERITY

Trifonov is best known for his works from the late 1960s until 1981. The Soviet critic Vladimir Gusev discerned how the author's earlier narratives had suffered from a glut of superficial, "horizontal" description, while his later writing benefited from a deeper, "vertical" way of portraying. Trifonov's prose now had fewer images but endowed them with rich, multiple meanings.[34] At the same time, the author's personal life was in tumult. Following his estrangement from Nelina, he married editor Alla Pastukhova (1968); after this relationship ended the writer had a son with Trifonova, a novelist who was his common-law wife. Beginning with *The Exchange* (*Obmen*, 1969), his widely read *povest'* about trading apartments and compromising morality, Trifonov's writing concentrated on the fractured ethics of the Moscow intelligentsia. Yet even within this focus his work was surprisingly diverse; for instance, Turkmenia was the setting for much of *Taking Stock* (*Predvaritel'nye itogi*, 1970), a novella about a translator escaping a crumbling marriage by fleeing to Central Asia. Trifonov died in 1981 after complications from an operation related to kidney cancer. His last project has mystified critics. In the most comprehensive Anglophone study of the author, David Gillespie speculates that Trifonov was preparing a manuscript on prerevolutionary Russian radicals and German Lopatin, who belonged to the People's Will terrorists that Trifonov praised in his novel *Impatience* (*Neterpenie*, 1973). Trifonova, however, maintains he was interested in the infamous Evno Azef, whose double-crossing of Tsarist agents and revolutionaries embodied the insincerity that disturbed her late husband.[35]

Trifonov's prose became the writing of middle age, reflecting the intelligentsia's realization that the idealism of Soviet culture was diminishing. His balding husbands and pudgy wives resembled those in films such as *Autumn Marathon*, where a philandering intellectual tries to replace his spouse with a younger woman. *Telesnost'* was a way to "take stock" of one's life; this key phrase from the 1970s compared past and present to determine what had gone wrong. On the surface the Brezhnev era enjoyed a higher standard of living than previous decades, thanks to rising oil prices and the stability of almost two decades under a single leader. Sociologist Anna Paretskaya outlines how the culture of late socialism condoned individualism and self-reliance in consumption, tacitly promoting private interests over the collective and eschewing the intelligentsia ethos of helping others. Soviet scholars such as S. Ikonnikova and V. Kobliakov legitimized material well-being if it helped "the personality's spiritual development" (*dukhovnoe razvitie lichnosti*). This phrase relied on Marx's base and superstructure model of culture, where the world of objects and consumption supported the realm of emotions and ideas. A sociologist at the time noted that the USSR's way of life should keep pace with increased availability of goods. Oushakine gives a more honest assessment: late socialism tried to make consumption a logical, orderly process but could not agree on society's needs, let alone change consumer behavior.[36]

After the mid-1960s Trifonov viewed consumption as categorically negative and the author crafted his prose to reflect this. His change of opinion

Introduction

had three causes: Trifonov's associating Stalinism with greed as well as oppression, his new awareness of technology's invidious influence, and realizing that he himself had been corrupted by state privilege. Late socialism vilified materialism as irrational and uncontrollable by the state. Already in the 1960s journalist and author Liubov' Kabo had bemoaned how *meshchanstvo* replaced "civic engagement" with greed, even alleging that it made people display one face in public and another in private. Natalya Chernyshova, in her cultural history of consumption, notes the intelligentsia's fear that its values (including *iskrennost'*) were threatened by grasping newcomers. However, as Trifonov's final works intimated, materialism originated at the beginning of the Soviet era with an older generation of *intelligenty*.[37] *Meshchanstvo* also raised concerns with gender. Dumančić explores how culture assumed urban women to be the primary consumers, as opposed to the increasingly passive Soviet man. Elena Stiazhkina illuminates one obvious reason for this difference: for decades the state had shifted responsibility for obtaining goods onto women, allowing men to be less involved. Trifonov's prose exposes how some characters benefit from the coldhearted acquisitiveness of their wives, while lamenting their spouses' insincerity and lust for things.[38]

Trifonov's late prose condemned Soviet society as immoral. Two autobiographical stories, "Memories of Genzano" ("Vospominaniia o Dzhentsano," 1960) and "Cats or Hares?" ("Koshki ili zaitsy?," 1981), used recollection to link *telesnost'*, material comfort, and insincerity. Adapting the work of Pierre Nora, scholar Ekaterina Novoselova argues that in Trifonov's late works the body is a "place of memory" for a past that Soviet culture tried to ignore. The first of these narratives occurs in the village of Genzano on Trifonov's initial trip to Italy, where he is fascinated by a local festival (and an Italian who had been a Soviet prisoner of war). The second story recounted how he reluctantly returns to Genzano during a later visit to the Italian capital.[39] The autobiographical narrator notes,

> I arrived in [Rome] eighteen years after I had been here for the first time. Then I had been thirty-five, I ran, jumped, played tennis, smoked, could stay up nights working. Now I am fifty-three, I don't run, jump, play tennis, don't smoke and can't stay up nights working. . . . Then everything astounded me, I wanted to notice everything, remember everything, and I was tormented by the desire to write something lyrical about all this, and now nothing astounds me and I do not really feel like writing. There are many reasons for this. I will not go on about them. I will just say that life is the gradual loss of what astonishes.[40]

14 Introduction

Absence and loss define Trifonov's second trip. The narrator mocks his earlier, naïve desire to create "something lyrical," which has been replaced by the sad awareness that "what astonishes" is gone from life. The passage of eighteen years is one factor; more important are the "many reasons" left unsaid. Elsewhere the story emphasizes yellow colors, suggesting that the narrator is in the autumnal epilogue of his life: what was important has already transpired and can be neither reclaimed nor redeemed.[41] By 1978, when "Cats or Hares?" takes place, Trifonov was living with his third wife, regretted his pro-Stalinist *Students,* and was worried that technology and consumption were debasing society. In the first (and best) monograph on Trifonov, Natal'ia Ivanova notes the similarities between this story's narrator and the unhealthy protagonist of his most famous work, *House on the Embankment* (*Dom na naberezhnoi,* 1976). The author did not suspect he had only three years left alive.[42]

These two stories contain multiple layers of time: "Cats or Hares?" comments on "Memories of Genzano." This narrative in turn briefly mentions the future author drawing a picture while in fifth or sixth grade, the approximate time of Valentin Trifonov's arrest. "Cats and Hares?" is thus a doubled recollection, referring to visiting Italy as a younger man and to the year he lost his father. The story insinuates that the author's increased prosperity cannot compensate for past trauma. Despite Trifonov arriving in Rome wealthier and more famous than in the 1960s, his disillusionment and tired body demonstrate that such an opportunity is empty without the "astonishment" that gives meaning to life. The writer's physique hints at what the author hesitates to admit: his best years are over and little time remains. As Nora observes, the body has a memory and "inherent self-knowledge" that do not lie.[43]

Corporeality and consumption defined *byt* for the author and his era; the way we read Trifonov shows how we interpret everyday life as an underlying force from Stalinism to the 1980s. Iurii Lotman, a contemporary of Trifonov, gives a prosaically poetic description: "*Byt* is the ordinary flow of life in its real and practical forms. It is the things that surround us, our habits and everyday behavior. *Byt* surrounds us like air and, like air, is only noticed when it is spoiled. . . . *Byt* is thus always located in the realm of practice; it is above all the world of things."[44] *Byt* encompassed the "ambiguity" and "flexibility" that Bren and Neuberger espy in consumption; daily life in the USSR involved tactics and subterfuge to obtain deficit goods and negotiate relationships. Attacks on everyday life intensified during the

Brezhnev years as fears about *byt* combined anxiety over changing gender roles, increasing urbanization, technology, and consumption, all topics that critics connected to Trifonov's late prose. Yuri Andropov himself commented that the author's works needed more discussion of Party policies and less emphasis on daily life. Soviet culture saw the quotidian as an overwhelming world of things threatening to subsume meaningful existence (*bytie*).[45]

In Trifonov's prose *byt* included the material world of bodies and things but also implicated morality. The author maintained that the everyday was too important to dismiss: "*Byt* is a great test. One should not talk about it with scorn as the lower half of human life, unworthy of literature. For *byt* is ordinary life, a test by life, where the new morality of today appears and is put to the test." *Byt*, Trifonov clarified, was both "ordinary life" and "the new morality of today." Elsewhere he argued that "*byt* is low [*nizmennaia*] life, material, and *bytie* is elevated [*vozvyshennaia*], spiritual. But people live simultaneously in both lives." He could not decide whether *byt* was the lower half of existence, redeemed by *bytie*, or whether it and *bytie* were equal partners in shaping life. The tension between *byt* and *bytie* runs throughout Russian literature and stems in great part from the intelligentsia's abiding suspicion of the material world. Pomerantsev, for instance, urged authors to improve *byt* and thus vanquish it. Trifonov, however, was unusual in worrying that the physical nature of everyday life would overtake the very process of writing, an anxiety that matched his generation's fears over the prominence of consumption.[46]

Critics at the time scorned Trifonov's emphasis on the everyday, preferring his historical commentary to what they mislabeled as *byt*'s banality. They either denigrated the quotidian or assumed it was a steppingstone to loftier topics, as when the Russian critic Igor' Reif commends Trifonov for expanding *byt* to the size of *bytie*. From this viewpoint, the quotidian is small, trifling, and lacks scope.[47] Ironically, it was the canny editor Anna Berzer at *Novyi mir* who applied the label of *byt* to Trifonov's later prose, believing that packaging *The Exchange* as "merely" about daily life would distract censors from its themes of marred morality. In the 1960s–1970s critics saw the everyday as a necessary toxin, harmless in small doses but lethal when contaminating the "important" themes of Russian literature. Lev Anninskii, one of the era's most perceptive critics of Trifonov, praised the writer's prose for transcending the physical to embrace the spiritual. Trifonov's portrayals of *byt* were an example for other writers of the era (*shestidesiatniki*) such as Vladimir Makanin and Natal'ia Baranskaia; the latter published her groundbreaking *A Week Like Any Other* in the same year and journal as *The Exchange*.[48]

Dedkov praises Trifonov for portraying *byt* as heavy with the weight of the past. This resembles Nora's belief that memory is physical, rooted in the objects and gestures that for Lotman comprise the quotidian. A Russian critic who lived in Moscow in the 1970s extols Trifonov's picture of life in the capital: the writer conveys a "general sense of tiredness" that sticks to all who encounter it. In his prose the everyday is objects but also the memories and feelings that coalesce around them.[49]

Trifonov understood that everyday life was an important way to remember history; seemingly minor details pointed to the trauma that Stalinism inflicted. The minutiae of *byt* reopened old wounds as characters recalled (or tried to forget) their role as victims or accomplices. As Cathy Caruth outlines, trauma is an event whose significance comes after the fact: "to be traumatized is precisely to be possessed by an image or event."[50] Trauma is both the initial incident and reaction to it. In Soviet culture, focusing on mourning was a response to political repression; Alexander Etkind notes that grieving involved obsessively returning to the tragedies themselves. In Trifonov's late works, the everyday was a new way of looking at the USSR's history: *byt* was both mundanity and horror, where apparently innocuous objects recalled the destruction of lives. Images of food, a character's boots, and other fragmented details become markers of violence.[51] They accompany the silence that historian Jay Winter pairs with a culture's reaction to trauma. In Soviet society this meant avoiding difficult moments in the past, for example, Stalinism. Dmitrii Bykov praises Trifonov for raising silence to the level of poetics and evoking what has been lost. As Tvardovskii noted in his diary, to ignore Stalin's terror would be like a family living in a room underneath which a murdered relative was buried. The family never discussed the crime, but agreed to not kill anyone else. This horrific image demonstrates how trauma is both an event (the murder) and a process (the family's refusal to mention the crime). Putin's war with Ukraine provides a similarly macabre metaphor. Maksim Trudoliubov, a scholar decrying the 2022 invasion, calls Russia a society trapped with the skeletons of a Stalinist past it never confronted.[52]

Memory, trauma, and silence have a strong presence in Trifonov's prose from the Brezhnev era but appear in his earlier writing as well. After 1953 he described the problems of recollection in physical terms that suggested both unease with the material world and the problem of understanding the past. The author's most famous work, *House on the Embankment*, opens with a narrator noting that the characters would not even recognize their younger selves.

> Not one of those boys is alive today. Some were killed in the war, some died of sickness, some disappeared without a trace, while others, though still alive, have turned into different people; and if by some magic means those different people were to meet their past selves—in their cotton twill shirts and canvas sneakers—they would no longer know what to say to them. I fear, in fact, that they would not even guess that they were meeting themselves. Well, to hell with them, if they're so imperceptive. They have no time to spare, anyway; they have to hurry on, to swim with the current, paddling with their hands, farther and farther, faster and faster, day after day, year after year: the shores change, the hills recede, the forests thin out and vanish, the sky darkens, the cold sets in, they have to hurry, hurry—and they no longer have the strength to look back at what is behind them and fading away like a cloud on the edge of the horizon.[53]

Memory drowns within the force of forgetting, a power expressed through the material world. The landscape changes, erasing former landmarks. Weather turns from the warmth of childhood, with its "cotton twill shirts and canvas sneakers," to an ominous present where "the cold sets in." Friends and rivals have vanished and those who survived cannot identify their former selves. This is the opening of a novella that recounts how the scholar Glebov tries to forget those he betrayed in the 1930s and 1940s. The passage touches on many of the themes in Trifonov's late prose: losing friends, youth, and even one's sense of self to the trauma of Stalinism. *House on the Embankment* conveys this through objects big and small, including clothes, the shore, and the water that represents time. In Trifonov's prose it is not ideas that direct existence but the crushing magnitude of the material. Sometimes, however, things recall events the characters and their culture have tried to forget. Maya Nadkarni, in her anthropological study of Hungary, discusses how remains of the past become "matter out of time," reshaping and challenging collective concepts of trauma. In *House on the Embankment* and Trifonov's other late works, objects do something similar, revealing memory to be ordinary and physical yet uncontrollable and disturbing.[54] Recollections reveal dissimilar viewpoints; this is fitting for an author who first justified then undermined the Soviet approach to the past. Such diversity challenge a monolithic approach to history, an opposition key to village prose writers as well (Trifonov admired the *derevenshchiki*, who shared his belief in sincerity and suspicion of the material world).[55]

During Stalinism and the Thaw Trifonov hoped *iskrennost'* could bolster and revive society; his Brezhnev-era prose abandoned this dream. In doing so, he exemplified the disillusionment of the intelligentsia, which after the Prague Spring realized that sincerity no longer had a place in public life. Solzhenitsyn urged his fellow citizens to "live not by lies." Trifonov more quietly rejected the state's cynical call for unity between word and deed even as it practiced deceit.[56] In his late works *iskrennost'* was also imperiled by a culture of consumption. As Alekseyeva notes, by the 1970s the intelligentsia was wary of the NTR's effects on society. The material world even tainted the process of depiction: Trifonov's prose showed that he worried whether one could describe consumption without being overwhelmed by it. Was it possible for a writer to control representation so that he, in Pomerantsev's words, remained an author and not a compiler? Could one honestly recall a past that questioned the sincerity of the present? Trifonov's late prose raised questions that undermined the basic assumptions of Soviet literature and society.[57]

Beyond Victim or Apologist

Trifonov's writing garnered an astounding amount of secondary literature in the USSR and beyond. These responses, however, usually focused on his Moscow prose in the Brezhnev era. Within this narrow scope some Soviet critics derided his supposedly excessive interest in *byt*. Others (particularly in the West) reduced the author's oeuvre to a critique of Stalinism or a shift from "supporting" to "attacking" the Soviet regime. These viewpoints did clarify some features of the author's best-known works yet ignored his earlier prose, unusual focus on Central Asia, and multifaceted interest in the material world. In the West, Gillespie and Josephine Woll published comprehensive studies of Trifonov in the early 1990s, reading his fiction in light of the historical and political crises destroying the USSR. Building on their analyses, my study links Trifonov's prose to the role that consumption, bodies, and sincerity played in Soviet culture.[58]

Critics' responses to Trifonov have several interrelated themes. The first is the intelligentsia; by late socialism this group saw itself as preserving knowledge, ethics, and a vision of the world independent from the state. In everyday life *intelligenty* acted selflessly and scorned material reward. These

Introduction   19

traits were, of course, more mythological than real. Trifonov was essential to this image of the intelligentsia, which he defines as a purely Russian phenomenon.[59] The author observes, "An *intelligent* is what we call a person who has spiritual qualities [*dushevnymi kachestvami*] such as selflessness, conscience, the absence of the desire for material gain [*zhazhdy nazhivy*]. An *intelligent* simply cannot be someone who is trying to get ahead, who wishes to get more than his share from life. In my understanding *intelligentnost'* is three concepts together: education, spiritual qualities, and understanding of the world."[60]

The intelligentsia must have knowledge but also "spiritual qualities" that match its interest in ideas. These oppose "material gain"; the group endorses thought over objects and avoids getting more than one's "share." Sincerity for Trifonov is connected to the intelligentsia's "conscience" and enlightened kindness. His writing demonstrates that consumption undermines the realm of ideas and ethics that *intelligenty* uphold. Tat'iana Trifonova, the author's sister, remarks how, when she visited Prague, her brother urged her to bring back banned Russian books instead of jeans or dishes. This reminiscence furthers the author's reputation as an *intelligent* who valued the written word over material goods.[61]

Trifonov's statement on the intelligentsia is a rare instance of him showing readers how to live, as opposed to his more common portrayals of moral compromise and greed. The author's demand that the intelligentsia live by positive values echoes Solzhenitsyn's famous distinction between "real" *intelligenty* and those "smatterers" corrupted by the state.[62] Marina Selemeneva, the most talented Trifonov scholar since perestroika, argues that the author was an atheist yet possessed an intuitive morality thanks to Russian literature and the intelligentsia. While critics have exhaustively analyzed Trifonov's conflicted image of *intelligenty*, their discussions center on his later narratives and ignore the group's role in his pro-Stalinist novel.[63]

Another commonplace of critics is the dichotomy of official/unofficial literature. The author complained about the Western tendency to pigeonhole him as a "government" or opposition writer, an unhelpfully simple designation.[64] Writing in the 1990s, Mark Lipovetsky and Naum Leiderman remark that politics guided how Russian critics evaluated Trifonov: while in the Brezhnev years conservatives attacked him for emphasizing *byt*, after the collapse of the USSR some liberals snubbed Trifonov as representing the communist regime. Trifonov's biography and the fate of his prose demonstrate that such labels are misleading: *Students* was applauded by the state, yet many of his later works were delayed by cautious editors and censors.[65] Trifonov's books sold on the black market for three times the regular price; Solzhenitsyn and Lev Kopelev esteemed his prose. As a child of the elite, Trifonov benefited from the system, lost family members to the purges, benefited again as a young man (winning the Stalin Prize), then became disenchanted while enjoying the privileges of a published author with global fame. In the 2000s Russian/Eurasian studies has rightly eschewed the division of culture into conformist or unofficial spheres, a designation Alexei Yurchak undermined with his study of the last Soviet generation.[66]

A third mainstay of critics is the atonement trope, which links *Students*, *The Bonfire's Glow*, and *House on the Embankment*. These three works respond to Stalinism in ways that illuminate changes within Trifonov and his society: the first admired Stalin, the second documented Valentin Trifonov and other purge victims, the third revisited the plot of *Students* with sympathy for the repressed. Trifonov noted that later in life he was afraid to pick up his debut novel; the author also confessed that he was frightened when writing about his father. In his post-1953 works several characters lose this parent during the purges. Valentin Trifonov's death was trauma he could never move beyond, leading him to view the past as an unstable, malevolent influence on the present. This appears through characters resembling Hamlet, a symbol of yesterday haunting those who try to deny its trauma.[67]

Another theme in criticism is Trifonov's linked works. *Students* is connected to *House on the Embankment* and *The Bonfire's Glow* is paired with *The Old Man* (*Starik*, 1978), a fictional account of a Red Cossack in the Civil War. Critics' responses focused most on *Students* and *House on the Embankment*, glossing over the first novel in favor of emphasizing the later (and better) work. Anne Dwyer makes the intriguing but debatable claim that reading *Students* through *House on the Embankment* renders the author's first novel subversive. Ivanova saw a shift from superficial depiction (*Students*) emphasizing appearance to more profound description in his late narratives. This observation paralleled Gusev's argument that Trifonov's prose moved from "horizontal" portrayals to a more selective yet skilled use of images.[68]

There is a third, overlooked pair: *Slaking the Thirst* and *Taking Stock* are both devoted to Turkmenia. The first novel awkwardly combined enthusiasm for the future with dread over the past; the second found hope in neither yesterday nor tomorrow. My study builds on all these patterns in criticism, connecting them to Trifonov's interest in sincerity, bodies, and consumption.

The shared historical periods of his narratives (the Civil War, Stalinism) underline how the aftershocks of trauma—the repeated return to a troubling event—guided Trifonov's career.

No new substantial monographs in English on Trifonov have appeared since the 1990s; I address this lacuna while delving into his underexamined Stalinist and Thaw works alongside those devoted to Central Asia as edge of the Soviet empire. My book combines a chronological approach with a thematic one, following how Trifonov's prose commented on bodies, consumption, and sincerity as Soviet culture tried to remake humanity and its objects in the image of a brighter tomorrow. Chapter 1 focuses on the writer's Stalinist prose. *Students* tried to reconcile sincerity with support for lies and oppression: totalitarianism imposed its own (terrifyingly false) conception of *iskrennost'* on Trifonov and his characters. Their bodies evinced sincerity or duplicity, a key feature that continued into his later works. Critics were drawn to descriptions of everyday life in *Students*, beginning the connection between Trifonov, *byt*, and objects that persisted for decades. In postwar society consumption was either the just reward of serving the state or a hollow accumulation of unearned goods.

Chapter 2 investigates how Trifonov's overlooked Thaw works, including *Slaking the Thirst*, shifted from belief in technology and the radiant future to a "thin present" overshadowed by the trauma of the past. *Under the Sun*, like *Slaking the Thirst*, conjoined Central Asia to the USSR's presumably better future. Trifonov's portrayal of the region's vast desert, however, signaled that humanity cannot manage its own destiny, let alone the environment. The chapter then examines *The Bonfire's Glow* as an effort to connect sincerity, memory, and history while the Thaw came to a close.

The third chapter centers on Trifonov's Moscow novellas, which were written in the late 1960s-mid 1970s and established his place in world literature. Examining the role of bodies and consumption provides new insights into narratives such as *House on the Embankment*. In these works the present is under the long shadow of the past; *byt* implies muted trauma as well as daily struggles. Chapter 4 explores Trifonov's final narratives from the 1970s to 1981; in this prose fragmented memories replace hope for a better tomorrow. Works such as *The Old Man* demanded a sincere approach to the past yet showed that such a view was impossible: Trifonov likened examining history to crawling into catacombs, a subterranean symbol of the intelligentsia's buried hopes. I examine *Impatience*, his novel praising the assassination of Alexander II, and relate this to 1970s terrorists, whom Trifonov scorned as embodying insincerity promoted by technology. The chapter looks at *The Abandoned Home*, a collection of autobiographical stories about traveling abroad. Characters in his Brezhnev-era prose had differing levels of sincerity; at first there appeared to be a generational divide (selfless revolutionaries versus their greedy successors). However, *House on the Embankment* and *Disappearance* revealed the roots of corruption to extend from the very beginning of the Soviet experience. His final works were not merely a summation of the author's oeuvre but portrayed how the NTR and consumption eclipsed *iskrennost'* in late socialism.

The conclusion explores Trifonov's effect on other writers, including I. Grekova (pseudonym of Elena Venttsel') in the 1970s. In perestroika and the 1990s liberal Liudmila Ulitskaia and iconoclastic Liudmila Petrushevskaia continued Trifonov's style, themes, and Moscow setting. Trifonov has a contested presence in Putin's Russia, a society that has abandoned the liberal values the author supported in his later years. Since February 2022 the discourse of hatred, cult of military strength, and demands for complete loyalty have made Russia resemble the Stalinist era pictured in many Trifonov works. His inclusion in the country's most popular biographical series shows relevance and marketability as the nation increasingly evokes the Soviet culture that so worried the writer.

1

A Radiant Future of Things

Trifonov's Stalin-Era Prose

In 2018 the Memorial human rights organization erected a plaque on the outskirts of Moscow. The marker stands not far from the dacha Trifonov purchased to remind him of the happiest years of his life: the period before his parents' arrest. Decades later the writer's widow discovered that the writer's father had been buried nearby. Trifonov unknowingly passed his grave when driving to the property bought with the money from *Students*, which received the Stalin Prize from the leader ordering his father's execution. In February 2022, four days after the beginning of the war against Ukraine, the Moscow prosecutor's official "liquidated" Memorial. The phrase, recalling Stalin's destruction of internal enemies, was one of the signs that honest discussion of the past was no longer permissible.[1]

These chilling coincidences tied to Trifonov's dacha are the lingering trauma of an entire society; they also underscore that his first works are essential to understanding how bodies and objects came together to shape postwar Stalinism. Trifonov's early prose assumed ideas and the material world worked in tandem to promote sincerity as a societal virtue. It was during Stalinism, an epoch of total falseness, that Trifonov began to value *iskrennost'*. His initial writings, from the end of the 1940s to the early 1950s, responded to significant cultural changes: recovery from war, the anti-Jewish campaigns, and the first traces of reforms that would come after 1953. Scholars have traditionally seen late Stalinism as a period where ideas served oppression as the state subdued newly annexed territories and coopted (or destroyed) the intelligentsia. However, there was another side to this era: the complex, understudied role of the material world. The author's first works revealed, often inadvertently, how *telesnost'* and things could reinforce or

24 A Radiant Future of Things

subvert official policies. His early prose was not a rough draft of his later, better writing. Instead, these largely forgotten narratives offer new approaches to a period that is itself marginalized. As Dobrenko observes, scholars more often focus on the purges of the thirties, the Great Patriotic War, or the Thaw. Reading Trifonov allows us to investigate this overlooked era. More importantly, his first writings reveal a basic problem that post-1945 culture failed to solve: how could those building communism enjoy a better life yet ensure material comfort did not overpower ideals? Chapter 1 explores how the young author unsuccessfully confronted this quandary, which would confound him and his society for the next decades.[2]

BODIES, OBJECTS, AND ILLUSORY *ISKRENNOST'* IN LATE STALINISM

Beginning in the 1930s, socialist realism illustrated how corporeality guided by the correct ideas must transform society. Physicality loomed large in late Stalinist culture, counterbalancing the era's shifting ideological campaigns. The period, continuing the logic of the 1930s, demanded that healthy and productive bodies reflect citizens' sincerity: appearance should indicate essence. The film *Fall of Berlin* (1949) envisioned Stalin defeating fascism and securing peace. While many of the non-Russian soldiers perish, the two lovestruck protagonists are unharmed, ready to marry and produce future citizens. Natasha, the heroine, retains her statuesque form despite being in a concentration camp; hero Alesha is a Stakhanovite steelworker-turned-soldier. The film exemplifies how Stalinist cinema used hyperbolic masculinity to underscore the need for obedience and virility.[3] Vladimir Dobrovol'skii's novel *Three Men in Gray Overcoats* focused on veterans in a central Russian city rebuilding their university—the fourth main character, a wounded soldier, is nursed back to normalcy and will soon join their ranks. The work implied that those who are politically reliable but temporarily separate from the collective will reunite with their comrades to ensure the country's recovery.[4]

As Kaganovsky observes, the most famous example of the postwar body was the legless pilot Meres'ev in Boris Polevoi's novella *Story of a Real Man*; the plot celebrates his triumphant return to the air force thanks to a woman's love, prosthetic limbs, and determination. In late Stalinism, repairing the individual body symbolized the recovery of the body politic; faith in tomorrow, alongside the material and moral support of the state, made anything possible.[5] Society ignored the malnourished, maimed bodies of those in the gulag. Likewise, the 1946–47 famine, which killed between one and two million people, was absent from Trifonov's early work and public discourse as a whole. Instead, films such as Ivan Pyr'ev's *Cossacks of the Kuban* featured burly men and comely women who were well-fed and eager to expand their collective farms. This vision tried to supplant a ruinously low standard of living, which some lawmakers under Stalin hoped to alleviate even as others increased the burden on *kolkhozniki*.[6]

For many in the USSR priorities changed as the country emerged from war. Historian Juliane Fürst observes that after 1945 young people chose consumption (not ideology) as the main way to express identity. According to the fantasy promoted by Soviet advertising, shortages simply did not exist. Vera Dunham, in her pioneering study, identified a "Big Deal" between consumer and state: the regime compensated the subservient, whose possessions gained positive meaning from their owners' support for Stalinism. Those who were sincere would accrue the benefits of *iskrennost'*, with sincerity defined by the mendacious regime. Trifonov was a key supporter and beneficiary of this social contract, which claimed to provide material comfort in the present yet promised even more abundance in the future.[7]

This new focus on objects created a host of problems. The intelligentsia worried consumption would erode morality and threaten sincerity, ignoring the larger issue that the *intelligenty* were now intellectual vassals of the state. Red Army soldiers occupying Eastern Europe were enraged by the higher standard of living in defeated Germany and 'liberated' Poland. At the same time, consumption became a new arena for international competition: the state wanted to make the superiority of socialism evident in everyday life, a stance that helped explain the first signs of a shift from heavy to light industry.[8] A draft law in 1947 argued for more apartments, expanding the automotive industry, and creating public dining facilities—these steps heralded Khrushchev's more famous (and successful) Thaw reforms. Yet hunger, poverty, and new waves of arrests and deportations kept much of the populace destitute.[9]

Advances in science seemed to validate the USSR's leap from agrarian empire to industrial superpower. Scholars usually date the scientific-technical revolution from the late 1950s, with the launch of Sputnik and advent of nuclear energy, automation, and consumer electronics. However, the first Soviet nuclear weapon was tested in late Stalinism, created in part thanks to gulag labor and a pliant technical intelligentsia. Ulitskaia, examining the roots of consumption, looks back at the postwar years with fascinated

26   A Radiant Future of Things

horror: "Physics, chemistry, and biology got involved, medicine expanded, with all its wonderful accomplishments in dentistry, cosmetology, and surgery. Psychology raced ahead with convincing arguments. Many ways were thought up for a person to express love for himself."[10] The cult of technology and consumption developed hand in hand.

Literature offered a parallel vision. Scholar Nataliia Kozlova explores the popularity of socialist realism, whose readers devoured novels because of their descriptions of the material world, not their ideological content. Her analysis builds on Dunham's argument that what people valued was the chimera of domestic comfort, privacy, and (limited) wealth. All of these were a haven from the trauma of wartime and the difficult life after victory. Kozlova modifies Dunham's argument, clarifying that socialist realism was a "projection of desire" or even acted as "collective therapy." Its fictitious vision of the world reassured Soviets that eventually they too would have the private apartments, stylish clothes, and knickknacks crowding the pages. Late Stalinism's relationship to things was an important chapter in the USSR's long battle with the material world; the Party and intelligentsia proclaimed ideas to be more important than objects. Readers, however, reached the opposite conclusion.[11] The state again demanded sacrifices as the country recovered from war, repeating a refrain heard since 1917—Soviet consumption was a narrative of waiting. Kozlova underscores that literature reiterated this message, implying that readers should forgo comfort until the arrival of communism. Her argument, combined with Katerina Clark's theses on socialist realism, asserts that late Stalinist writing promised material abundance as well as ideological consciousness. Trifonov's first novel relies on these assumptions.[12]

Students dominates this chapter not because it is a sterling example of literature like the writing of Mikhail Bulgakov or Boris Pasternak. Instead, the novel helps us read the surprisingly fraught relations between bodies, things, and sincerity in the era of "conflictlessness," a period when all serious problems had supposedly been resolved. *Students* began Trifonov's obsession with *iskrennost'*, which directed his critique of Soviet society for the next thirty years. The plot's details about sports, love, and *byt*'s objects give a new perspective on the USSR where, as Lewis Siegelbaum outlines, private life was less a defined space than an interconnected series of layers.[13]

Students follows how Vadim Belov returns to Moscow after the Great Patriotic War and enters a teaching institute only to be disappointed. He hopes to educate the next generation of readers, a mission central to the intelligentsia. However, appropriately named Professor Kozel'skii is an un-inspiring teacher who turns out to be a cosmopolitan and toady to the West (*nizkopoklonnik*). Vadim's closest friend, Sergei, is another problem: fellow students condemn his selfishness and careerism and he retreats into em-bittered isolation. As these events are riling the collective, Vadim discovers that his girlfriend Lena is a frivolous materialist, far less worthy than the sincere and hardworking Olia. The work concludes with Kozel'skii no lon-ger teaching, Sergei admitting his errors, and Vadim and Olia taking in the May Day fireworks as they plan their future. Tomorrow is bright for these young members of the Stalinist intelligentsia.

Discussing the novel in 1950, Trifonov alleged that Kozel'skii was based on several academics attacked for formalism and cosmopolitanism. Actual scholars who resembled this character suffered persecution, which explains in part why the author later wrote *House on the Embankment* as a sort of repentance. Medvedev remarks that some colleagues defended Kozel'skii's real-life prototype, but *Students* omitted this moment. Critics at the time lauded the professor's accusers, praising Trifonov for being in touch with the epoch and extolling him as a son of the Stalin era, a horrifying compli-ment given his father's execution.[14] Responding to the novel, a group of students assumed that it could still be revised and noted shortcomings in the current variant. By implication *Students*, its creator, and the USSR itself were all growing and improving, much like the young bodies of the book's characters. The critic S. L'vov reminded readers that study is also a form of labor; this logic, relying on the metaphor of learning as physical activity, rendered Kozel'skii as dangerous as any saboteur on the factory floor.[15] There is a darker way to interpret the novel. Among Kozel'skii's errors is writing a book entitled *The Shadow of Dostoevsky*. While the professor's study recog-nizes the leading role of Russian writing, focusing on this particular author in the postwar era signaled antipathy to socialism. *Students* misses the irony of the reference to Dostoevsky in the final years of Stalinism, a time when Vadim, like Raskol'nikov, believes 'everything is permitted' in the service of the word-idea.[16]

Students, written during Stalin's final purges, the last Soviet famine, and the aftermath of war, sublimated the nation's trauma through confidence in youthful bodies and material prosperity. Unlike Trifonov's later prose, which took a more critical stance, his first novel portrayed objects as ambiv-alent. Sometimes they evinced technological progress and constituted earned reward; at other moments they implied *meshchanstvo* and insincerity. What remained constant in *Students* was how a thing's moral status derived more from its owner than from the thing itself.[17]

LOVE AND THE FRIENDSHIP OF BODIES

It is unsurprising that the author's first novel privileged youth, a core feature of the postwar genre of student novellas (*studencheskie povesti*). Trifonov later noted that while writing *Students* he felt as young and strong as the times; in the late 1940s he did not realize that Soviet culture needed such self-assurance to distract from war and oppression.[18]

Students began Trifonov's enduring fascination with sports, a crucial part of his reputation in Soviet culture. Sergei is a more attractive version of protagonist Vadim, with broad shoulders and a forehead creased by wrinkles from challenges met during the war. In one of the novel's climactic scenes, he scores the winning point for the institute's volleyball team, signaling that Sergei has returned to society. This moment symbolized bodies working together for corporeal and ideological fitness. B. Platonov, writing shortly after the novel appeared, complained that it should discuss literature instead of volleyball. He failed to understand the role of athletics and, more importantly, made an allegation that would recur for the next thirty years: Trifonov is an author of the petty and physical.[19]

Sergei's body demonstrates how his missteps are serious but will not prevent him from contributing to society. The erring student even confesses to Vadim that he suffers "without people, without a collective." While estranged from his fellow students, Sergei gets the flu and chain smokes, selling a rare Flaubert book to buy cigarettes. Earlier in the plot it is his nagging mother who causes the young man to fall ill, despite him being healthy during the war. Presaging the Thaw's worries over imperiled masculinity, the novel implies that isolation and overbearing women threaten men as they adjust to peacetime life.[20]

When his former girlfriend demands that Sergei be punished for abandoning her when he thought she was pregnant, Vadim responds: "There are no two-faced people [*liudei s dvoinym litsom*]. In the end everyone only has one face. The real one . . . which is more difficult to see."[21] His peers force Sergei to change his actions and Vadim uses the logic of Stalinism to underscore the era's definition of *iskrennost'*, wherein the disparity between public and private behavior must be eliminated. *Students* asserted that characters' actions should mirror their thoughts, with both emphasizing the intelligentsia's duty to help the country. Unmasking Sergei's "real" face recalls historian Oleg

A Radiant Future of Things

Kharkhordin's observation: by the late 1940s the state no longer needed to police citizens because they had assumed this role themselves.[22] Decades after Stalinism, Soviet critic Anatolii Bocharov argued in an interview with Trifonov that *Students* was "sincere" by the standard of the Zhdanov years. The author quickly changed the subject, wishing to discuss neither his first novel nor its connection to *iskrennost'*. Trifonov had come to realize that Vadim's public denunciations of Sergei and Kozel'skii violate a crucial tenet of sincerity: not being false to others. Stalinism's urge to root out and destroy enemies negated the altruism underlying *iskrennost'* and intelligentsia behavior.[23]

While Sergei's redemption transpires within the masculine arena of competition, images of young women connote other expectations. On the crisp winter day when Vadim meets Olia, she "bent over lithely to fasten her skis, and when she straightened up Vadim was suddenly aware of the slender, graceful lines of her figure, emphasized by the snug-fitting sweater." Her physical activity and study of forestry accentuate harmony with the countryside; she combines the fit Stalinist heroine and nineteenth-century "Turgenev maiden," a young woman who is intelligent but modest, cultured yet loves the outdoors. This combination embodied the contradiction of a society that celebrated women's ties to the same natural world it subdued in the 1930s.[24]

Olia's sexuality is appropriately demure, fitting Stalinism's aversion to the overtly erotic. However, Vadim notices that she has outgrown her old housedress and cannot bend over comfortably, hinting that her body is as appealing as that of Lena, his first love interest. Both women have the prominent breasts signaling fecundity and prosperity (as opposed to the reality of malnourishment and privation after the war). *Students* offered a corporeal equivalent of the wish-fulfillment scenario Kozlova sees in socialist realist prose: through these characters readers can picture the bodies they desire but do not yet have.[25]

Students concludes with Vadim and Olia gazing confidently at the future that is unfolding before their eyes:

> "Are you happy for me, Vadim?" she asked, her voice still lower. Of course he was! For her sake, and for his own, too—for not having been deceived in her. . . . Right over their heads the flares burst, lighting up the embankment with an orange glow. For a long, long time they stood in silence, watching the fountains of multi-coloured lights go up into the sky, and come down to the ground, or fall into the river with a sizzling sound. Everything turned pink and blue and gold, and for a moment it was as light as day.[26]

The couple's happiness is made "as light as day" by the May 1 fireworks over Moscow. With this closing scene Trifonov's novel reiterates its message: love is a sincere union where strong bodies evince the right ideas.

The physique of other ethnicities indicates their integration into Stalinist society. *Students* briefly depicts characters from the periphery, the geographically and culturally distant parts of the Soviet empire. These personages were less full-fledged individuals than caricatures; critics for their part conflated Trifonov's Russian and Soviet identities without examining the muted tensions between his Russianness and how the USSR's largest ethnic group dominated others. Vadim's friend Petr Lagodenko is a Ukrainian naval veteran with a passion for Russian literature. Lagodenko's interest in these writers suggests that authors of his own ethnicity do not merit serious study, a telling stance in the years when Russian forces brutally subdued Western Ukraine. However, Lagodenko's love of books is secondary to his respect for physical strength.[27] After insulting Kozel'skii during a meeting, he is reprimanded by the Komsomol. This seemingly minor episode points to a larger but unacknowledged postwar problem: how could veterans be made to obey peacetime authorities? *Students* suggests that masculinity, especially that of non-Russians, must be directed by the Party, lest those such as Lagodenko stir up what one critic labeled "partisan chaos" (*partizanshchina*). Trifonov depicts the former sailor as well intentioned yet lacking the disciplined consciousness of a positive hero.[28]

The Uzbek Rashid Nuraliev is another classmate whose identity symbolizes his region's function in Soviet culture: "Vadim had already made friends with this black-haired, swarthy youth, who had broad shoulders, and the powerful hands of a hereditary tiller of the soil. Vadim liked his high-cheekboned, cheerful, typical countenance, his invariable good humour, his smile displaying all his gleaming teeth, white and strong, like corn on the cob. Rashid wanted to know everything at once and in detail, and was never afraid of seeming ignorant or ridiculous, bombarding all and sundry with his questions, but never making himself tiresome."[29] The Uzbek student is straightforward; like Lagodenko, he lacks guile and acts with *iskrennost'*. His description has strong colonial overtones: Rashid's "powerful hands" come from picking cotton before he came to Moscow. Even at the institute he remains a subaltern, eager to learn "everything at once" from his better-educated comrades. Neither Rashid nor Vadim can escape the legacy of Russian domination in Central Asia. During a visit to the Tretyakov

A Radiant Future of Things   31

Gallery, the two gaze at Vasilii Vereshchagin's painting *Surprise Attack*, which portrays Russian soldiers caught off guard during a campaign near Bukhara.

> Vadim and Rashid stood long before this terrible picture. And each of them thought inwardly: that tall soldier with golden curls and no cap, standing rooted to the spot with drawn sword in front of his comrades, might have been Vadim's grandfather, and that oriental warrior with the black beard and green turban, rushing upon him with a face distorted by rage, and brandishing his blade for the fatal stroke—Rashid's grandfather. . . .
> It had all happened only seventy years ago—just the span of a man's life.
> "It's an ancient picture," said Rashid respectfully. "Strictly historical." He made a clicking sound with his tongue.[30]

Examining Vereshchagin's 1871 painting with its portrayal of bloodshed, Rashid's response reveals that representation matters: how artists depict their themes determines the nature of that reality. Vereshchagin's Turkestan cycle, including *Surprise Attack*, critiqued the inherent violence and death of war. However, in *Students* this message is lost within the narrative of Russians trying to pacify a savage East that is "distorted with rage." The subject matter fits a pattern Dobrenko sees in late Stalinism, an era obsessed with glorifying Russian history and castigating enemies. Rashid's love of the USSR implies that first Russia and then the Soviet state prevailed thanks to military might and civilization.[31]

In its socialist incarnation the Russian state conquered Central Asia a second time, imposing collectivization and an alien ideology under the guise of modernization and liberation from "backward" traditions. Vadim's thoughts suggest that now enmity and strife have been replaced with peace and unity; bloody conflicts between ethnicities are only found in the museum (a location that underscores the exotification of the East). The narrator, however, vacillates between two opposites: the realization that the conquest was not so long ago ("just the span of a man's life") and Rashid's dismissal of the painting as "ancient," "strictly historical," and thus safely in the past. Later in the novel Rashid makes a playful reference to Russian domination, suggesting that the Uzbek student is familiar with those who resent Moscow's power (but he does not). This mention and the scene in the Tretyakov established an unfortunate paradigm for Trifonov: his writing depicted

32   A Radiant Future of Things

those from the periphery via the assumptions of the capital as center. Such a portrayal stemmed from the centripetal structure of Stalinism and imperial policies before it. Rashid's identity is explained to readers first through *telesnost'* (the hands and shoulders of a digger) and then through a painting that recalls the violent relationship between Russia and Central Asia. As with Lagodenko, the young Uzbek man is defined more by flesh than mind.[32] The bodies of Lagodenko and Rashid follow the maxim of national in form, socialist in content. They reiterate Russian clichés about their regions: Lagodenko is hot-tempered and Rashid is an earnest cotton picker. Both have come to Moscow to bolster their intellect, merging with the friendship of peoples that the state controls. Lagodenko and Rashid are subordinate to their Russian friends yet share their sincerity, displaying this through physique.

FRUSTRATED ROMANCE AND FALSE PHYSIQUE

In *Students* the *telesnost'* of problematic characters is more intriguing; their physical appearance imparts moral and political shortcomings. The novel relied on the era's need to compulsively differentiate the positive/sincere from the negative/insincere, then repeat this difference via the iconography of socialist realism: what is praiseworthy or harmful must be pictured at the level of corporeality, dress, and possessions as well as ideas. Lena, the female negative character, is strongly distinguished from Olia. To some extent this comes from women's polarized depiction in Russian literature, which envisioned them as nearly perfect (Aleksandr Pushkin's Tat'iana Larina) or seriously flawed (Tolstoy's shrewish Betsy Tverskaia). Lena embodies this lack of subtlety. From the beginning Vadim's first girlfriend mixes sexuality and materialism: she is tall, striking, and offers Belov perfume on a date. As the audience admires her at the theatre, the scene recalls Hélène Kuragina's beauty in *War and Peace*: "People began turning round to look at Lena, some with curiosity, others with disapproval. But they all went on looking—the men gazing long into her face, the women chiefly studying her dress. Lena did not seem to notice their glances, but Vadim felt mingled embarrassment and pride. It was delightful to be sitting next to this beautiful girl, who attracted such general attention."[33]

Men stare at Lena's "face" (a coded reference to her breasts) and women admire her "dress"; she is an object of desire for both sexes. Vadim is flattered by the reactions but the allusion to *War and Peace* bodes ill. Lena as Hélène typifies an insincere, aristocratic corporeality lingering in Soviet

Moscow. Her crass sensuality, packaged in a sophisticated wardrobe, is alien to a Stalinist heroine such as Olia. At a housewarming party in Lena's parents' new (private) apartment, she and Vadim argue and he watches her reflection in a shiny lampshade; a discolored tooth mars his girlfriend's beauty and hints at internal flaws. Light refracts off one of the objects in Lena's home, emphasizing a defect Vadim previously did not notice. As with Vadim and Rashid in the museum, the novel emphasizes the process of representation. This fleeting focus, which accentuates how the author shapes the physical world through depicting it, is a rare instance where *Students* differs from other postwar works.[34]

Stalinist critics ignored this facet of the novel, instead railing against Lena's superficiality. These accusations began with *telesnost'* then impugned the vapidity behind it: detractors complained that the future teacher was neither seriously involved with the institute's extracurriculars nor particularly interested in studying. Iurii Karasev, for instance, seethed that Lena's academic goal was merely "to become a woman," which implies beauty, greed, and apathy as she prepares to snare a successful husband.[35] Many readers worried that such people favored *meshchantsvo* over the honest work of building socialism. One sniped that Lena's frivolous nature and coquetry became *poshlost'* and emptiness. These were serious allegations: for the intelligentsia *poshlost'* reduced the ideal of love to the desires of the flesh. Likewise, these assumptions paired women with a sexualized behavior and consumption that were incompatible with Soviet culture; this disturbing pattern continued in criticism of Trifonov's prose throughout his life.[36]

Early in the novel Vadim compares his romance with Lena to the fatal frustration felt by doomed lovers: "Some old author had written: 'Love is wanting what is not there and does not exist' [*togo, chego net i ne byvaet*]. That is the way it always was—the Montagues and Capulets, Madame Bovary, Anna Karenina. For them love was life and life was torment. And the tragedy . . . was that, in fighting for their love, they fought for their life. That was how it was earlier, in those distant times."[37] Drawing on the literary references favored by *intelligenty*, Vadim notes that love was an uncontrollable force in "distant times," inspiring great writing yet making characters' lives "torment." In the words of the (uncredited) author Ivan Bunin, love was loss, the inability to have what one wants. Vadim phrases his lament in a manner that unwittingly complicates Stalinism's schematic view of human nature. First, Vadim cites Bunin, an émigré author who was taboo as any sort of authority. The young man likewise sees himself in a host of characters whose suicide shows that passion overpowers rational choice and free will. The novel quickly forgets this troubling definition of love, thanks the relatively smooth courtship between Vadim and Olia. The plot reworks Bunin's formulation into "Love is wanting what is not there yet, but which will inevitably come." This personalizes the masterplot of socialist realism, rewarding positive characters with happiness. Vadim and Olia's children will expand Stalin's Great Family, creating another generation where able bodies and conformist minds work together to support the state. What is more interesting is how *Students* pairs desire and consumption in Trifonov's oeuvre: both are an attempt to gain what one does not possess.[38]

Like Lena, Kozel'skii combines *telesnost'* and a love of things. Vadim, scrutinizing the antagonist's appearance, is suspicious after the scholar denigrates the importance of contemporary (Stalinist) literature. Dismissing the professor as a "poser," Vadim clarifies: "He's just playing at it, everything in him is for show. His noble gestures, his pipe, his distinguished grey locks, his knowledge—he even shows off his knowledge. He arrays himself in knowledge as he does in that fitted waistcoat of his, with the red bone buttons."[39] Knowledge becomes simply another accessory for Kozel'skii, no more meaningful than his "fitted waistcoat," a garment evoking effete aristocracy. The professor contaminates ideas with possessions; both are "for show." The pipe is a particularly galling detail. In the late 1940s it recalled Stalin's favorite accessory, symbolizing contemplation that leads to action as the *vozhd'* first defeated fascism then rebuilt society. Kozel'skii, however, profanes this object by embodying the gilded greed of the Russian nobility. During an exam, as Vadim answers a question on the populist poet Nikolai Nekrasov, Kozel'skii plays with his pipe. This reaffirms the ideological distance between the two—the young man admires the democratic-revolutionary traditions of Russian literature, while the professor secretly scorns socialism. Vadim and Kozel'skii emphasize the conflict between young and old that was a staple of *studencheskie povesti*. The professor participates in society, reaps its rewards, yet cares more for his pipe and "red boned buttons" than for Russian literature. Kozel'skii lacks sincerity and his perfunctory service to the state does not warrant such a wardrobe.[40]

Kozel'skii has another vexing commonality with Lena: neither is devoted to their avocation, which is teaching the next generation about Russian literature. Lena is uninterested in politics while Kozel'skii sees society as merely the provider of his privileged position. Like Vadim and Olia, the two are physically attractive. However, Kozel'skii's and Lena's appearances do

A Radiant Future of Things

not match up with their inner thoughts. *Students* abhors this gap between external form and internal essence; it contradicts the era's insistence on a sincerity in which body and mind are united.

SPECTERS AND THE LIVING DEAD

Trifonov's Stalinist works contain another, far less visible category of *telesnost'*: the traumatized body. Its strongest presence is in his overlooked early story, "Winter Afternoon in the Garage" ("Zimnii den' v garazhe," 1946), a sketch that is unremarkable except for its discussion of the Holocaust. After the liberation of Odessa, the Jewish worker Misha learns the Nazis have killed his relatives. His supervisor shares the man's sorrow, recalling that he witnessed such "sincere" suffering at the front as well. The brief remark legitimates Misha's grief because it is shared by soldiers, as opposed to civilians. The story implies that the protagonist's *iskrennost'* extends to his habits as a consumer: Misha does not use his access to special military supplies but instead relies on rations. "Winter Afternoon in the Garage" also quietly challenges Stalinism's minimizing of non-Russian deaths in the Great Patriotic War. The story broaches the fate of Jews in a work published the year before the anti-cosmopolitan campaign began. Misha sees no point in living—his absolute despair undermines the hope in the future dominating *Students*.[41]

Trifonov's first novel highlights the bodies of its living characters; those who perished in war are all but forgotten. Vadim's father was a school principal who died in December 1941 defending Moscow (as opposed to during the disastrous initial months of the invasion). He is the first in a series of intelligentsia characters who refer back to the author's own father. Vadim and his family used to live on Bersenevskii Embankment, where the Trifonovs resided before his parents were purged and the family was evicted from the House on the Embankment.[42] The similarities between Vadim's and Trifonov's fathers emphasize what Etkind sees as central to mourning Stalin's victims: a "recurrent response to loss that entails a symbolic reenactment of that loss."[43] Trauma that could not be voiced in public—a father murdered in the 1930s—was a common Soviet experience that resurfaces in Trifonov's works. *Students* camouflages the "traitor" Valentin Trifonov by depicting his fictional counterpart as a casualty of war, continuing a lie Trifonov had made about his father dying at the front when the future author entered university. Beth Holmgren notes that grieving those lost in the conflict with Hitler was sometimes code for remembering victims of the gulag; the novel replaces one stigmatized trauma with another, culturally validated one.[44]

Aside from brief mentions of Vadim's father, *Students* ignores those killed or injured between 1941 and 1945. Ivanova comments on the frequent sight of maimed veterans in postwar Moscow but Vadim apparently overlooks them while admiring the many pretty women near Red Square. His observation is frightening for what else it does not see: the absent husbands, brothers, and sons who died at the front or were in the camps. This conveniently selective focus comes in part from Trifonov's own experience. Too young to have fought in the war, he was more familiar with efforts to rebuild. On a deeper level his early prose was incapable of confronting the purges because of the secrecy and shame surrounding his father's execution.[45]

Students does, however, have hints of Hamlet, a traumatized character type that will become more pronounced during the Thaw.[46] Vadim resembles the Prince of Denmark before Shakespeare's protagonist realizes the horrors of present and past. Trifonov himself had supported the system that murdered his father, even winning the Stalin Prize. Yet Hamlet's doubts, introspection, and rejection of falsehood had no place in socialist realism, which believed in certainty and determination as traits creating a better tomorrow. Shakespeare's character was derided during the era, which saw his doubt and passivity as anathema. Kevin Platt points out that silence was the main response to the traumas of Stalinism, especially before 1953. Vadim's father is a mute memory that cannot voice the unsettling implications of its spectral presence in the novel.[47] In *Students* physique illuminates essence as bodies convey what culture deemed important. This scenario, however, could not be permitted for the dead and the maimed. If Trifonov had focused on how war and terror disfigured *telesnost'*, he would have insinuated that violence defined and deformed existence after 1945, clouding hopes for the better future Stalinism promised.

Technology, Luxury, Loyalty

Trifonov's early works offer a comforting vision where things serve socialist humanity. Technology transforms human experience for the better, a stance that continues the myth of "flesh to metal" that Rolf Hellebust defines as central to Stalinism. Consumption and technology join to improve *byt*; to symbolize this, *Students* opens with the growth and modernization of postwar Moscow. After five years in the military Vadim returns to his native city, rides on a new, shiny trolley, and admires one of the (extremely rare) cars in the capital. He is astounded by a streetcleaner: "A thing like a gigantic blue beetle came round the corner, its watery wings extended. Each wing consisted of millions of drops, and shone with all the colours of the rainbow. As the chariot of rain crawled slowly on, it left behind it a wave of coolness." Technology is remaking everyday life and these innovations have a common benefactor, as the narrator implies in a later passage: "The genius for leadership, the ability to inspire others with lofty aspirations and to lead them onward, was the greatest of all gifts."[48] This opinion is shared by Vadim, an exemplary child of the Great Family who believes Stalin has protected this metropolis and will now improve it thanks to the nascent NTR.[49]

One of Trifonov's first stories, "In the Steppe" ("V stepi," 1948), depicts life far from Moscow. Veterinarian Varia comes to a remote sheep station in Kazakhstan and quickly gets used to the noise of the flock, comparing it to the rumble of production on the factory floor. This unlikely association fits into the Stalinist cult of industrialization, hinting that the NTR will transform even this agrarian outpost. The story underscores that the periphery must be remade in the image of the capital. As with the characterization of Uzbek student Rashid, this narrative assumes that Soviet modernization brings prosperity and culture to Central Asia—there is no hint of the 1.5–2 million Kazakhs who perished during collectivization. The story also has a hidden and disturbing biographical referent: Trifonov's mother, trained in animal husbandry, helped create a new breed of sheep during her years in Kazakhstan's Akmolinsk camp for wives of enemies of the people.[50]

There were other ominous aspects to Trifonov's early images of technology and the NTR. The Stalinist critic Drewnowski, himself a part of the totalitarian machine crushing postwar Poland, denounced Kozel'skii in *Students*: the professor gives robotic descriptions of literature better suited for mannequins than students. Drewnowski argued that in the hands of the right-thinking (Stalin), knowledge melded human and machine to improve the world. Enemies of the people, however, could misuse it to warp future generations. Such potential harm qualified the beneficence of technology, even as the NTR raised the standard of living and helped the USSR compete with the West.[51]

In *Students* characters' homes also augur a better tomorrow but raise questions Trifonov did not intend. In a flashback, the narrator recounts how Vadim stops by his family's room as he heads for the front, intent on avenging the death of his father. The young man affectionately gazes at their modest furnishings: "Everything was as he had left it: the books on their shelves, the piano with the embroidered runner on the top, the old bronze clock, and his bed, neatly covered with a green blanket. Lifting the napkin off a plate on the table, he revealed a bit of dry bread, an onion and an egg shell."[52] The novel devotes a few scant sentences to these possessions, yet they elicit strong emotion. Vadim already misses the communal apartment he may never see again, as well as his mother (who is at work), and the memories connected to his father. The room's things exude familiarity, warmth, and the sincerity that comes from good taste and honest functionality. Even the piano with its "embroidered runner" is a homey comfort that shows the material advantages accessible to all. There is nothing superfluous in this cramped but welcoming space. The narrator later observes that Vadim, unlike some children of loving mothers (Sergei, Lena), was not spoiled during childhood.[53]

Vadim's apartment is an intelligentsia idyll, where things are firmly subordinate to the ideals of those who possess them. Each object has a meaning that derives both from its function and from its owners' contribution to the collective. Vadim is preparing to follow in his father's footsteps and become a teacher; his mother is an engineer. Their belongings are, according to the totalitarian mindset, the sign of a better life they will have thanks to loyalty and labor. Such rhetoric of deferring happiness fit the epoch's focus on the future, the intelligentsia's suspicion of the material world, and the state's inability to provide for citizens in the present.[54]

Students devoted more attention to Kozel'skii's apartment, beginning Trifonov's enduring concern with living quarters as a problematic part of consumption. Obvious contrasts, whether between bodies, apartments, or ideas, were a crutch for the superficial description of Trifonov's early works and the Manichean thought of Stalinist culture. Kozel'skii and Vadim both live in *kommunalki*, yet this similarity is subsumed by distinctions that announce divergent worldviews:

> Everything in [Kozel'skii's room] spoke of a tranquil, comfortable [*komfortabel'noi*], bachelor life. The room was study, drawing room, library, and bedroom in one. The entire floor was covered by a thick Persian carpet. The handsome old writing table, the armchairs, and the bookcase were all of mahogany. A television set on a low table. An electric heater. A tennis racket in a press. Two light, three-kilogram dumbbells on the window sill, and next to them a longnecked bottle of brandy. And a pier glass [*zerkalo*]—a flawless, shining pier glass between the windows. The dainty, voluptuous oval seemed to have found its way from some lady's boudoir into the bachelor quarters of this scholar and sportsman.[55]

The professor's room conveys the allure of the material world; the description quickly abandons verbs and allows objects to take over. The fine furniture presumably graced the much larger apartment Kozel'skii enjoyed before the revolution. A pier glass reflects the professor's "voluptuous" nature, just as Lena's corruption is mirrored in the lampshade Vadim notices after they argue. The professor's place is "comfortable," connoting suspect sumptuousness instead of earned prosperity. Late Stalinist student novellas condemned wealth when characters also violated the maxim that only the devoted and hardworking received luxuries. One critic at the time, foreshadowing later attacks on Trifonov's prose, referred to Kozel'skii's apartment as outmoded *byt*. This judgment conflated consumption, banality, and the dangers of the prerevolutionary intelligentsia maintaining physical symbols of their former power.[56]

Opulence per se is not a vice in *Students*. This is made clear when Vadim is stunned by Lena's apartment during their first date. The young man "was absorbed in a minute examination of the mauve wallpaper, the lamp shade hovering like a rosy cloud over the table, the massive side board, the piano, on the top of which stood a host of knickknacks. His attention was caught by a book, also on the top of the piano, with an old-fashioned 'marbleized' binding, and a ribbon bookmarker."[57] The scene overwhelms Vadim and the reader with a cornucopia of details as objects elaborate the era's message: conditions may be difficult now but will soon improve. Unlike in Vadim's room, here the piano is not a marker of the intelligentsia but a sign of prosperity alongside the elegant wallpaper and "ribbon bookmarker." Vadim spends as much time thinking about Lena's home as about Lena herself. This is the first instance when a Trifonov character connects sexual desire with having the material comfort that his love interest enjoys.

The novel, however, unintentionally questions the moral status of such luxury. *Students* links Lena's privilege to her mother; Al'bina Trofimovna fritters away time with her daughter's well-off friends (she does not need to work). As Slavist Xenia Gasiorowska pointed out, associating women and material comfort was a dubious trope in the era's prose. It is Lena's father, a factory manager, who receives the perks doled out by the state and thus spoils both wife and daughter. Vadim immediately likes the older man's weathered face, which implies a working-class background, a sincere interest in helping the country, and thus justification of his wealth. *Students* does not mention another factor: supporting Stalin has secured his position (and kept him and his family from arrest). Instead, the novel implies that Lena's father has earned the right to luxury but his wife and daughter have not.[58] Lena's family complicates the already tangled relations between objects and ideas. Vadim comes to disdain the materialism of his former girlfriend, yet the system he supports encourages cupidity by rewarding her father. The novel cannot admit the hypocrisy of an allegedly egalitarian society where some (Lena's family) profit from others' labor. *Students* has glimpses of the corruption that comes from consumption but its author could not see that greed was a central feature of postwar culture. Doing so would have meant rejecting Stalinism and questioning the efforts of his father's generation, which tried to create a classless society indifferent to the world of things. Trifonov failed to unknot the problem of Soviet consumption, passing it on to his later works.

Together *telesnost'* and objects shaped late Stalinism. Emboldened by the beginning of the NTR and a false sense of righteousness, Trifonov's early characters devoted themselves to the present and future. Their bodies, things, and ideas reinforced the unity between physicality and ideology that the era demanded. *Students* assumed Vadim and Olia were sincere and would receive the boons granted to those whose private thoughts corresponded to public obedience. Their *iskrennost'* was the product of a dishonest society, where oppression posed as unity and the better life promised to all was given to a few. The intelligentsia in Trifonov's early works either supported the state or, as Kozel'skii shows, was removed from society. After 1953 his prose continued to use bodies and consumption to reflect on *iskrennost'*, even as sincerity came to mean rejecting the Stalinist past.

2

Enthusiasm and Ambivalence

Trifonov and the Thaw

Just after the end of the Thaw in the hallway of *Novyi mir* Iurii Trifonov saw Solzhenitsyn, whom he described as having the "face of a prophet." The future Nobel laureate admired the younger author, lauding him as one of the most influential writers of the era and praising his support for Tvardovskii when the editor was ousted. There was, however, another telling meeting. In 1967 Trifonov visited the Kremlin to meet Anastas Mikoyan, a former Politburo member whose service extended from Lenin to Brezhnev. The two discussed the Civil War, which Mikoyan had witnessed and Trifonov depicted in his recently published novella, *The Bonfire's Glow*. Solzhenitsyn and Mikoyan were the antipodes of dissident and state-controlled culture at the end of the 1960s; Trifonov's good relations with both signaled his contradictory role within a society itself divided by the Stalinist past, the volatile present, and an uncertain future. The author's writing demonstrates that these changes extended far beyond literature or policy. His prose during the Thaw provides new ways to examine the era by understanding how bodies and consumption affected sincerity.[1]

Scholars see the period from Stalin's death until the end of the 1960s as a series of ideological swings between liberal reform and conservative regression, an approach Stephen Bittner notes in his skillful analysis of the Moscow intelligentsia. The Thaw has provoked intense debate, yet academic discussion centers primarily on clashes within literature, the arts, politics, and historiography. There was indeed a collision of ideas between poets and physicists, as well as those who supported or opposed Khrushchev's mercurial policies. Culture cautiously critiqued Stalinism, seeing sincerity as a mandate to transform society and honestly recall the past (within limits).

42 · Enthusiasm and Ambivalence

Liberal Soviet critics believed they were reclaiming the legacy of Lenin, which the cult of personality had distorted. De-Stalinization tried to exorcize the ghost of the recent past and prove the USSR was once again a model for humanity.[2]

Trifonov's prose depicted these views but focused on conflicts within the material world as well. Relying on continuities and ruptures before and after Stalin's death, his writing pictures how bodies and technology literally and symbolically built the Thaw. In his 1950s–1960s works *telesnost'* is at times young and confident, recalling the protagonists of *Students*. Other characters have been physically and metaphorically mutilated by the system that Trifonov's first novel had praised. Consumption is a more subtle presence in his Thaw works, either subsumed within scientific progress or eschewed in the struggle to build communism. Golubev notes that post-Stalinist culture connected identity to making objects; Trifonov's prose shows that objects made people by shaping their views of the world. The author deliberately envisioned the struggle with the totalitarian past in strikingly material terms but did not understand the ties between Stalinism, the NTR, and the obsession with consumer goods.[3]

This chapter assesses bodies, consumption, and *iskrennost'* in Thaw culture, then looks at Trifonov's prose as he moved from the 1950s and a cycle of short stories about Turkmenia to his novel *Slaking the Thirst*. Other than critics from the region themselves, few have examined the author's sustained focus on Central Asia. Near the end of the Thaw Trifonov published *The Bonfire's Glow*, a nonfiction novella about Valentin Trifonov, which Ivanova and Woll have discussed through its links with history. I focus on how this work treats the problems the material world creates for those who try to understand the past. The chapter concludes by examining "It Was Noon in Summertime," an understudied story that the author labeled a transition to his later works.[4] For Trifonov the 1950s–1960s alternated between hope in the future and realization that the present could not escape the past. Sometimes this vacillation was unintended; at other times it was an explicit theme. The author's own life was far from stable: his first marriage dissolved during the Thaw and he married Pastukhova in 1968. Trifonov's works emphasized the physical as well as the ideational and depicted the distant vistas of the USSR more than the cozy apartments of the Moscow *intelligenty*.[5] The Thaw ended with the invasion of Czechoslovakia, a disturbing event Trifonov heard about at the dacha with Tvardovskii. Both men embodied what Bykov critiques as bravery within boundaries carefully policed by the state. After

Enthusiasm and Ambivalence 43

the Prague Spring these controls tightened. Vail and Genis observe that, by the conclusion of the sixties, the intelligentsia's hope that the USSR was building communism became the realization that the state was consolidating empire.[6]

INHERITED OPTIMISM AND AN UNSETTLING PAST

During the Thaw, conceptions of the body were divided into two polarized categories: resolute builders of socialism and survivors of trauma. The film *Spring on Zarechnaia Street* matched an idealistic (female) teacher and an enthusiastic (male) worker, a pair familiar from *Fall of Berlin* and Soviet culture's stock gender roles. *Lenin's Guard* blended shots of excited youth with the Moscow streets: these images assumed a society reinvigorated after war and Stalinism.[7] The traumatized body, however, undermined this vision. Solzhenitsyn's *One Day in the Life of Ivan Denisovich* featured a protagonist scarred by injustice; in the same year Andrei Tarkovskii's film *Ivan's Childhood* portrayed a teenage scout executed by the Nazis. Focusing on the miserable minutiae of the front, it exemplified what art historian Lida Oukaderova sees as the Thaw's shift from ideology to objects and minor details over panoramic vistas. Trauma lacked a telos: unlike in *Fall of Berlin* or *Story of a Real Man*, there was neither redemptive victory nor a miraculous recovery. As Woll notes, after 1953 many protagonists of war films returned home yet wished they were dead.[8]

Some works implied that cautious discussion of past violence was now a part of Soviet culture. Caruth observes that a traumatic event is not understood when it first occurs; instead, victims repeatedly experience what happened. Her analysis fits the Thaw's recurring yet incomplete discussion of Stalinism—the cult of personality haunted those returning from camps and exile. Hamlet was one of the era's most important symbols, as Grigorii Kozintsev's film adaptation proved.[9] This version of Shakespeare's play implied that the liberal intelligentsia was both the offspring and repudiator of Stalinism. Etkind states that *intelligenty* grappled with this paradox, given that "as Hamlet shows, recognizing a ghost does not rob the ghost of its otherness." Admitting the horrors of the past was not enough to overcome them. The traumatized body, a spectral presence before 1953, took on flesh and blood as the Thaw portrayed Stalin's victims. Conservatives dismissed Hamlet as defeatist and passive, echoing similar complaints during Stalinism.[10] Evgenii Evtushenko's poem "The Heirs of Stalin" worried that the dictator's supporters still had power. Hamlet was their opponent: he symbolized the intelligentsia's *iskrennost'* but also its ambivalence and weakness. As Rutten argues, sincerity brings with it doubt and suspicion (two defining traits of Shakespeare's character). Trilling noted that Hamlet was a sincere character who "feels not less but more than he avows." In the Thaw this surplus of feeling added to the emotional depth the era lauded as honest.[11]

New images of sexuality mixed optimism and trauma. In Grekova's story "Summer in the City" a single mother discovers her daughter is planning an abortion, prompting memories of how during Stalinism she tried to end the pregnancy that gave her daughter life. Grekova moved discussion of desire beyond procreation or marriage. As with trauma, representation of sexuality was no longer determined by the goals of the state.[12] Instead, *telesnost'* was a more autonomous presence, directing attention away from lofty ideals and toward everyday experience.

Byt now underscored the urgency of consumer demands. In 1962 the Party predicted that the current generation would live under communism; material comfort was a central part of reaching utopia.[13] The stakes for failing to provide a better standard of living were high. First, the coming of communism would be postponed. More importantly, the food riots in Novocherkassk showed the immediate danger of shortages. Finally, as Reid and others note, surpassing the US's standard of living was now an essential part of Cold War rivalry. After Stalin's death, historian Gleb Tsipursky summarizes, the USSR saw itself as the vanguard of "socialist modernity": the country was an advanced, progressive society that had reclaimed its Leninist roots and could provide for its citizens.[14] Yet more possessions were not the answer. Vail and Genis explain that the USSR tried to increase prosperity while shunning *meshchanstvo*. As in late Stalinism, consumption was politically charged. Now, however, the terms were reversed: *Students* pictured a world where only the loyal should be rewarded. Kabo asserted that it was actually the "cult of personality" that promoted *meshchanstvo* over "being a citizen." For liberals Stalinism connotated greed as well as a threat to socialist values.[15]

The Thaw followed the 1930s-early 1950s in assuming technology was a positive force in culture. The world was enthralled by Gagarin's space flight, the result of the Sputnik program. Reid argues that the state wanted people to access technology in *byt* as well.[16] Yet not all innovations were equal, as Grekova's novella *Ladies' Hairdresser* (1963) revealed. The protagonist is a single mother who runs a computer institute and befriends a hair stylist. In the plot the NTR is innovative (computers advance the boundaries of science) but disappoints (it fails to produce enough chemicals for hair salons, even in Moscow). *Ladies' Hairdresser* outlined the contradictions of 'better living through chemistry,' where technological innovation failed to boost the consumer goods sector.[17]

In the 1950s–1960s science was a collective effort and collectivist dream, sidestepping fears that the objects it created could harm society. The state tried to ensure a better life for individuals while pursuing largescale projects such as the space and arms race. As under Stalin, technology supposedly heralded a better tomorrow; things served humanity and advanced its ideals. Technology ignited the debate between poets and physicists at the end of the 1950s. Critics praised it as proof of the (limited) disputes now permitted in the USSR. Presented as the dialog between art and the natural sciences, this discussion overlooked the two groups' similarities. At a basic level, poets and physicists were contributing to the building of communism. Both also assumed that science should exploit the material world, whether through building dams and canals or by chronicling these feats. Ilya Ehrenburg differentiated the country's scientists from their Western counterparts; the latter, the writer remarked, were tainted by Hiroshima and materialism.[18] Grekova's story "Beyond the Checkpoint" supported Ehrenburg's assumptions. It pictured sincere young *intelligenty* in a secret institute where the results of their work (presumably for the military) are less important than the creativity involved. The Thaw continued the cult of technology, ignoring Soviet science's ties to the arms race.[19]

Historian Susan Costanzo examines how the NTR intersected with the Thaw's "culture of feelings," with *iskrennost'* chief among them. As Pomerantsev's article established, sincerity now meant rejecting the cult of personality.[20] During the Thaw anti-Stalinists saw themselves on the right side of history; they believed sincerity and Khrushchev's policies would lead the USSR into the future. This view, Kozlov and Gilburd explain, guided *shestidesiatniki* such as Trifonov, who were "civicminded" in a way that promoted Leninist democracy over Stalinist hierarchy.[21] During the Thaw the author believed *iskrennost'* to be the force behind society's transformation through the material world. However, Trifonov did not realize that he envisioned *telesnost'*, technology, and sincerity in ways that repeated many Stalinist assumptions while repudiating the repressive policies of the previous era.

Visiting Tomorrow: Trifonov's Turkmenia Stories

Trifonov tied the Thaw to Turkmenia in ways that reveal how Russian ideas about the region directed the Soviet experience. He portrayed Central Asia

46 Enthusiasm and Ambivalence

in physical terms (images of the body and technology); these portrayals first appeared in *Under the Sun*, short stories that shaped his anti-Stalinist novel, *Slaking the Thirst*. Both celebrated Khrushchev's plans to control the natural world, a continuation of 1930s policies. The *rasskazy* and *roman* focused on the Karakum Canal, a grandiose, environmentally catastrophic project to irrigate Turkmenia with water from the Amur Darya River. As with *Students*, these works are not well written but are important because of what they impart about Soviet culture.[22]

Trifonov's fascination with Turkmenia began in the 1940s at the Gorky Literary Institute. The author recalled sitting in Konstantin Fedin's seminar: "Maybe it was unconscious. Maybe it was the atmosphere we breathed in during those seminars—of travel, romanticism, searches for authenticity [*dostovernosti*]. Konstantin Georgievich wrote and related much about maps. About his love of poring over them. The Caspian, Krasnovodsk, the desert around Kazandzhik, the Valley of Atrek—how I explored them and touched them while still sitting in Moscow!"[23] Even before writing his first novel, the author dreamed of "authenticity" in an era of lies, exploring with his mind's eye the desert and Caspian shore. The USSR's hinterlands had already influenced Trifonov's life and that of his relatives: his mother was imprisoned in Kazakhstan from 1938 to 1945. After the revelations about his father's identity, Trifonov traveled to Turkmenia and, in the words of his widow, attempted to make Central Asia "his own" while differentiating *Slaking the Thirst* from his first novel.[24] As the stereotyped Uzbek character in *Students* shows, Trifonov was unaware of the problems inherent in a Russian depicting Central Asia in such tritely offensive terms. *Under the Sun* and *Slaking the Thirst* contain disturbing assumptions about Central Asia, progress, and Russians' right to speak about those on the periphery of the Soviet empire.[25]

Under the Sun enlists workers and technology to demonstrate the sincerity of the younger generation. In "Bako" the narrator praises the growth of a western Turkmen oil town: "Streets appear, buildings sprout up with apartments no worse than Moscow's, with balconies, gas, electricity. And in the courtyards between the buildings camels wander, calling out to one another in their strange, squeaky voices. . . . And people come from all over: Turkmens, Russians, Kazakhs from tiny villages [*kibitochnogo 'kazakh-aula'*], Azeri oil workers, Jews, Ossetians, Persians and Latvians—they all somehow resembled one another. . . . This is the way people become similar, creating something great together: a new religion, a revolution, or a new small city."[26]

The paragraph proffers platitudes about the periphery. New apartments "not worse than Moscow's" exist alongside camels as living symbols of the orient. It is "oil workers" who bring the gas and electricity to this town; the NTR and technical intelligentsia are remaking Turkmenia. Those in the city have varying ethnicities yet "somehow resembled one another"—according to the 'friendship of peoples,' the construction effort subsumed all differences. These men and women became a single-minded whole, united by belief in the system. Trifonov was seduced by this new version of certainty; under Stalin the goal was destroying the opposition and protecting the USSR, in the Thaw it was constructing communism. Critics at the time had mixed opinions about *Under the Sun*. For Z. Finitskaia, the stories suffered from lack of scope and could not move beyond the lives of individuals; I. Iakimenko, however, lauded them for connecting the prose and poetry of life, a pairing that contrasted the banality of *byt* and higher meaning of *bytie*. Both critics defined literary merit by joining the specific (a new oil town) to something larger and more meaningful (how the USSR was reinventing itself).[27]

"Bako" contained some personages that detracted from the positive image of the NTR. The main character's wife is a Russian of German ancestry who has had many abortions; this implies that Turkmenia is growing yet those who live there cannot support a large family. Technological progress has outstripped the infrastructure needed for daily life, a problem that began with Stalinism and lasted throughout the Soviet period. The narrator also briefly mentions Valentina Semenovna, a "lonely, middle-aged woman, thrown into this region by the vicissitudes of fate" [*prevratnostiami sud'by*]. She reads French, adores the modernist poet Innokentii Annenskii and, readers may assume, shares something with the protagonist's spouse: Stalinist repression brought her to Turkmenia. These two women indicate how socialism's successes mask a low standard of living and the legacy of trauma.[28]

The story "Hourglass" ("Pesochnye chasy") offers a more intriguing vision of Central Asia. Its autobiographical protagonist stands near ancient ruins in Turkmenia, pondering the rise and fall of empires. Noting that his time to die is still distant, he conveys confidence in the personal and national future. The narrative becomes more complex when it turns to the old man guarding the site. This minor figure cannot provide any information about the place's history. Instead, he complains about the delay in getting pension paperwork from his former kolkhoz; as Gillespie states, struggling with difficulties in the present forces the old man to ignore the past. "Hourglass" draws on the Thaw trope of the little man (*malen'kii chelovek*) abandoned by the system Stalin set up.[29]

The story's deeper meaning is more foreboding. The narrator muses: "When you walk down a dune, your leg sinks up to the ankle in sand. It is like walking in water. The white sand quietly rustles and flows, sliding down in layers. I feel as if I will be transported into eternity, swimming in the sands of an enormous hourglass. Civilizations and kingdoms, hordes of conquerors, peoples as numerous as the sands—all ground up by time, all turned into quietly rustling, white, silent sand."[30] The narrator is no longer gathering information about how technology changes this mysterious land. Power over the desert dissipates as the "rustling" but "silent" sands render the protagonist small and lost in "eternity." His hopes, and the Soviet attempt to control the future, will be covered by the drift of time. "Hourglass" is profoundly divided between the young protagonist's faith in tomorrow and the past of shifting sands.[31]

The collection's opening and closing stories focus on the desert, which Trifonov's autobiographical narrator sees first from an airplane and depicts as brown, dead, and threatening. One of the other passengers comments that soon this wasteland will be used for agriculture. After landing the narrator realizes there is nothing stronger than human nature, implying that the irrigation project will conquer the region. The last story in the cycle, "Under the Sun," concludes with the protagonist once again seeing the desert as he departs for Moscow. This time the Karakum Canal glimmers like a steel rail as it cuts through the sand. Comparing the new waterway to train tracks suggests the romantic images of the 1930s and projects such as Turksib, which connected Central Asia to Siberia. Time appears unidirectional and firmly under Soviet control.[32] However, the desert that opens and closes *Under the Sun* reifies a cyclicality that will outlast the narrator, canal, and socialism as a whole. Slavist Ewa Nikadem-Malinowska likens the Karakum to a black hole, which swallows thoughts and even memory. As in "Hourglass," the desert is a powerful symbol of all that is beyond human control as the arid expanse becomes the graveyard of technology and its masters. Despite Trifonov's efforts to assert otherwise, the desert shows that the Russian/Soviet center cannot impose progress on the Turkmen periphery. Instead, it is the periphery that directs how those from the center experience time. *Under the Sun* was more than a loosely linked series of impressions extolling modernization: the stories harbored subtle but deep concerns about the physical world burying human efforts in the sands of time.[33]

Enthusiasm and Ambivalence 49

The Thin Present: Between Past and Future in *Slaking the Thirst*

Trifonov's second novel built on the paradoxes of *Under the Sun*. *Slaking the Thirst*, the first long work Trifonov published following *Students*, appeared thirteen years afterward. Writer Fedor Abramov praised *Slaking the Thirst* for its landscapes and people, an observation that shows the myriad ties of Soviet literature: a leading voice in village prose commented on a Moscow author who depicted Central Asia.[34] This acclaim suggested there was more to *Slaking the Thirst* than uneven artistic merit (Trifonov later noted that the novel did not deserve the praise it received). Its two parallel plots were embedded in the triumphs and travails of the Thaw. One, recalling the production novel, extols those digging the Karakum Canal. The second storyline centers on conflicted journalist Petr Koryshev, a member of the intelligentsia; his father was executed in 1937 but now he eagerly reports on the canal's construction. Both plots intersect when Koryshev defends the canal's boss, the talented but unorthodox Ermasov, against Stalinist political opponents. 1956 and the Twentieth Party Congress dominated the novel; most of the plot transpires a year later, with an epilogue taking place shortly thereafter. These storylines work poorly together but their clumsiness exemplifies the contradictions of Thaw culture as it tried to reconcile Stalinism's aftershocks with the NTR's promises of tomorrow.[35] The present is trapped between these two moments; in Trifonov's novel it is merely the temporal battlefield on which an unresolved past threatened the future. This is most evident in the epilogue, which attempts to merge both plots: Ermasov has finished work on the canal and Koryshev is a published author. Critics at the time were unconvinced by this convergence and decried the ending as artificial.[36]

Current events have a strong presence in *Slaking the Thirst*; Cold War competition and de-Stalinization have replaced the dangers of toadying to the West that preoccupied *Students*. Koryshev is quizzed about the recent Picasso exhibition in Moscow; canal workers debate which Western nation is to blame for the Suez crisis. The construction project itself symbolizes time as progress: one Turkmen critic from the 1960s claimed the novel depicted irrigation as the common goal for his Soviet republic.[37] The novel follows the Karakum project as excavators and engineers advance into the desert, where arcane debates over construction become existential questions. The production plot adopted the arrogant optimism of socialist realism, which believed the USSR could and must remake humanity and nature for a brighter future.

50 Enthusiasm and Ambivalence

Slaking the Thirst conflates the NTR, progress, and superiority over the natural world. While flying over the Karakum an engineer curses the desert as a scoundrel whom he could beat into submission with fifteen bulldozers. The violent language of the boast evokes an unsettled past: before the Karakum there was Stalin's failed Main Turkmenistan Canal. As a scientist makes clear in the novel, the desert must be controlled; if not, the Karakum could expand, the Caspian Sea could shrink, and even the distant Sahara could grow and thus make Europe hotter.[38] This is a sadly prescient claim given climate change and the destruction of the Aral (but not Caspian) Sea, with the second catastrophe a result of the canal itself. Trifonov's early works assumed nature to be the enemy of the NTR and its linear conception of time; the canal represented Soviet culture channeling the flow of history to serve the needs of socialism. Trifonov did not realize that exploiting the environment was the ultimate form of consumption.[39]

The ending of *Slaking the Thirst* is less certain in its assertions. After enumerating various successes in the novel's epilogue, Koryshev describes his own mixed feelings: "No, I didn't feel bored. There just arose some sort of longing for hope [*tomiashchee chuvstvo nadezhdy*] and desire to get a glimpse of what is in the distance. . . . This is what happens when you part for a long time, forever, and a new life glimmers before you, and it is as if the old one remains behind a glass door: people are moving around, talking, but they are almost not audible."[40] Koryshev starts with a nod to the future as he envisions looking into the distance, "longing" for the optimism of "hope." However, this devolves into a sense of loss. The past is locked behind its "glass door," as unreachable as Koryshev's murdered father. There is no sense of the present in the passage. What is happening now is only a transition between yesterday's trauma and an uncertain future.

Builders of Communism, Victims of Stalin

Images of the body at first seem simplistic compared with Koryshev's musings. Soviet critics praised the novel's focus on the enthusiastic younger generation (one entitled his review "The Youth of the Soul"). Another asserted that the author's personal history was the biography of his time: now Valentin Trifonov's death became a symbol of the Thaw, erasing his son's previous support of Stalinism.[41] The canal's builders have the certainty and strength that Thaw culture carried over from the 1930s–1940s. Fit physique, the narrative suggests, means sincere devotion to transforming Turkmenia. Marina, one of those working on the canal, is twenty, blue-eyed, and "tall, with big

Enthusiasm and Ambivalence 51

shoulders, a sunburnt, simple face. . . . She looked older than her years—her face was like a girl's but her figure was full, powerful, like a young married woman [*kak u dobroi molodukhi*]" with "high breasts under her shirt." Marina's solid build, resembling that of Olia in *Students*, implies unyielding energy for the Karakum project. As in Trifonov's first novel, *telesnost'* follows the ideals of socialist realism. Marina eventually parts from her greedy husband Nagaev when he refuses to repair a burst dam without extra pay. She then has a miscarriage when she helps with the breach, symbolically sacrificing her unborn child to help the nation.[42]

In the novel the body justifies Soviet policies in Central Asia. Bairim is Nagaev's apprentice but used to be a shepherd and, as the narrator observes, resembles a camel. A Komsomol member, he has married recently and misses his bride's "timid breasts" and "eyes wet with tears," but more often he dreams of levers on the excavator that symbolizes the NTR. Koryshev feels a strange annoyance when Bairim's father-in-law spouts banalities about the canal.[43] The father-in-law is later implicated in killing Bairim and attempting to sell his own daughter, now widowed, to receive a second bride price. Koryshev wonders what motivated the murder: wealth, love, or something that only the East comprehends. Trifonov is not interested in understanding his Turkmen characters. The unfortunate end of Bairim and his bride is a well-worn trope of Soviet orientalism; the reader is furious that backward customs linger within socialist modernity. The couple's fate justifies the need for the state to transform private life and thus civilize the actions between bodies. Presumably this goal will be achieved when the canal is finished—the novel implies that technology will alter human behavior as well as the desert.[44]

The primitive East is not the only threat. *Slaking the Thirst* envisioned Stalinism and its legacy as a disease afflicting both characters and the body politic. Koryshev is discouraged when he is slow to be hired as a journalist: he is still suspect despite his father's rehabilitation. The protagonist laments that he cannot eradicate the "self-doubt" that plagues him "like a virus" (readers discover these problems even before learning Koryshev's name). He contemplates the relationship between time and death after an onset of panic, realizing that "these episodes are familiar. It seems to me that they come from time. Usually we don't feel time, it flows through us unnoticed, but sometimes it gets caught on something and for a moment we are terrified: it is like the approach of death. But then it goes away, like an attack of asthma."[45] Koryshev's "virus" causes "episodes" that make him equate the passage of

52   Enthusiasm and Ambivalence

time with mortality; he is the first Trifonov character to fear that the past robs the present of meaning, a worry that is expressed through the body.[46]

Koryshev's biography resembles Trifonov's own in terms of *telesnost'*, trauma, and history. The protagonist recalls standing outside a Moscow prison in 1938, trying to glean news of his father. Later Koryshev complains that time has little meaning because "real life" ended for him at eleven when the NKVD seized his parent. Since then his existence has been "unreal" as he and other victims of Stalin try to rectify what cannot be corrected. This feeling exemplifies Oushakine's description of responses to trauma: survivors and relatives try to re-create a sense of wholeness that compensates for what they have lost. Koryshev is Trifonov's second Hamlet figure. Unlike Vadim in *Students*, he recognizes the horror of what has happened. This version of Shakespeare's character is paradoxical, combining recognition of previous tragedy with optimism for the future.[47]

Journalist Denis Kuznetsov has a more harrowing past and is ultimately destroyed by trauma. He has been away from his family for sixteen years because of war, imprisonment by the Nazis, then being a refugee until a Soviet amnesty allowed him to return. His wife is remarried, his son has forgotten him, and Kuznetsov's mother dies of shock after receiving a letter from him. Time has stolen youth and happiness, leading Koryshev to comment: "it was impossible to demand anything—what can you demand from time?"[48] This succinct statement combines resignation and recognition of injustice. Kuznetsov perishes while trying to plug a leak in one of the canal's dams. Thaw critics praised him for giving his life to save the project, yet there is a less positive interpretation: Kuznetsov dies as he lived, drowned by the fascist and Stalinist systems that took meaning from his life and then life from his body.[49]

Slaking the Thirst, Sincerity, and the Torrent of Time

For *Slaking the Thirst* mourning the past and building the future are inseparable from *iskrennost'*. In Ashkhabad the protagonist follows a spirited exchange linking literal and metaphorical thirst; after praising the Karakum Canal the discussion turns to truth and justice: "Do you know how Turkmens quench their thirst? Just listen: to begin with they quench the 'little thirst,' two or three small glasses, and then, after eating supper, the 'large thirst,' when they'll finish off a whole teapot. And a man coming in out of the desert is never given a lot of water. Just a little bit at a time." "Otherwise

Enthusiasm and Ambivalence

it will make him sick," said Platon Kir'ianovich. "It won't make anyone sick! That's nonsense! I don't believe it," said Tamara excitedly. "How can there be too much truth [*pravdy*]? Or too much justice [*spravedlivosti*]?"[50]

Construction is equated with rebuilding truth and justice, values central to how the Thaw intelligentsia saw sincerity. The passage was a favorite for 1960s critics because it highlighted Trifonov's enthusiasm for *iskrennost'* as a principle purportedly shared by all in Soviet culture. The scene also drew attention to the secondary meaning of the novel's title: quenching moral thirst by renouncing Stalin. It is a physical image (drinking) that provides the metaphor that conveys these axioms of Thaw society.[51]

Koryshev for his part is obsessed with justice. Near the end of the novel, he publicly declares his love of *spravedlivost'* when Ermasov is investigated following a hostile newspaper article. This persecution, with its whiff of Stalinist attacks on enemies of the people, provokes Koryshev to defend those who act boldly and oppose rigid thinking. The protagonist declares, "There is nothing more dangerous than dogma: religious, philosophical, or even in the form of planning an irrigation canal." At this moment the production plot and Koryshev's storyline converge. Both oppose "dogma," which hinders constructing communism as well as the canal and evokes the cult of personality. At the same time, this moment in the plot resembles speeches in *Students* where characters denounce their peers and professor. The similarity illuminates how Trifonov's early prose joins sincerity to justice as a societal virtue, whether this involves Vadim "unmasking" Kozel'skii or Koryshev decrying the brutality of this same process. The author himself was unaware of this commonality.[52]

The novel worries that *iskrennost'* along with justice is under attack. Cynical journalist Sasha Zurabov voices a thought that will run throughout Trifonov's prose in the Brezhnev era: everyone has become used to lies. Another character connects dishonesty to cronyism, blaming Stalinist attitudes for the delay in publishing Koryshev's article on the canal: "There is momentum [*inertsiia*]. There are old acquaintances, there is the habit of working in the old way: without asking anyone for advice, without explaining, in a way that . . . is undemocratic." "Momentum" is a crucial word in this novel, implying that the falsehood of Stalinism is invisible but still powerful. Society must oppose this force and return to the 'democratic' norms of socialist culture.[53]

Elsewhere the novel identifies a similar but less politicized problem. While listlessly reading Plutarch's account of the Parthians, Koryshev worries about

54 Enthusiasm and Ambivalence

his own fate: "It seemed to me that I was losing time, lagging behind, I was dying. Dead [*Pogib*]! If I don't start something very soon and do some serious work—write about something I at least know, my life, Turkmenia, about how time can fracture [*lomaetsia vremia*], how some people come and others go and how I turn around and around in this current as it rushes along amid the noise and the din—if I don't start to simply take down notes, take down notes every day, I am dead, dead!"[54]

The "momentum" of the previous discussion is now "the noise and the din" of an uncontrollable flood. The past inundates the present with a "current" that "rushes along" and threatens to carry off Koryshev. This is a key image for *Slaking the Thirst* and Trifonov's post-Stalinist prose. Throughout the novel the narrator compares his personal life to this same "current." Having sex with his girlfriend, he thinks that the flow is sweeping him along like a speck. Later, wondering if he should end their relationship, he decides not to act, noting that the torrent is carrying him once again. Critics at the time misread this as Koryshev overcoming the Stalinist past. They failed to see a key problem. Koryshev fears the rush of time can be neither stopped nor resisted, just as Trifonov was uncertain that we can control our own life or history.[55]

Trifonov's second novel takes place in an era overshadowed by yesterday and tomorrow. Koryshev and Kuznetsov are consumed by the trauma of the purges and war, while the Karakum Canal promises a better day to come. *Slaking the Thirst* preserved the terrifying right to judge that *Students* established but now turned its wrath on Stalinism. The novel likewise continues the cult of technology, assuming the NTR would remake both the landscape and the mindset of Turkmenia. Characters' bodies evinced enthusiasm for the canal or bemoaned the lingering effects of repression as the novel's faith in the future competed with worry over the past.

Illuminating *Iskrennost'* in *The Bonfire's Glow*

In 1966 Trifonov published a *dokumental'naia povest'* about his father commanding Red forces in the Don, Caucasus, and Ural regions during the Civil War. As Trifonov explains at the beginning of the novella, his father had wanted to write an account of the Red Army (which Valentin Trifonov helped found). However, his arrest caused this task to fall to his son, who hoped to clear his father's name. In the process Trifonov examined how authors depict history by gathering and manipulating materials from the past. *The Bonfire's Glow* is a product of trauma, allowing the writer to explore issues he was too young to discuss with his father. In the 1990s Trifonov's sister would voice her frustration in a much starker manner, asking readers why their father had dug his own grave by protesting Stalin's disastrous policies. Trifonov did not see the similarities between this novella and *Slaking the Thirst*; both works featured sincere believers, the promise of a better tomorrow, and devotion to a common cause. These created terrifying results: the dying Aral Sea and the bloody beginning of the Soviet state. The two narratives unintentionally indicted the intelligentsia, which Trifonov believed to have supported first the revolution and then the state's assault on the natural world.[56]

The Bonfire's Glow was Trifonov's first major work to entirely focus on the past. As Clemens Günther explores in his dissertation, the novella follows Thaw assumptions that historical truth could be determined and conveyed to the reader. The era believed that sincerity can and must guide understanding of what has come before. Unlike in *Slaking the Thirst*, *iskrennost'* is not embodied in muscular workers building the future. Instead, it must be located by sifting through the physical evidence left by history. Trifonov's narrator outlines the problems of working with the sources he has gathered.[57] He notes:

> All of this began after reading papers that were found in a trunk. Within them facts nestled, they smelled like history but because these papers were preserved by accident [*byli sluchainy*], they were kept in a haphazard way and in them the life of [Valentin Trifonov] was glimpsed in excerpts, bits and pieces, and sometimes what was most important was missing and the insignificant came to the forefront. Because of this, in what is written below there is no well-constructed story, genuine grasp of events, enumeration of important names necessary for a historical account, and there is not the sequential structure needed for a biography.[58]

Objects impede our understanding of the past. Disorganized and scattered, the evidence must be carefully reconstructed to make sense of the "bits and pieces." The start of *The Bonfire's Glow* points out the need for careful arrangement, as opposed to the simple amassing of "facts" that "smell like history." In reality Trifonov researched these materials in an archive: the trunk as prop heightens the drama of discovering the documents and the need for the author to transform them into a coherent vision of the past.[59]

Trifonov was desperate to redeem his father's name yet had to rely on records that created their own difficulties. The narrator ponders this when discussing documents that now seem important: "Time and space sometimes make into art that which was not art—for this reason I think time has a strange power: the gift of making things into art [*dar khudozhestvennosti*]. Diaries, letters, business correspondence, trial records and military reports take on an unexpected quality with the passage of years. Poetry appears in old and simple words, uttered in passing long ago just to get something done."[60] "Simple words" and mundane missives become "art," a curious transformation that comes from probing the objects of bygone years. One person's words "uttered in passing" become "poetry" to later generations. This is inevitable but has disquieting implications for those investigating the past: what survives is special yet also distorted. Memories of history, Trifonov suggests, are inherently selective, preserving only the fragments that withstand "the passage of years." The material world can mislead the unwary author or scholar.

Thaw readers and writers argued for a more objective approach to the past. One critic demanded a truthful account of Valentin Trifonov's career, believing his son's archival research and the passage of time would help this cause. However, accuracy was not enough. In a recent study, Viacheslav Sukhanov asserts that this novella's ethos of honesty comes from organizing sources into a narrative: it is precisely Trifonov's skill as an author that creates a sincere approach to the past. Sukhanov assumes that this arrangement of the facts was motivated by the altruism and compassion that Russian culture pairs with *iskrennost'*. The critic ignores the implications of this claim: emotion is not the enemy of truthfulness. Instead, the problem is emotion that is directed toward the wrong end, as when Stalin stoked hatred against his enemies, including Valentin Trifonov.[61]

The writer was far from neutral as he depicted a father whom he lost as a boy, then betrayed by writing *Students*, and now eulogized. *The Bonfire's Glow*, an extended conversation with the dead, has strong overtones of Hamlet considering his father's murder. It is no coincidence that Ivanova ties this image to a central question for Trifonov: "to be or not to be?"[62] *The Bonfire's Glow* lets Trifonov speak for his father's ghost as the son tries to work through a trauma that encompassed his entire generation. The alternative would be a kind of second death for Valentin Trifonov, as the narrator in *The Bonfire's Glow* laments: "That which time has killed is killed forever and that which lives on lives a surprising, changed life."[63] In the context of Soviet culture this language was literal as well as metaphorical—the dead were destroyed once more when no one remembered them. What "lives on" was altered; what was not recalled never existed. The son did not know where his father was buried yet linked him to the spirit of the revolution, writing a documentary novella to serve as his gravestone.

Conflagration gives *The Bonfire's Glow* its title, showing how Trifonov increasingly used the physical world to pair history with trauma. The narrator opens and closes the documentary novella by describing an overpowering blaze that spread from the Civil War to the ensuing Soviet era. Gathering materials for the book, Trifonov noticed: "They were all tinged with red, a reflection of that huge, humming bonfire in whose flame Russia's previous life burned to ashes." At the end of the work, the narrator concludes: "And the bonfire rumbles, blazes, and lights up our faces and will light up the faces of our children and those who come after them."[64]

The optimistic closing of *The Bonfire's Glow* evokes the romanticism of the Civil War, the sincere enthusiasm of the Bolsheviks, and assumes that the revolution has outlasted the Stalinist attempt to smother it. This was an appealing image for Trifonov and Thaw culture as a whole. Both the author and his era assumed the Leninist course was correct, with the cult of personality a temporary albeit terrifying digression.[65] Dobrenko gives a less optimistic reading: the blaze's glow is the last light of revolution, dying amid the darkness of Stalinism. Indeed, the revolution's flames "burned to ashes" Valentin Trifonov and others who ignited them. Using fire as a metaphor raises a series of problems for Trifonov. First, Dedkov extols the Thaw precept that people must control history instead of being consumed by it. The novella, however, demonstrates that history's momentous events are deliberately begun yet overwhelm their masters. Using an elemental force as a comparison, Trifonov inadvertently implies the USSR has failed to control the material world or even its own ideology: the flame Valentin Trifonov started became the conflagration of Stalinism. This image of burning, along with time as current in *Slaking the Thirst*, symbolized Trifonov's worry that his culture could not direct history. Its failure will leave humanity at the mercy of the inexorable forces that *Under the Sun* also portrays.[66]

Trauma creates a series of significant silences in *The Bonfire's Glow*. Trifonova noted that the novella's final section had to be cut because it detailed how Valentin Trifonov helped choose the location of the Lubyanka Prison. Likewise, there is no description of Bolshevik reprisals against the Don Cossacks, despite this very subject being a major theme in *The Old*

58   Enthusiasm and Ambivalence

Man, a later novel by the author. Trifonov, like many *shestidesiatniki*, was the child of a true believer and thus could not challenge the foundational myth of the USSR: the Leninist state was just and did not create its horrific Stalinist epigone.[67] Trifonov's *dokumental'naia povest'* was less document than hagiography as the son assembled, omitted, and transformed the facts of his father's life. *The Bonfire's Glow* served as an exemplary Thaw narrative in its pathos of sincerity, Hamletism, and belief in the future by condemning the past. However, conflagration as a central image questioned whether Soviet culture could come to terms with its history.

"It Was Noon in Summertime": Journey into Trauma

Trifonov's little-studied story "It Was Noon in Summertime" ("Byl letnii polden'," 1966) was a major shift in the author's prose, anticipating the intelligentsia's retreat from public participation into private disappointment after the Prague Spring. Similar to *The Bonfire's Glow*, it depicted the past as trauma but deliberately implied that such tragedy was insurmountable. In the plot Ol'ga Robertovna returns to her native Baltic city, a problematic area for Soviet culture. Unlike in Turkmenia, modernization could not justify Soviet occupation of this periphery, long seen as more Western than Russia.

Remarking that she should have come twenty years ago, Ol'ga Robertovna laments that she no longer has any friends there. She is in the city for an exhibit commemorating her husband and has not visited since 1917, when as a young worker she helped the revolution. The struggle to establish the new Soviet state is followed by imprisonment and then rehabilitation for herself and her husband, who died suddenly in the 1930s and thus escaped arrest (his glasses, beard, and fighting on the southern front recall Valentin Trifonov). Ol'ga Robertovna's son killed himself in 1939, the year of the non-aggression pact giving the Baltics to the Nazis; some acquaintances moved to Russia during the Civil War and others perished in a ghetto. The Baltics become a locus of the combined tragedies of Stalinism, Nazi occupation, and the passage of time.[68]

The last page of the story provides a powerfully brief summary of Ol'ga Robertovna's suffering under Stalin. She recalls

> the sweet smell of tobacco mixed with quiet conversations so that the children could not hear but the children knew, and once [her husband] said "Get ready. It will happen to me, too" but it did not happen to him but to her; he died unexpectedly in their private apartment on Vozdvizhenka and she

discovered three years later when she was in the Far East that he had died; her forebearers had passed on their slow Baltic blood, her hands were not afraid of work and became crooked like those of a hired laborer, she worked, bore [*vynesla*] everything, returned, her son was gone, her daughter looked at her with alien eyes and addressed her with the formal "you," and she bore that, too, bore that whole long road, which had begun here in this dusty courtyard, hot from the sun, littered with scraps of clasps, and she had crossed through [*peresekla*] that courtyard.[69]

This telescoped personal history encompasses the fate of her generation. Like Valentin Trifonov, Ol'ga Robertovna was a sincere supporter of the revolution. Because they were Old Bolsheviks she and her husband thought he would be arrested but instead she was; he died suddenly (as did Trifonov's uncle in 1937). She learned of his death while in the gulag; when she returned her son was gone and her daughter was estranged. Ol'ga Robertovna "bore that whole long road" of loss, imprisonment, return, and isolation. Her hands are "crooked" because of working in the camps, where her "slow Baltic blood" and strong constitution helped her survive. Ol'ga Robertovna displays the *telesnost'* of trauma, which Trifonov conveys with a few subtle words. "It Was Noon" provides a first, compactly brilliant example of years passing in the space of a single paragraph; such deep brevity is a hallmark of the author's late works. This story evinces that Trifonov has moved from what Gusev labels the "horizontal" description of his earlier writing to the richer, "vertical" description of his Brezhnev-era prose. Dedkov praises the "verticals" in Trifonov's later prose as roads that guide the reader into history. By comparison the abundant details and long passages in *Students* and *Slaking the Thirst* are bloated and superficial. This new economy of prose appeared alongside a shift from the future to the past as Trifonov and his society lost faith in their brighter tomorrow.[70]

In the story's final paragraph, Ol'ga Robertovna has returned to Moscow. Waiting in line to buy milk, she tells a neighbor only that it rained when she was in the Baltics. This coda, also a feature of Trifonov's late prose, reasserts what Ivanova saw as the reality of daily life. "It Was Noon" was his first work to combine history and *byt* as two inevitable, interconnected factors shaping experience. Ol'ga Robertovna is simultaneously a widow, Old Bolshevik, gulag survivor, mother, and one of the many women standing in line. The banal conversation in the epilogue indicates that society is no longer interested in the trauma of the past.[71]

Ol'ga Robertovna's recollections suggest that the intelligentsia realized it had become the hostage of its own empire. The protagonist helped create the state that imprisoned her and destroyed her family.[72] Unlike Koryshev or the narrator of *The Bonfire's Glow*, she does not assume that sincerity and justice will triumph. Her small victory is one that is private, not public—she has "crossed through" the horrors of the twentieth century and "bore everything" without being destroyed. This survival is all *intelligenty* can hope for at the end of the 1960s. "It Was Noon" negated the Thaw's optimism, search for sincerity, and hope for the future. Ol'ga Robertovna knows that only individual memory can honestly address history and the path she has traveled. Her tired body hints that tomorrow can no longer compete with the past.

Trifonov's prose showed that the Thaw was shaped by the material world as well as ideas. Both he and Soviet culture attempted to cautiously investigate history while preserving faith in what would come next. The effort had mixed results—belief in the NTR and socialist superiority existed alongside fear that the natural world might defeat both this generation and humanity as a whole. Trifonov revealed the 1950s and 1960s to be a fragile era defined by the trauma of yesterday and a tomorrow that was far from certain.

3

Empire of Objects

Sincerity and Consumption in the 1970s

"What is happening to the moral content of humanity? For some reason it seems that *Homo sapiens* is becoming deformed, that is, in some way changing its form and maybe its essence under the influence of wars, terror, hunger, aviation, television, nuclear weapons and an abundance of frills. But some main principle remains!"[1] In a letter to West German author Martin Walser, Trifonov lamented the broad changes in humanity during the 1970s, pairing technology and consumption's "abundance of frills" with the mechanized brutality of the twentieth century. He speculated that people's basic nature was unchanged but then continues: "In our country people aren't afraid of what will happen tomorrow, which means that there is [no longer] this important stimulus for slavery [*rabstva*]. But what can be done about slavery of a different type: the slavery of moral poverty [*bezdukhovnosti*]? Of belching on a full stomach? Of indifference and disinterest toward everything that does not involve one's own precious persona?"[2]

Trifonov implied that the forced obedience of the 1930s–early 1950s had vanished yet "moral poverty" remained. "Full stomachs" rendered values less important than things; this corporeal metaphor reflected the problems of a society that had traded the "slavery" of Stalinism for the chains of consumption. The letter to Walser argued that the greatest conflict was not the ongoing Cold War; instead, it was the battle between humanity and a worldview dictated by objects, complacency, and greed.

Trifonov's prose provides new ways to examine the years from the Prague Spring to the early 1980s. Scholars often take a polarized approach to this era, condemning it via terms such as "Stagnation" or seeing the period as the USSR's golden years and the source of nostalgia for the socialist past.

62   Empire of Objects

Yurchak has a more useful stance, exploring how the intelligentsia retreated from sterile public culture into a surprisingly rich and variegated private life. During this epoch the USSR moved from looking toward the future to contemplating the past, even as the state silenced discussion of many topics (Stalinism, wartime losses and collaboration, ethnic minorities' oppression). For the intelligentsia a relatively high standard of living coincided with fears that morality had been sacrificed for goods and services. Trifonov's late prose broke new ground by suggesting that the roots of this problem were in fact formed decades before.[3]

My study devotes two chapters to the Brezhnev years, allowing for focused analyses of Trifonov's extraordinary output from the end of the 1960s to his untimely death in 1981. The author concentrated on the intelligentsia, searching for its causes of corruption even as he helped define the group's identity. Chapter 3 looks at his works from the late 1960s until the mid-1970s; these examine a present that was fully determined by the past. I first survey the ways that bodies, consumption, and sincerity shaped the era, then look at the author's best-known works: the Moscow novellas he published from 1968 to 1976, including his masterful *House on the Embankment*. The *povesti* had a huge impact on late Soviet writing: they portrayed *intelligenty*, concerns with everyday life, and protagonists whose moral shortcomings arise from greed. Both Chapters 3 and 4 delve into history and *byt* to understand how the material world threatened culture and people's attempts to understand the past. From the late 1960s onward, Trifonov consciously crafted works that showed how aging bodies, sincerity (or lack thereof), and consumption distorted characters' lives and Soviet culture as a whole. This intentional critique, as opposed to the false certainty of Stalinism or the ambiguity of his Thaw prose, bolstered the literary merit of his late writing.

Critics from 1968 to the present have described how this prose envisioned history as the battle between remembering and forgetting, whether on a collective or personal level. I expand on this approach, identifying *iskrennost'* as the core component of memory.[4] By the end of the Thaw the author no longer believed society could channel the flow of history; the next five years of his writing revealed that even honestly recalling the past was difficult. One reason was the USSR's refusal to discuss Stalinism, an omission that for Platt defined the era's approach to what had come before. The fragmentation of time was another problem. Unlike his writing from the 1940s– early 1960s, Trifonov's later works illustrated a today that no longer led to tomorrow—instead, history overshadowed the present and threatened the

Empire of Objects 63

future.[5] In this prose, everyday life provided small moments of truth that shed light on personal and national history. During an interview the author observed how past and present come together to create "what we swim in every day, every minute" while acting as "the thread connecting time" and "the nerve of history."[6] This was not the march toward communism proclaimed first by Stalin and then by Khrushchev. Instead, in Trifonov's writing past and present combined uneasily within *byt*, which itself was part of the uncontrollable current of time.

TAKING STOCK OF MIDDLE AGE: BODIES AND THINGS IN LATE SOVIET CULTURE

The Brezhnev years depicted bodies that were growing older as the USSR entered what leaders optimistically dubbed the "era of developed socialism." Films such as *Moscow Does Not Believe in Tears* looked at how youth's sexuality gave way to the quieter passions of middle age, where a stable family was the reward for believing in the promises of a better tomorrow. Baranskaia's *A Week Like Any Other* showed how newlyweds' desire dissolved into the routines of marriage, which demanded wives sacrifice for husbands and children. *Telesnost'* conveyed the costs that came with moving from idealism to the resignation of middle age. Critics even claimed that Trifonov's 1970s characters had bodies that could no longer feel joy. Urbanization, higher divorce rates, and increased access to education lowered population growth among the intelligentsia. The state worried that birth rates among Slavs were falling behind those in the Caucasus and Central Asia: Russians could become the minority in their own empire. As during Stalinism, procreation was politicized as a matter of national importance.[7]

The scholar Ol'ga Klimova, analyzing films in the Brezhnev era, outlines how bodies reified the power dynamics between young and old, parents and children, state and citizens. Youth lamented the lack of reliable advice on sexuality; for instance, the Russian translation of an East German manual for newlyweds counseled young people to choose reading or sports over carnal pleasure.[8] *Telesnost'* also reflected the upheavals that defined the Soviet Union. Village prose authors such as Valentin Rasputin used the battered bodies of older characters to eulogize a culture destroyed by modernity and collectivization. His *Farewell to Matyora* compared aging women to their beloved village; both were doomed by a society fixated on technology and wealth. Grekova explored the wounded female body and psyche in *The Ship of Widows*. She, Rasputin, and Trifonov established that the state's assault on corporeality was a legitimate theme for mainstream literature if the critique was limited and grounded in the past. This was a crucial precedent after 1968. The writers' connections between history, *byt*, trauma, and *telesnost'* influenced culture's sense of the past for decades to come.[9]

In the Brezhnev era the intelligentsia benefited from what James Millar terms the "Little Deal," where the state created a rising standard of living, especially in Moscow and Leningrad.[10] Alekseyeva, examining trends in interior design, noted a "rehabilitation of the object world" that allowed people to decorate without being called materialists. Oushakine discusses how campaigns against *veshchizm* (love of things) signaled that rational consumption was permissible but a passion for material goods was not; the boundaries between these two were unclear.[11] In the Brezhnev era, objects conveyed a social message that was more important than their price: deficit goods, jeans brought back from the West, and East German furniture conferred style and prosperity. During the 1960s there was a worry that objects' significance could outstrip their usefulness. Trifonov, like many in the intelligentsia, saw this as a threat to morality.[12]

The slowly increasing access to foreign goods furthered fear that consumption was changing relations between people and objects, as Viktoriia Tokareva's short story "A Japanese Umbrella" humorously suggested. Waiting to buy the eponymous item, the narrator realizes that "the people and things had changed places. The things had stretched out in a long line and were choosing people. The people were sitting in the kind of cardboard boxes that you pack televisions in, sticking their heads out and breathing in the fresh air."[13] There is a troubling reversal of animacy in this scene: objects become more alive than their owners. Increasingly prosperous consumers and a trickle of Western goods made *meshchanstvo* a prominent issue for intelligentsia and Party alike. Kabo had earlier characterized this problem as a contradictory condition where consumers were educated yet did not act accordingly. Ikonnikova argued that the right type of morality and behavior must accompany the USSR's improved level of material comfort. Trifonov's late prose explored the opposite tendency, which critics coined *nedochuvstvie* (insufficient feeling). This flaw conjoined greed, self-interest, and disregarding others. In his Moscow novellas, everyday life was the arena where *nedochuvstvie* and *meshchanstvo* bested morality. During Stalinism *meshchanstvo* had signaled disloyalty and a fondness for bourgeois values, while the Thaw had rejected it as a holdover from the cult of personality. Chapters 3 and 4 argue that the Brezhnev era, which deemphasized open conflict, critiqued *meshchanstvo* as a problem in the present but ignored how it came from those who gained power in the 1920s–1930s.[14] Worries over gender combined with anxiety over consumption. Stiazhkina notices that late Soviet culture condemned some women as *meshchanki* while labeling materialistic men as "soulless philistines" (*bezdukhovnye obyvateli*). The latter were passive and weak, an assumption reinforcing fears of "soft" men that dated back to the nineteenth century.[15]

The NTR, propelled by the space race and an increase in consumer electronics, played an ever more prominent role in consumption and the Cold War. Literary scholar A. Metchenko highlighted the political stakes when he asserted that Zbigniew Brzezinskii wanted US computers to control the world: socialism must not fall behind capitalist technology or the consequences would be dire. *Ivan Vasil'evich Changes His Profession* took a more lighthearted approach to the NTR. The film portrayed technology as a part of *byt* when its protagonist builds a time machine that brings Ivan IV to 1970s Moscow. The NTR's supporters maintained that technology met increasingly diversified consumer demand, applauding how it aided the "sphere of moral consumption" (*sfera dukhovnogo potrebleniia*). Such phrasing was anathema to skeptics such as Trifonov; "moral" behavior and "consumption" were mutually exclusive concepts for many *intelligenty*.[16]

Television was a special source of worry for the intelligentsia. By 1975 74 percent of Soviet households had a set; Golubev notes that doctors fretted the populace was suffering from "telemania." In the late 1960s Trifonov questioned the long-term effects of television, believing viewers were unknowingly "experimenting" on themselves (a concept drawn from the NTR's lexicon). Later in this same article, where he discussed the advent of broadcast sports in the USSR, Trifonov claimed that television may even shorten our lives. *Moscow Does Not Believe in Tears* linked television to vapid duplicity, while Grekova's *intelligenty* derisively ignored the "box." Television, these critiques conveyed, imperiled the real culture the intelligentsia lionized.[17] Even reading was under threat. Trifonov lamented that people were interested more in acquiring volumes than in reading them. Some consumers even bought books to match the décor of their apartments, including the television set now enthroned at the center of domestic life.[18]

Trifonov went so far as to pair television with the rise of terrorism. An avid consumer of news about the West, the author was horrified by Carlos the Jackal and the Baader-Meinhof Group. Those committing violence, he maintained, craved publicity from a culture that treated them like "film stars" because the media and terrorists had become "Siamese twins." Anninskii agreed, explaining that such extremists needed the (Western) press and a passive television audience—without them, he concluded, terrorism would vanish. This flawed assessment aligned with fears that the NTR had rendered people lethargic and even incapable of determining right from wrong. Anninskii explicitly employed the rhetoric of consumption, showing how Trifonov attacked terrorism as a "product" packaged for consumers. Trifonov claimed that the consequences of terrorism could be catastrophe; the author mentioned 175 attempts by terrorists to obtain nuclear material. Technology, he asserted, lowered moral barriers to violence and increased the consequences, a combination that could destroy the world.[19]

The intelligentsia feared that this changing environment threatened sincerity. As Vail and Genis explain, after the Prague Spring its members realized they were under attack by state policies. Living through crisis was part of the group's identity. Likewise, as Rutten reminds, *intelligenty* had long worried about imperiled *iskrennost'*.[20] Trifonov's letter to Walser, however, imparted a new urgency as consumption increasingly eclipsed ideas. Oleg Altaev (pseudonym of dissident Vladimir Kormer) believed that the NTR had already seduced the intelligentsia. Trifonov implicitly agreed when he asserted that the label "intelligentsia" had been too broadly applied: it was not enough to be highly educated. What was needed was the right morality.[21] Many in the Brezhnev era feared that Soviet society had exchanged the vitality and enthusiasm of earlier decades for insincerity, *meshchanstvo*, and apathy. Trifonov's prose hinted that the problem was more serious and complicated than a generational shift in values.

THE EXCHANGE AND TAKING STOCK:
BYT AND THE MORAL BACKWATER

Trifonov is best known for his Moscow novellas, works set mainly in the Soviet capital. Together these powerful narratives showed how the past configured the present, a truism that Trifonov reconceptualized by connecting daily life to the material world in a manner that diminished hope for the future. Unlike his writing from the Stalinist and Thaw periods, these novellas had what Gusev praised as a more profound, 'vertical' use of details; there were fewer descriptions but each was more effective. Minutiae were the foundation of *byt* in the *povesti* but at times also evoked memories that characters tried to forget. The outsized role played by the material world in

Empire of Objects

67

the process of recollection was itself a problem. If objects motivate the sense of the past, then the consumption that Trifonov laments in his letter to Walser controls yesterday as well as the present and tomorrow.

Critics fixated on the Moscow novellas' vision of *byt*. This was shorthand for focusing on 'unworthy' banality, yet everyday life allowed Trifonov to depict the morality behind it. Ivanova was one of the first critics to understand this; she perceived that the petty props of life in fact revealed characters' essence. Sukhanov, writing almost two decades later, builds on her statement and proclaims that Trifonov depicted the death of the soul. My study assumes that materiality was more than a collection of inert objects— the Moscow *povesti* narrated late Soviet culture as a war between things and morality, with the material world victorious.[22]

The first of these novellas, *The Exchange*, secured Trifonov's fame as the leading figure in the city prose (*gorodskaia proza*) movement. The *povest'* follows how the engineer Dmitriev, pressured by his wife (Lena), trades apartments and in the process deeply offends his ailing mother, an Old Bolshevik *intelligentka*. In the novella the quest for material comfort leads to loss of sincerity (the "exchange" in the work's title). This process occurs gradually throughout Dmitriev and Lena's marriage and results, as one critic claimed, in the couple switching morality for material comfort. The novella revolves around objects, including imported furniture and the middle-aged bodies of the protagonists themselves.[23] The narrator relates how "Dmitriev and Lena slept on a wide ottoman of Czechoslovakian make, luckily purchased some three years before, which was an object of envy among their acquaintances. . . . In the evening when they were lying on their Czech bed—which turned out to be not very durable, quickly getting rickety and squeaking with every move—Dmitriev and Lena always listened a long time for sounds . . . trying to figure out whether their daughter had gone to sleep or not."[24] The couple at first rejoiced over their fortunate "purchase," an "object of envy" that lacked the quality expected of a fashionable import. The ottoman becomes the physical and metaphorical location of tense, hushed arguments and, less frequently, quiet sex. Dmitriev, via the third-person narrator, notes that Lena's body makes the ottoman "crack under her weight" despite his wife lying down as gingerly as possible. The impractical bed symbolizes a marriage founded on material things well before the ill-fated idea to exchange apartments. Both spouses weigh more than when they first met. In the novella this is not simply a part of aging but a corporeal clue that Lena and Dmitriev carry an unacknowledged burden of moral compromise.[25]

The Exchange became a literary sensation. Readers stood in line to check out journals where the Moscow novellas were published, while critics were sharply divided. M. Sinel'nikov, for instance, assailed the author's personages as "not quite *intelligenty*" (*nedointelligenty*) and "philistines" (*meshchane*). These labels, ironically echoing Trifonov's own stringent ideas, assume the intelligentsia cannot be defined by a love of things. Furthermore, according to this logic, portraying *byt* was only justified because it highlighted the evils of consumption. This approach reduced Trifonov to the level of journalist and ignored how the *povest'* pictures an intelligentsia mired in the materialism.[26]

In their attack on *byt*, critics assumed female characters were obsessed with the world of things. Sinel'nikov labels Lena a "conquistador in a skirt." Yet the critic also notes how Dmitriev and his relatives benefit from her and her father's businesslike approach to problems such as fixing the dacha's septic system and installing a telephone. Selemeneva is more accurate. She outlines a continuum of female characters in Trifonov's late prose, from the "pragmatic" and "grabbing" to the selfless. This latter extreme contains those who are "almost holy fools," including Dmitriev's lover Tania, who loans him money out of kindness and pity. Such women suffer from male dishonesty and sacrifice themselves for others. The "grabbers," by contrast, include Lena and promulgate a *poshlost'* that opposes intelligentsia values. Despite some critics' ideas to the contrary, Trifonov's writing demonstrates that consumption is a sin of both genders.[27]

The second Moscow novella, *Taking Stock* (*Predvaritel'nye itogi*), receives more attention in this chapter due to being the last work among Trifonov's understudied Turkmenia narratives. Its title connotes a process of reflection that begins in the past but indicts the present as Gennadii Sergeevich flees his second wife and adult son in Moscow to translate a poem in Central Asia. Lack of *iskrennost'* is the transgression driving him to a region he dismisses as a literal and metaphorical backwater. Kirill, who has inherited has father's dishonesty and his mother's materialism, scorns his father for publishing "junk."[28] The protagonist himself does not speak Turkmen and, more to the point, knows that the poem is worthless; he is completing the translation for the money and to escape his family. Gennadii Sergeevich's actions constitute a literary version of the crass consumption that *intelligenty* abhor.[29]

As in *Slaking the Thirst*, the Turkmen are one-dimensional even when at the center of Gennadii Sergeevich's attention. Thinking about Yazgul, the wife of the caretaker who runs the rest home where he is staying, Gennadii Sergeevich muses that her face is old and worn from raising children:

> Her arms, however, which are usually bared to the elbow, look young and strong. And probably her body too, with its big stomach and heavy-hanging breasts just barely outlined under the folds of her *kuynak*, is still young and full of life. . . . Once, thinking about Yazgul, I had trouble falling asleep. It even frightened me a bit—though what did I have to be frightened about at this point? Actually, what I felt was a momentary flash of bitterness. A man becomes aware of his age only belatedly. It's the same way with a wife's infidelity: you don't suspect a thing, and everyone else already knows all about it.[30]

Yazgul is older than his wife, Rita, but her exotic dress and "young and strong" body excite him in a way his spouse does not. The protagonist's inner monolog and the novella's plot suggest that desire for Yazgul stems from his own fear of aging. Gennadii Sergeevich bitterly reflects on his own family. While his son criticizes his father for being a poor translator, Kirill nonetheless covets the jeans and records his father's salary and connections provide. Gennadii Sergeevich is disgusted by this hypocrisy; Ivanova believes that he should reflect on the father-son relationship instead of judging his child as a *meshchanin*.[31]

Taking Stock emphasizes Gennadii Sergeevich's crisis through an unusual variant of the water imagery that runs through many Trifonov works. In yet another moral lapse, he has sex with the young nurse, Valia, whom Yazgul and her husband adopted. At the same time, Gennadii Sergeevich slips into a memory of himself and Rita on a boating trip early in their marriage. At first the scene is nostalgic and comforting, but its conclusion resembles the pressures crushing the protagonist from the novella's beginning.[32] The first-person narrator observes, "The water was still warm, but the air seemed to disappear and there was nothing to breathe. The water was choking us. It was that same staircase on which I always felt myself suffocating. For some reason I had to keep climbing higher and higher—just one more step, just a little more effort—but there was simply no air."[33] Lying with Valia merges into being on the river with Rita, an initially soothing vision that soon becomes the literal and metaphorical suffocation threatening Gennadii Sergeevich.

The past overtakes the present; a moment of philandering pleasure devolves into a memory of his wife and the family crises bringing him to Turkmenia. Valia for her part is an episodic but significant character. The nurse explains to Gennadii Sergeevich that Yazgul is more important than her biological mother, adding that "relatives are those who do good things" (*Rodnye liudi—kto dobro delaet*). These simple words are one of the keys to Trifonov's late prose: kindness, the bedrock of sincerity, creates its own type of kinship. Valia's pronouncement is anomalous for being a positive example of how to live, instead of the numerous negative actions the writer's Brezhnev-era works portray.[34]

Moral failures are this novella's chief anxiety. Insincerity fouls Gennadii Sergeevich's alleged honesty as he enumerates errors as husband, father, and friend. His confession, however, is less atonement than gambit for sympathy. Lipovetsky and Leiderman discern that *Taking Stock* represents an intensification of the corrupting process Dmitriev undergoes in *The Exchange*.[35] Woll notices that Gennadii Sergeevich suffers from twenty years of the compromises Dmitriev fears, with this sickness taking corporeal form. The body does not dissemble, and Gennadii Sergeevich laments that he looks a decade older than his forty-seven years.[36]

The protagonist comes back to his wife and son; as one critic commented, the husbands in Trifonov's prose have nowhere else to go with their bad hearts and high blood pressure. The ambiguous epilogue makes it clear that the reconciliation is temporary. A few months after Gennadii Sergeevich returns from Turkmenia, he and Rita vacation near Riga. At the end of the novella the protagonist drily summarizes: "August turned out to be beautiful—sunny and clear, and not too hot. I took long walks every day and, as always, the Baltic climate had a healing effect: I was able to breathe deeply and evenly, my blood pressure went down to normal, and at the end of our stay I got hold of a racket and even played a little tennis."[37] His tone is hopeful yet reminds readers of the preceding narrative's connections between infirm bodies and inner death. Ivanova points out that Trifonov believed that the protagonist would die at the novella's conclusion, but then the author reconsidered. Gennadii Sergeevich must not perish—death would be too easy an escape from insincerity. Selemeneva expands on this, asserting that Trifonov critiques an intelligentsia whose members are spiritually dead yet feigning life. With these grim diagnoses the novella fits into a theme running throughout the Moscow *povesti*: the future no longer has meaning.[38]

Empire of Objects

The Long Goodbye and *Another Life*:
Moscow and the Material World

The Long Goodbye (*Dolgoe proshchanie*, 1971) also portrayed ethical crises rooted in the past. The novella chronicles the career of actress Lialia Telepneva as she chooses between two lovers, the calculating Smolianov and seemingly more moral Rebrov. The first of these two men, Ivanova notes, "knows how to live," which in Trifonov's writing denotes an unethical drive to consume all one can. Rebrov resembles the classic Moscow *intelligent* (or, rather, how the group sees itself): he is introspective, haunted by failure, and uninterested in the material world.[39]

The *povest'* contains a minor scene that illuminates the problem of describing the body and depicting trauma. Rebrov catches himself thinking about the appearance of his in-law Tamara Ignat'evna: "how repulsive a person's face must be examined under a magnifying glass, all its pores, little hairs, the unevenness of the skin. . . . And all we do is examine under a magnifying glass. Every minute, second, magnified a thousand times. But we need to look at all of time—years and everything. Then there would be no hate."[40] Rebrov realizes he should not find Tamara Ignat'evna "repulsive" since earlier the narrator implies that her "unevenness of the skin" comes from harsh winters in the gulag. These details, enlarged through focusing on the body, show the dangers of considering *telesnost'* without its context. Suffering has made Tamara Ignat'evna physically unappealing yet worthy of compassion. This passage exemplifies how the physical world reveals the soul. Tamara Ignat'evna's pores, hairs, and skin are the opposite of the firm young bodies in *Students*: one is evidence of victimhood, the other is a strength that oppresses Tamara Ignat'evna and others.

The past shapes characters in ways they do not understand. In the closing lines of *The Long Goodbye* Lialia likens the growing Soviet capital to her vanished youth. She is now the privileged wife of a military officer and long ago abandoned Rebrov, who is an influential script writer dating a woman young enough to be his daughter. Both main characters exemplify the connections between insincerity, consumption, and corporeality. Rebrov's self-satisfied *telesnost'* contrasts with the battered body of Tamara Ignat'evna; Lialia little resembles the naïve actress who defended herself against sexually predacious men. Their physique supports Gillespie's belief that the protagonists have abandoned what gave them meaning earlier in the novella.[41]

Another Life (*Drugaia zhizn'*, 1975) has a more thoughtful protagonist but still grapples with reconciling sincerity and material comfort. In this retrospective narrative scientist Ol'ga Vasil'evna remembers her marriage to historian Sergei before the heart attack that killed him. Ol'ga Vasil'evna is the character most closely allied with the NTR yet she elicits sympathy as the plot follows her grieving and recollections. The protagonist's discipline, biochemistry, is new to Soviet culture. Ol'ga Vasil'evna is searching for the chemical conditions for incompatibility and her project centers on what the novella calls a "single idea," a premise that ignores the multifaceted meanings inherent to existence. *Another Life* implies that connections come not from molecular bonds but the ties that bind. Love and *iskrennost'* render Ol'ga Vasil'evna a positive character despite material success and ties to technology.[42] She worries about the applications of her field, speculating that the unscrupulous could manipulate others through the biological basis for emotions. Given the state's use of drugs to torture dissidents, her fear is well founded—however, Trifonov's prose studiously ignored how Soviet science furthered political oppression in the 1970s.[43]

This novella characterizes the past and its trauma in remarkably physical terms. Sergei focuses on history's material nature but is not a materialist. He believes in a series of links between yesterday and today that present numerous interpretations, as opposed to the Marxist-Leninist view of history as moving steadily toward communism. Sergei jokingly refers to his research as "digging up graves," a visceral phrase foregrounding the role of violence as he investigates the 1917 revolution. For the scholars S. Eremina and V. Piskunov, Sergei gives voice to the dead, who carry the memories of the past (and sometimes were the victims of oppression). The critics' approach fits with Etkind's ideas on mourning, where those who survived must speak for the deceased. Sergei refuses to adhere to the code of silence that surrounds the excesses of the early Bolshevik years—this is one reason he never completes his dissertation.[44]

Consumption also plays a role in the *povest'*. When Ol'ga Vasil'evna's mother and stepfather Georgii Maksimovich move into a new apartment, their furnishings are transformed: "everything that in the old house had seemed like junk here acquired a special, expensive look of old-world distinction." Beginning with *Students*, Trifonov established the apartment as a semiotically charged locale that reveals much about its occupants. Georgii Maksimovich is compromised by his material possessions precisely because of the "old-world distinction" gained in their new context; the objects and their owner have changed to better fit in with what surrounds them.[45] This moment evokes an intriguing tenet that Trifonov borrowed from Tolstoy.

Discussing the famous author, Trifonov concurred with his assertion that we must change ourselves before remaking society. Otherwise, Trifonov noted, it will be "as if I plan to renovate my apartment and begin to live according to my conscience, but in the meantime, while there is dirty wallpaper and old furniture, I have the right to live in a bad way. And it ends up that wallpaper is to blame for a man's bad actions."[46] This observation crystallized Trifonov's concerns over the world of things. He rejected the idea that objects determine the "spiritual strength" of humanity and, in doing so, reiterated the prerevolutionary intelligentsia's scorn for the material world. This is particularly striking when discussing a private apartment; as Boym notes, this type of living space connoted privilege (especially in Moscow).[47]

A formerly talented modernist who turned to hackwork, Georgii Maksimovich escapes the scorn Trifonov metes out to those swapping sincerity for success. This anomalous treatment is because he is a caring stepfather to Ol'ga Vasil'evna. As with Valia in *Taking Stock*, his characterization underscores that kindness is the basis for meaningful relationships. Through Ol'ga Vasil'evna and Georgii Maksimovich, *Another Life* shows that Trifonov's critique of consumption and worry about the NTR have limits. The two characters evince how both issues can coexist with sincerity if *iskrennost'* prevails: their lives are not dictated by the objects they have accrued. *Another Life* rewards these efforts. In the epilogue Ol'ga Vasil'evna gets a rare chance at a second love, suggesting that her future still has meaning. This gift is far more valuable than the dubious material comfort Lialia and Rebrov have procured by the end of *The Long Goodbye*.[48]

HOUSE ON THE EMBANKMENT: CONSUMING SINCERITY

The most renowned of the Moscow novellas is *House on the Embankment*, which brought Trifonov prominence well beyond the Soviet Union. The framing plot of the novella takes place in the 1970s, when Vadim Glebov has become a successful literary critic and even travels to the West. Most of the novella, however, recounts flashbacks to the life of Glebov and his friends. The first of these segments takes place in the late 1930s and the second portrays some of the friends as students at a Moscow literary institute in the late 1940s, when Glebov contributes to the denunciation of Professor Ganchuk, his mentor.

Glebov's past implicates the fate of the Soviet intelligentsia. As Dwyer explores, *House on the Embankment* returns to the premise of *Students* but replaces Vadim Belov's righteous persecution with Vadim Glebov's reluctant

74   Empire of Objects

participation as enemies attack the professor.[49] Both works connected bodies and consumption to problems with *iskrennost'* at the level of individual and society. It is no coincidence that in *House on the Embankment* immoral characters overshadow their positive counterparts. Readers discover the caring and honesty of Glebov's fiancée (Sonya), for instance, through how Glebov takes advantage of her. This protagonist is an older, cynical version of Vadim; insincerity and love of things have transformed Glebov from a hungry, thin student in the late 1940s to a successful but bloated literary critic in 1972. The years between have left their mark as the past defines the physique of the present.

> Almost a quarter century ago, when Vadim Alexandrovich Glebov was not yet balding and fat, with breasts like a woman's, flabby thighs, a big paunch and sloping shoulders, which obliged him to have his suits tailormade instead of buying them off the rack (while his jacket size was fifty-two he could barely squeeze into pants of size fifty-six, and sometimes had to get a pair of fifty-eights); when he did not yet have bridgework in both his upper and lower jaws; when the doctors had not yet noted the irregularities in his EKG that indicated cardiac insufficiency and stenosis of the coronary arteries; when he was not yet a martyr to morning heartburn, dizzy spells and general listlessness; when his liver was still working normally and he could eat fatty foods and greasy meat, drink as much wine and vodka as he liked without fear of the consequences; . . . when tormented by insomnia and the wretched inadequacy of youth, he dreamed of all the things that later came to him—but which [now] brought him no joy because achieving them used up so much of his strength and so much of that irreplaceable something [*togo nevospolnimogo*] that is called life: in those days, almost a quarter of a century ago, there had been Professor Ganchuk, there had been Sonya, Anton, and Lev Shulepnikov, all of them Vadim's neighbors.[50]

Young Glebov had a "strength" marked by masculine hunger that drove him to consume as much "fatty meat" and "wine and vodka as he liked." Now he is cursed with "breasts like a woman's, flabby thighs," and clear indications that his virile days have passed. He needs to have his clothes specially made (Soviet fashion tried to disguise the overweight male form). Time is not the reason the protagonist is ill at ease with his body. The culprit is the avarice that took over his youth. Glebov's love of things is written on the flesh; the protagonist's physique shows that *byt* is physical (bad teeth, expanding

Empire of Objects 75

waistline) yet also contains the moment when one loses the "irreplaceable something that is called life." It is the body that provokes the underlying question: how did the natural desires of a young man mutate into immoral consumption? The protagonist is desperate to forget Professor Ganchuk and Sonya but *telesnost'* will not let him. As with the description of Gennadii Sergeevich, the physical form reflects ethical ailments. Corporeality in this novella recalls Nora's discussion that the body has its own memories and does not lie.[51]

While critics focused on *byt* in Trifonov's picture of Brezhnev-era Moscow, flashbacks to Stalinism show how everyday life stimulates the young Glebov's appetites. He, like Vadim in *Students*, connects sexuality to getting what one lacks but covets. He first becomes interested in Sonya after a drunken party in the late 1940s where a guest wonders whose girlfriend she is. It is at the Ganchuk family's dacha that Sonya and Glebov have sex for the first time; Glebov notes to himself that her body belongs to him now (she was a virgin before). As Selemeneva and Ivanova argue, the protagonist's desire is based on getting what others have, in this case Sonya's comfortable life.[52]

Their relationship flounders when Glebov borrows a friend's apartment for their trysts. Gone are the spacious confines of the dacha. Instead, "there was a cafeteria underneath and the smells seeped up through the floorboards, and sometimes when the restaurant staff mounted a campaign to exterminate the cockroaches, the place reeked of disinfectant and the apartment was threatened with a plague of cockroaches fleeing from destruction— in that grubby bachelor's pad Glebov experienced the first attacks of loss of self-confidence, of inability to understand his own feelings, or, put more simply, of postcoital depression. . . . There were times when he couldn't come [*ne doplyval do berega*], despite protracted and exhausting efforts."[53]

The smells of cafeteria cooking—as well as the occasional influx of insects—decrease Glebov's interest in Sonya, leaving him sometimes sexually frustrated. His desire is a function of setting. At the dacha his status as future son-in-law (and thus rightful owner of the country house) is a powerful aphrodisiac. In the borrowed apartment, by contrast, he is left with only one possession: Sonya, who is not enough. Wanting what is unavailable motivates Glebov's acquisitive nature and thus his erotic desire; this drive is incompatible with the cockroaches and cooking smells of late-Stalinist Moscow. Altruistic Sonya hesitantly wonders aloud if Glebov needs another woman but the *povest'* demonstrates that the problem is rooted within the main character.[54]

76　　　　　　　　　　　　　Empire of Objects

Greed and envy mold Glebov as lover and consumer. This invidious process begins in the 1930s. As a child, the protagonist makes an astounding discovery when he has tea with his friend Shulepnikov's mother:

> [Alina Fedorovna] could prod a slice of cake with a fork and push it away, saying, "This cake is stale"—and the cake was removed. When this happened for the first time, Glebov was secretly amazed. How could a cake be stale? It struck him as an absolutely stupid idea. Cake was a rarity at home; it appeared only on someone's birthday, it was quickly eaten, and it never occurred to anyone to say whether it was fresh or stale, because it was always fresh, deliciously fresh, especially the gorgeous kind decorated with roses made of pink frosting.[55]

The cake carries a significance that lingers longer than the object itself. Glebov is "secretly amazed" when he discovers a new aspect of a food he, like most in the 1930s, rarely encounters. For him it is a luscious edifice "decorated with roses made of pink frosting"; such ornate construction suggests the saccharine splendor of Stalinist architecture. Alina Fedorovna is one of this era's elites, a connoisseur with demands that match the power of her NKVD husband. In the novella the details of everyday life are not inert, but significant markers of identity. Glebov already understands this. He needs to adjust to the more prosaic conditions in his own (communal) abode upon returning from his friends' apartments.[56]

> After a visit to the [House on the Embankment] he at first used to feel somehow depressed whenever he suddenly saw, as if he were a stranger, his little lopsided building with its yellowish-brown coating of stucco; whenever he climbed the dark staircase, where you had to go carefully because the steps were broken in places; whenever he approached the front door, dotted with nameplates, inscriptions and bells like an old patched blanket; whenever he plunged into the many-layered kerosene-smelling atmosphere of the building, where something was always bubbling in a saucepan and someone was always boiling cabbage; whenever he washed his hands in the bathroom, where movement was difficult because of all the planks that covered the bathtub . . . but gradually it all subsided, softened, and ceased to upset him.[57]

In *Students* Vadim is not ashamed of the room he shares with his mother. *House on the Embankment*, however, examines the resentment of those who

Empire of Objects

cannot wait for their reward in the radiant future. Glebov approaches his apartment building as a stranger, first noticing its "yellowish-brown" color then making his way inside until he reaches the bathroom, a storage space with various objects stacked on the unused tub. Along the way he must readjust to the smells of kerosene and shared quarters "where something was always bubbling in a saucepan." These odors, as well as the cooking and baking that produce them, are absent from Shulepnikov's apartment. In that place only the result is visible: the cake that consummate consumer Alina Fedorovna rejects. At home the smell of boiling cabbage is particularly prominent for Glebov (this is far from surprising, as it is a mainstay in portrayals of *kommunalki*). Even in an olfactory sense the House on the Embankment influences Glebov's sense of his life; cake contrasts with the less-pleasant odors of the communal kitchen. These remind the protagonist that he lives in a different, more claustrophobic world than Shulepnikov. Such realizations will later make Glebov, already envious, prone to the series of compromises that shatter the lives of the Ganchuks. The aroma of the edible object stimulates the mingled hunger and jealousy controlling the protagonist since childhood. Glebov is primed to become the grasping *meshchanin* that Trifonov abhors.[58]

In the late 1940s this becomes more evident. Merging with the voice of the protagonist, the narrator uses a strangely naturalistic image to recall Glebov's role in ousting Ganchuk from the institute:

> It is all so long ago now, it has all become so blurred and distorted, fallen apart like a piece of old, rotten fabric that it is hard to remember what really happened. Why did this happen, why that? Why did he act like that and not differently? Only trivia survive, fixed in the memory: they are imperishable, immortal. . . . Trivia: the sight of Professor Ganchuk greedily eating a napoleon in a café on Gorky Street after the meeting at which he was destroyed. Glebov had happened to pass by and had seen him through the window.[59]

The past is built on things (the café, Ganchuk's napoleon) but is not something solid on which the present can rest. Instead it is "rotten," ready to disintegrate, at least for those who attempt to forget. The mind can excise larger issues but preserves "trivia," such as the napoleon. This detritus of *byt*, however, draws Glebov back to larger problems: the betrayal and moral compromise that come from the ravening envy of his youth. In her discussion of memoirs written by *intelligenty*, Irina Paperno explains that it is

78   Empire of Objects

precisely these intimate, material details that aid recollection of personal and collective catastrophe.[60] Nadkarni makes an analogous point: the small odds and ends of everyday life form "remains" that stubbornly persist despite efforts to forget them. The image of Ganchuk's napoleon is one of these—it is important enough to return to in more detail later in the novella. During this second mention the narrator underscores that watching Ganchuk eat is one of the few episodes Glebov recalls (or chooses to recall) from this time.[61]

Glebov didn't know that the time would come when he would try not to remember everything that happened to him in those days, and no doubt he didn't know either that he would come to live a life that *did not exist* [*zhivet zhizn'iu, kotoroi ne bylo*]. And suddenly, through the window of a café on Gorky Street, near Pushkin Square, Glebov saw Ganchuk. He was standing at one of the little tall tables where you drink coffee, and was greedily eating a [n]apoleon, holding it in its paper napkin with all five fingers of his hand. His fleshy face, with its pink folds of skin, expressed pure enjoyment as it moved and twitched like a well-fitting mask, the whole skin from jaw to brow vibrating with pleasure. Ganchuk was so absorbed in the sweetness of the cream and the thin crispness of the strips of pastry that he noticed neither Glebov . . . nor Shulepnikov . . . . Yet a half-hour ago this man had been destroyed.[62]

Ganchuk's face resembles a "mask," while his real persona expresses an animal delight in the napoleon. This is a voyeuristic look at the man whose career Glebov has just helped to end. The protagonist for his part has long been interested in fine food, which fuels resentment of those such as the professor. Due to its insignificant, material nature, the napoleon is one of the rare moments that survives Glebov's elision of the past. As Platt notes, the protagonist frantically tries to erase his recollections of late Stalinism, yet the details of Ganchuk's face remain precisely because they are physically striking and seemingly unimportant.[63]

As the professor's pastries suggest, Glebov's victims are also enmeshed in love of the material world. Iuliia Mikhailovna, Ganchuk's wife, is a committed communist. She reproaches Glebov for his fascination with the family's dacha and refrigerator, musing that this *meshchanstvo* encompasses his entire generation. Iuliia Mikhailovna maintains that she could be just as happy living in a hut (but resides in a luxurious apartment). Ganchuk himself has retreated from the brutal simplicity of the Civil War; his maid Vasena ironically notes that Glebov serves as his bodyguard when the professor goes out for a walk in his expensive fur coat. During the campaign against Ganchuk, his opponents fixate on the ornamental figurines in his large study, especially the statuette of Baruch Spinoza. The Jewish philosopher is suspect both due to ethnicity and because he was not a "true" materialist. As the investigation makes clear, what the professor owns implicates his worldview. More importantly, Ganchuk's possessions suggest that Glebov's greed is a disease inherited from those he betrays. The young followed the precedent set by those who longed for a utopia of ideals but were seduced by the material world.[64]

This generational link draws on Trifonov's uneasy relationship with Dostoevsky. The nineteenth-century author had his own suspicions of the material world and was someone whom Trifonov admired yet struggled to understand. Envisioning the affinities between Glebov and Ganchuk, Trifonov unintentionally borrows from Dostoevsky. In *The Demons* Stepan Verkhovenskii leaves his son in the care of others and their dangerous ideas, choosing to educate Stavrogin instead. Petr Stepanovich then brings disaster to his town. The younger Verkhovenskii, like Stavrogin, has been infected by the same word-idea that begins with his father's muddled liberalism, mutates into socialism, and spreads to the would-be revolutionaries. Glebov is to blame for his actions, yet Ganchuk helped prime his ruthlessness.[65]

House on the Embankment compares the events surrounding Professor Ganchuk's downfall to an ancient city buried in the sands of time; its outline reveals terror and a "skeleton of actions" whose purpose can never be unearthed. The atmosphere during late Stalinism, the narrator continues, was one of "fear, dehumanizing, blind, formless, like a creature born in a dark basement."[66] History is subterranean, covered by layers hinting at dread and hindering understanding. This brief, oblique description attacks the paranoia praised by *Students* and exemplifies the subtle richness of the author's late prose. In an interview Trifonov said that for readers one word from the author is enough for them to write the rest of the scene in their minds. This key statement explains his brilliantly incomplete style of description (*nedoskazannost'*).[67] *Nedoskazannost'* is deceptive: the result of careful crafting, it appears effortless on the page and relies on readers to supply what is missing. In *House on the Embankment* details such as a pale face and military boots subtly convey that Shulepnikov's stepfather has been up nights interrogating prisoners. *Nedoskazannost'* comes from the process of writing

Empire of Objects

when the act of depiction, not what is described, controls the scene. One result of this careful process was Aesopian language, a style that Thomas Seifrid defines as "strategic nonarticulation."[68] Skillful half-communication helped the novella pass the censors, as did the gaps and hints that Platt examines. In one such scene, Kunik, Ganchuk's protégé, reproaches Glebov for remaining quiet instead of aiding the professor. The young scholar states that silence is a form of execution, maintaining that the absence of speech can be a form of betrayal (or a way of portraying such betrayal). More fundamentally, the work's *nedoskazannost'* reflects how Trifonov sees the shifting ambiguities of life itself. As Mikhail Bakhtin famously observed, existence is an unfinished process and literature should show this incompletion. Telling all and leaving nothing unsaid is both impossible and arrogant on the part of the author.[69]

The modest length of *House on the Embankment* and the other Moscow *povesti* proves Trifonov's mastery as he compresses experience into a small number of pages. These novellas reveal how yesterday shapes the present, limiting possibilities as consumption constrains characters' morals. Saggy stomachs and increasing waistlines imply that greed has left its mark on the collective body as well as individual characters. The Thaw hopes for *iskrennost'* as a national virtue were gone; critics' invectives against *byt* signaled that banality had vanquished *bytie*. After the Prague Spring, Trifonov viewed his homeland as an empire of things that had destroyed the future.

4

Utopia Lost

Sincerity and the Past in
Trifonov's Final Works

In the winter of 1980, Trifonov and his wife were in Budapest at a writer's conference, spending their free time watching films banned in the USSR. Alarming news came from Poland as the Soviet-backed state tried to stop the rise of Solidarity. Writing in his diary, the author predicted: "This is the beginning of the collapse of the socialist camp and maybe even the Soviet Union. By the way, this corpse will take a long time to rot."[1] In foreseeing the demise of the Eastern bloc and USSR itself, he used a bodily image to denote the death of socialist ideals. Trifonov understood that the Soviet experiment had not only failed to transform the world but was itself decomposing.

The last chapter of my study is the most heterogenous, investigating how Trifonov's five final works portray the antagonism between sincerity, *telesnost'*, and consumption in culture. While this writing appeared in the 1970s–1980s, its real subject was the past; plots were deeply retrospective, with most focusing on the Civil War and Stalinism. Gone was the hope in the future that guided *Students* and created the battle between yesterday and tomorrow in Trifonov's Thaw works. Selemeneva labels his final narratives "thinking prose" due to their concern with recollection and morality. Vladimir Amlinskii, writing in 1982, praised the author's turn to history. Trifonov's daughter states that her father had a new sense of responsibility for others after his mother's death in 1975.[2]

Chapter 4 briefly expands on the cultural trends that chapter 3 introduced. My study then pairs two Trifonov novels not usually considered together. *Impatience* is a work of historical fiction praising the People's Will for assassinating Tsar Alexander II. *The Old Man* recounts memories of the

81

Civil War. Appearing five years later in 1978, it attacks the bloodshed and misguided fervor that *Impatience* extolled. This chapter also examines the novel *Time and Place, The Abandoned Home* (autobiographical travel stories), and Trifonov's unfinished novel *Disappearance*. Critics have extensively discussed *The Old Man* and *Time and Place*, yet examining how all these works portray the struggle between *iskrennost'* and consumption gives new insight into late socialism. Trifonov's final narratives did not juxtapose a harmonious past and harmful present (as happened with village prose, for instance). Instead, they hinted that Soviet society was marred by greed, trauma, and insincerity from the first years of its existence. Trifonov's popularity and carefully oblique prose ensured that many in the USSR could read this subtle yet damning judgment.

The late 1970s–early 1980s were an era of superficial stability increasingly undercut by crisis. The rise and (temporary) fall of Solidarity in Poland, the 1979 invasion of Afghanistan, and Reagan's election all worried authorities. Soviets were incensed at the US boycott of the 1980 Olympics and, like their American counterparts, feared the intensified Cold War rhetoric between Moscow and Washington. The Brezhnev years ended with renewed shortages and realizations that the last decade's relative prosperity had vanished. Sociologist Ol'ga Gurova notes that in the early 1980s invectives against materialism disappeared from state discourse due to growing fascination with imported goods: consumption had defeated those who attempted to regulate it. The film *Garage* wryly dramatized how greed and lies warped relations between coworkers. Chingiz Aitmatov's novel *The Day Lasts Longer than a Hundred Years* connected the arms race, Stalinist repression, and the destruction of memory in Central Asia. Both of these seemingly different works linked aging, loss of sincerity, and betrayal of ideals, continuing the "taking stock" of 1970s culture but with bleaker conclusions.[3]

Rapid technological changes had transformed daily life; Reid observes that the state wanted ordinary citizens to enjoy consumer goods created thanks to the NTR. TV and radio, along with books, were supposed to make high culture more accessible. Public discourse limited technology's problems to outside the Warsaw Pact. One Soviet critic explained that *A Clockwork Orange* illustrated how science and capitalism controlled the soul, neglecting the similarities between the film's proletarian protagonists and late socialist urban youth.[4] Trifonov's suspicion of technology had long been focused on the West, as in the story "Travnicek and Hockey" ("Travnichek i khokkei,"

1967). Visiting Vienna, the author was horrified yet titillated by watching *Doctor Goldfoot and the Bikini Machine*, where an evil genius created female robots that convinced men to give their wealth to the professor. For Trifonov the film epitomized the cynical exploitation of love, a phenomenon he also observed while watching prostitutes in the Austrian capital. During a trip to Kansas the author made an even more alarming observation: there was no one on the streets, only oversized American cars. He alleges that in the US things could replace their owners, hinting at humans' ultimate fate in the consumer age.[5]

There was another, less visible threat. In the 1970s the intelligentsia increasingly lamented how compromise, irony, and cynicism had become powerful enemies of *iskrennost'*. Sergei Dovlatov epitomized the era with his book, *Compromise*, which humorously recounted failed efforts to publish truthful newspaper articles. Dissident Boris Shragin was more explicit, arguing that seemingly small concessions to the state ultimately resulted in loss of self, a charge echoing Solzhenitsyn's and Kormer's belief that the intelligentsia had been corrupted.[6] Trifonov's works associated *iskrennost'* with a unity of behavior and action when both are grounded in kindness. Cynicism was its opposite; it exploited the chasm between belief and action. Grekova's academic novels such as *The Department* juxtaposed the sincerity and self-sacrifice of positive characters with their antagonists' careerism. Against this backdrop Trifonov's final works portrayed an intelligentsia disturbed by the NTR and the ways irony and cynicism were eroding *iskrennost'*.[7] His last narratives elaborated how memory and trauma formed around things, a process inherited from the writer's 1960s–1970s prose. Objects signaled the accomplishments but also duplicity of their owners; the twentieth century was shaped more by consumption and avarice than the collective altruism that socialism had promised. Building on his Moscow novellas, Trifonov's emphasis on the material nature of everyday life created a new way to explore the past: recognizing *byt* as the confluence between personal and collective history.

IMPATIENCE: FALSE CERTAINTY, DELUDED SINCERITY

Trifonov's later period included two novels that dramatized the costs of misguided sincerity. The first of these, *Impatience*, did this unwittingly through a rambling plot, poor artistic quality, and unreflective praise of the People's Will. Critics rightly hailed the second novel (*The Old Man*) as a perceptive, pessimistic commentary on the Civil War. These narratives contain contradictory efforts to understand the past yet both rely on the material world to do so.

Impatience opens with a lament familiar to Trifonov's readers: "Toward the end of the seventies, it became completely obvious to all contemporaries [*vsem sovremennikam*] that Russia was ill. They only argued about which illness it was and what could cure it."[8] Vladimir Novokhatko, one of the editors responsible for publishing the novel, decades later asserted that this malaise referred to the 1970s as well as the era of Alexander II. *Impatience* is the prelude to trauma; it recounts how People's Will member Andrei Zheliabov failed to assassinate the Tsar then demanded to be executed with those who succeeded. The novel has a series of subplots and a bewildering host of characters. Zheliabov's viewpoint predominates, with the spirit of history interjecting thoughts via the narrator. Despite this interesting device, *Impatience* cannot resolve a basic problem: Zheliabov, who was in prison, missed the successful 1881 murder of Alexander II. Grishnevitskii, who threw the second bomb and thus killed the Tsar, receives no character development due to being a minor figure in the movement. The young man responsible for the first bomb, Rysakov, was a novice who lamented getting caught. The bumbling nature of the assassination was a shaky foundation for this work of historical fiction. *Impatience* unwittingly renders the political murder a long, painful farce where experienced members of the People's Will fail but a neophyte succeeds.[9] Zheliabov proudly explains to the authorities the elaborate plans behind the regicide, which he wishes he could have committed. These details recall the excess description in *Students* and *Slaking the Thirst*. Trifonov's relapse into the "horizontal," superficial glut of details of earlier works has gruesome undertones as Zheliabov savors the preparations for assassination. Both Zheliabov and the protagonist of *Students* pervert *iskrennost'* by destroying their opponents in what they assume is a sincere quest for a better tomorrow. They believe the blind pursuit of utopia constitutes understanding history and substitute aggression for helping others.[10]

Trifonova tries to justify the theme and publication of *Impatience*. After the Prague Spring, she argues, her husband realized that the state would scrutinize prose about contemporary life; at the same time there was heightened interest in the People's Will. The subject matter allowed for some subversive material, and she adds that Vasilii Aksenov and Vladimir Voinovich also wrote for the Fiery Revolutionaries (Plamennye revoliutsionery) series that published *Impatience*. Listing these "anti-Soviet" authors is an attempt

Utopia Lost

to explain Trifonov's participation in the series and mitigate this novel's false representation of history.[11] As Jones more accurately notes, Fiery Revolutionaries hoped to engage ordinary readers and combat indifference to the past and Party ideology. (Publication of *Impatience* may have been aided by Trifonov's second wife, Pastukhova, who was one of the editors.) Pavel Khazanov discusses how culture's focus on the People's Will coincided with a fascination for the Decembrists: both groups provided (idealized) pictures of morally righteous revolutionaries. These were alluring to late Soviet readers increasingly aware that their own revolution had degenerated into consumption and cynicism. Novokhatko's commentary is more stark: the series tried to distract readers from contemporary problems, proffering a simplistic vision of the struggle that eventually created the Soviet state. Writers for their part called Fiery Revolutionaries a "feeder" (*kormushka*) because of its generous royalties. These varying assessments showed how Trifonov's own actions justified the author's fear that in the 1970s a full stomach was more important than sincerity.[12]

At times *Impatience* criticizes the People's Will, a group that Trifonov tried to distinguish from contemporaries such as Carlos the Jackal. Zheliabov's father-in-law decries Tsarist oppression but says the would-be revolutionaries are too radical. When Zheliabov announces he was imprisoned due to struggling for justice, another character warns that terrible things have been done in the name of this principle. Most interestingly, Alexander II bemoans old age, which he compares to a "well-executed siege."[13] The autocrat joins the ranks of Trifonov's male characters defeated by the passage of time. The People's Will, of course, ensures that the Tsar's end comes sooner than he had imagined.

One critic in the early 1980s praised the terrorists for being knights without fear or blemish, a cliché recalling accolades for Felix Dzherzhinsky. Yuri Slezkine points out that *Impatience* glorifies the same policies and lack of ethics that later destroyed Valentin Trifonov and many others in the House on the Embankment. The novel tries to introduce nuance into its praise of terrorism, but the result is a mere distraction from its legitimation of violence.[14] *Impatience* contradicted Trifonov's pronouncement in a 1978 interview that art must not act as a "prosecutor"; Zheliabov becomes not only prosecutor but also judge and (failed) executioner as he determines who should live or die. Like Vadim in *Students*, he is a sincere destroyer. In the context of Trifonov's oeuvre, *Impatience* is the prehistory of trauma with no sense of the assassination's consequences.[15]

This novel, like many of Trifonov's works, portrays the "current" of time as a physical and symbolic force. Zheliabov has a narrow view of history's flow, describing how he has moved in it like rainwater through a gutter, taking the only course possible. The revolutionary uses this elemental imagery to naturalize the attack on autocracy. In his mind, he follows historical inevitability as it flows toward revolution. 1970s critics praising the novel made two divergent assertions: V. Oskotskii claimed that Zheliabov, carried by the current of history, had no choice but to help with the assassination. Natal'ia Il'ina believed that within this same current Zheliabov made his own decisions. In Trifonov's post-Stalinist works history is an uncontrollable surge overpowering attempts to direct it. In picturing the past, *Impatience* was an exception to the thoughtful analysis of action, guilt, and responsibility in Trifonov's Brezhnev-era prose.[16]

As one critic has recently noted, Zheliabov scorns the terrorist Sergei Nechaev, then later emulates his inhumane philosophy. Trifonov himself admitted that, in trying to distinguish the protagonist from Nechaev, *Impatience* underlined their similarities. The author remarked that the assassination of the Tsar postponed the constitution that Alexander II may have planned to support (the novel notes that People's Will did not know of this possibility). In the same article Trifonov acknowledged the revolutionaries were too eager for change, making them devolve into "bomb-throwers."[17]

Critic Ol'ga Sukhikh observes that the failure of the People's Will underscored that violence cannot improve humanity, a realization that again links Trifonov to Dostoevsky. As with Ivan Karamazov's Legend of the Grand Inquisitor, the terrorists murdering the Tsar achieved the opposite of their intention. Ivan tries to shake his brother's faith yet solidifies it; Zheliabov wants to hurry history and instead delays it. Similar to Glebov in *House on the Embankment*, the actions of the protagonist evoke Dostoevsky's fears. In writing *Impatience*, however, Trifonov did not realize that these allusions undermine the novel's themes.[18]

Zheliabov draws strength from ideas that purport to explain how the past, present, and future interact. In a stilted scene the terrorist ponders how, "Actions, words, gestures, phrases all die—the only thing that will live forever, as long as humanity exists, is ideas. There are not many of them. They can be mistaken. But they are indestructible, they will arise again and again, in different forms but remaining the same."[19] He then excitedly explains the political program of the People's Will to Sof'ia Perovskaia, his fellow terrorist and lover. For Ivanova, such moments are a warning that ideas can take over consciousness, as in the biblical epigraph to *The Demons* where evil spirits drive swine to drown themselves. Zheliabov sacrifices his own and others' lives for ideas. *Impatience* mentions how, years before plotting to kill the Tsar, he abandoned his wife and children to join the revolutionaries. Trifonov, whose father was murdered by the state, lauded a parent who left his family to foment violence.[20]

The novel assumed communism to be history's endpoint, a teleological stance vindicating the assassinations and intrigues leading up to the October revolution. The delusional certainty that radicals can determine and control the flow of time created the next generation of violent revolutionaries, who unleashed the horrors that *The Old Man* depicts.

THE OLD MAN AND THE
TROUBLING STUFF OF HISTORY

The Old Man is a more sophisticated approach to trauma and its legacy as Trifonov takes stock of national history. In the 1970s Old Bolshevik Pavel Evgrafovich worries about his shiftless children and scrupulously recalls how during the Civil War he loved Asya and envied her husband, Cossack commander Migulin, who aided the Reds in the Don. What Pavel Evgrafovich forgets is the small but fatal part he played in Migulin's execution after the leader was wrongly accused of attempting to join the Whites. The novel is an example of what Oushakine terms "trauma-as-plot" (*travma-siuzhet*): the brutality of Reds and Whites shapes Asya, the narrator, and the work as a whole.[21]

Recollections of the Civil War start with Pavel Evgrafovich reading a letter from Asya. This is an old but effective plot device that employs objects to evoke memory, similar to Trifonov's claim that the materials for *The Bonfire's Glow* came from a trunk. Asya explains that she saw his mention of Migulin in a journal someone had thrown out. This detail adds to the tragedy of life: the heroic Cossack whom she loved has been discarded by a generation no longer interested in the Civil War. The 1970s plot, as with the frame narratives of *House on the Embankment*, depicts a world where bodies and consumption are more important than ideas. *The Old Man's* very title is pejorative, reducing the protagonist to a state of decline. Pavel Evgrafovich's children for their part are materialistic and uninterested in their parents' past. The character Kandaurov is a more odious example of immorality. When *The Old Man* first switches to his viewpoint, this literary scholar is forty-five but his body works flawlessly. He is lying to his wife about his affair with Svetlana, an intern who is twenty-three; he has sex with her because she reminds him of his own ambition. Even more than Glebov, this character shows that consumption and desire go hand in hand in Trifonov's prose. Before Kandaurov's trip to Mexico, doctors discover an illness that removes him from the narrative. Ivanova notes that his image is almost grotesque yet fitting: as the ultimate consumer of the "flesh of life," Kandaurov is betrayed by the body he lives to please. The novella's summary treatment of him is anomalous for Trifonov, underlining the author's derision for this character who combines insincerity with consumption. When Dedkov laconically summarizes that Kandaurov is a "modern" man, the critic conveys that Trifonov equates his era with the dubious pursuit of comfort.[22]

Pavel Evgrafovich is more complex, in great part because the past determines his present. For him "life turns into something strange, a duality: there is one life that is reality and a second one that is an illusion, memory-made, and they exist side by side, like a doubled image on a broken-down television set. . . . What is memory? Boon or bane? Why is it given to us?"[23] The television, Trifonov's most despised object, symbolizes the schism between memories and what actually occurred, between "reality" and "illusion." Recalling his youth in Petrograd, Pavel Evgrafovich describes memory as "a warehouse of unneeded things" that will eventually be "thrown out for good"—however, in a letter to Asya he notes that recollection takes on a life of its own, keeping one thing and discarding another.[24] Together these physical images show that memory is malleable and unreliable, a trope prominent in *House on the Embankment* and most other late Trifonov works. It is a graduate student at the novel's end who, researching Migulin, casually mentions that Pavel Evgrafovich forgot his role in destroying the Cossack when asked if the commander might be planning an uprising against his Bolshevik allies.[25]

Pavel Evgrafovich asserts that the *byt* of this bygone era matters because of the period's "sincerity" and the fact that it begot the USSR. This is the epoch of Valentin Trifonov and the decade that preceded the author's childhood. Yet, unlike *The Bonfire's Glow*, the novel critiques as well as lauds the Reds in the Civil War, an era that late Soviet culture saw as the historical embodiment of *iskrennost'*.[26] Pavel Evgrafovich depicts the conflict as lava that burned and drowned all in its path. However, within this flood one did not notice its heat. Gillespie aptly observes that this observation combines Trifonov's two overarching conceptions of history: fire and water. Selemeneva expands on this thought, stating that Pavel Evgrafovich is a pessimist for whom humanity is directed by powerful, elemental forces. I argue that

Utopia Lost

these material metaphors, which dramatize how history destroys its masters, were one of Trifonov's contributions to the Brezhnev era's circumspect debates over the past.[27]

The Old Man likens exploring history to venturing into catacombs, a frightening place where the past lies in wait. Ivanova notes that Trifonov's late prose digs deep into a character's "magma."[28] This word has several additional implications. First, the burning flow of revolutionary enthusiasm has ossified into a dark cavern that hides the past of individuals and the nation. This "magma" comes from the combined metaphor of lava and conflagration, which defined history in *The Old Man* and *The Bonfire's Glow*. The material world is oppressive, suggesting that unyielding forces—not the ideals of Party or intelligentsia—define existence. Pavel Evgrafovich struggles with this truth when, receiving a letter from Asya, he realizes she is still alive decades after the Civil War.[29]

> Time had caved in and buried her like a mine shaft burying a miner—and now how am I to rescue her? She is still alive, still breathing fifty-five years later, somewhere under the shale, under the lumps of unyielding ore, in the pitch-dark, airless *catacombs*.
>
> She was still breathing. But I thought she was dead. I ran into the house and the first thing I saw was a motionless whiteness on the floor, a heap of something white and rounded. Early dawn, half-light: I did not realize that it was a naked person on the ground. An absolutely naked woman.[30]

From the 1970s plot the novel suddenly drops reader and protagonist into the crypt of history, where Asya has somehow survived. Racing into a house during the Civil War, Pavel Evgrafovich discovers Asya nearly dead after being raped by bandits. She has become "a heap of something" indistinguishable from the rubble of the past, a reification of the trauma that accompanied the rise of the Soviet state. Migulin appears and takes her to safety, beginning the love affair that leads jealous Pavel Evgrafovich to help destroy the Cossack. The protagonist cannot admit that his passion was stronger than devotion to the revolution he deems sincere. He presents varying approaches to the conflict between Reds and Whites but omits his own culpability. In portraying Pavel Evgrafovich, Trifonov thus redirects Soviet literature's treatment of history, demonstrating that it is guided in great part by the desires of the body. This parallels the behavior of Glebov in *House on the Embankment*, where envy, greed, and lust lead the protagonist to destroy others.

In *The Old Man* and Trifonov's other late works there is another factor linking present and present: *nedochuvstvie*. Kandaurov embodies this sin, as does Pavel Evgrafovich through not recalling his part in destroying Migulin. Lipovetsky and Leiderman argue that *nedochuvstvie* is the real plot of *The Old Man* as the protagonist only gradually understands that it has marked his life. Unlike Kandaurov, he is a sincere supporter of the putative values of Soviet society (collectivism and helping the next generation). Yet he too has been contaminated by a lack of empathy, which first causes him to destroy Migulin and now stymies relations with his children. Awareness of this comes after the fact, a sign of how the past controls Trifonov's late prose. *The Old Man* quietly raises an alarming question: if even the scrupulously honest Pavel Evgrafovich has lost sincerity, what hope remains for society as a whole?[31]

The answer is concerning. Lipovetsky and Leiderman rightly claim the novel revealed the metastasis of historical "corruption," which started with the vicious tactics of 1918–21, then spread through Soviet history. Beginning with *Students*, Trifonov consciously used the image of illness to characterize his insincere characters: in his late prose the nation as a whole is ailing.[32] *The Old Man* leads readers to infer that the first years of Bolshevik rule helped pave the way for the purges of the 1930s (when the protagonist was briefly imprisoned). This succession discredits the Reds' role in the Civil War and continues a message underlying Trifonov's post-Stalinist works: terror is a constant in Soviet history. *The Old Man* was unusual in attacking both brutality and the uncompromising idealism that gave rise to it, a courageous move for a work of prose published during the Brezhnev era.[33] Zheliabov believes he can determine and control the flow of time. Pavel Evgrafovich lives through the consequences of this assumption: first he is part of the bloody Civil War then relives this trauma by venturing into the caverns of the past. Trifonov argued that art must dig out the truth. *Impatience* and *The Old Man* present history as a force that takes on material form (water, lava, catacombs). Construing the past in this manner, the author underscores the contradiction between ideas and the power of the physical world that thwarts them.[34]

Sincerity as Journey: *Time and Place*

Trifonov's last complete novel, *Time and Place* (*Vremia i mesto*, 1981), follows writer Sasha Antipov from youth in the 1930s through the war, Thaw, and then the Brezhnev years. The narrator begins the first chapter with a

Utopia Lost

question that is in fact an imperative: "Must one remember? . . . Must one remember an August that long ago melted away, like the trace of a plane in the blue sky? Remember people who evaporated like clouds? Pieces of the shore carried away by the current . . . ? About all of this? . . . Must one remember? God, how stupid, as if to ask—must one live? For to remember and to live is something single, blended, indestructible [*tsel'no, slitno, ne unichtozhaemo odno bez drugogo*], which together comprises a verb that has no name."[35]

This paragraph recalls the beginning of *House on the Embankment*, with its vanished landscape and clothes of childhood. While the *povest'* discusses those who would not recognize their former selves, *Time and Place* is dedicated to recalling the past. Following this command to remember are the last recollections Antipov has of his father before the parent's arrest in 1937. This event has sadly autobiographical overtones for Trifonov and his generation, suggesting that at moments *Time and Place* depicts the fate of the *shestidesiatniki* and, by extension, the late Soviet intelligentsia. In the opening passage objects (a plane, the shore) are in danger of "evaporating" or being "carried away by the current" of time that seizes those in Antipov's life. Memory opposes this destruction; it is "a verb that has no name" and evokes trauma but is a synonym of life. For Oushakine remembering the past compensates for the loss of wholeness, which in this instance refers to Antipov's (and Trifonov's) shattered childhood.[36]

In a key passage the narrator recounts how Antipov's mother returns from the camps.

> At the beginning of '46 Antipov's mother arrived and he had not seen her for eight years. When they had parted he had been twelve, pudgy, with curly hair, walked around the apartment in velvet shorts, did not wear glasses although he was nearsighted . . . and now Antipov was twenty, was a second-year university student, skinny, with broad, bony shoulders, wore glasses with ugly red-brown frames that his sister called "cockroach-colored," walked around the apartment in whatever he could find, in the remnants of a worn flannel ski jacket, in old man slippers, and when at ten o'clock in the evening his mother rang the doorbell on the sixth floor of a building she had never seen—while she had been gone the children had moved from the previous apartment to the one here, on the outskirts, with beating heart she listened to the thumping steps in the hallway, which seemed like the steps of an old man and she was afraid, because no one had written anything about an old man in their letters

and suddenly the door, with a click of the lock, opened and she saw in the half-darkened corridor the tall figure of a man in glasses, took a step back and gasped: "Shurka?" and Antipov saw a small woman in a quilted vest with a sad little canvas suitcase next to her on the floor, silently stared at the woman for a second, then stretched out his arms and said: "Mama?" And in their weak cries there was a questioning tone, but not because they had not recognized each other, although it would have been easy not to recognize each other, but because they had a momentary impulse to ask: How did it happen? How did this happen? And those eight years? And can we, my God, finally can we believe our eyes, arms, and lips? The mother felt how her son smelled like tobacco and the son noticed that his mother's face and clothing reeked of the train.[37]

Antipov's reunion with his mother is above all physical, involving "eyes, arms, and lips" as the two struggle to believe they are together again. This moment resembles two analogous scenes in "Cats or Hares?" and *House and the Embankment*. Those works contrast the protagonists' youthful physique with the tired bodies and failed morality of middle age. In this passage Antipov has suffered a different transformation. His change stems from the end of childhood after his parents' arrests: a happy, "pudgy" boy is now a "skinny" man with "broad, bony shoulders." In "Cats or Hares?" and *House on the Embankment* age and moral compromise are the culprits. Antipov's condition is part of trauma that he, as a child, could neither control nor avoid. His mother is also unrecognizable: in eight years she has become "a small woman in a quilted vest" with a lone suitcase. Readers know her clothes and luggage recall those released from the camps; this scene resembles the return of Trifonov's own mother from the gulag. Through passages emphasizing the body's changes, *Time and Place*, "Cats or Hares?" and *House on the Embankment* uses *telesnost'* to show how characters are the victims of forces they cannot control: political repression, corruption by the state, and the passage of time.

Trifonov remarked that *Time and Place* represented history as a "dotted line" (*punktir*), that is "pulsating, more alive than the solid line." As when decoding the description of Antipov's mother (quilted vest, canvas suitcase) readers must fill in the gaps, overcoming the silences and elisions connected with trauma that Soviet culture preferred to forget.[38] There were several reasons for this dotted line, which is a part of the *nedoskazannost'* in Trifonov's late prose. At one level, he preferred to guide the reader to the unstated truth (and avoid problems with censorship). The *punktir* also differs from the Marxist-Leninist concept of time as an unwavering path determined by the phases of class struggle. Most importantly, history as a dotted line made it less dependent on the physical world: readers had to actively interpret the past instead of relying on a mass of facts.

In *Time and Place* remembering and writing overlap as Trifonov blurs the craft of the author and historian. Antipov's novel perplexes publishers because of its many layers: the work chronicles Nikiforov, a self-doubting writer who has failed in life.[39] It is Nikiforov who gives the most striking symbol of history. He describes a stream diverted into a pipe as Moscow expands; the water is hidden underground but still flows, showing that history will continue despite efforts to control it.[40]

> From time immemorial a brook flowed in this soil of clay, but the city moved closer, and the brook became an obstacle. It became thinner and more shallow, and finally it was channeled into a pipe, soil was piled on top and a square built over it. The brook was gone, had disappeared forever. From the window of my building, on the sixth floor, I see the square and the lime trees that have grown tall, the fountain, the benches, and, on them the pensioners. Nobody remembers the brook which in old times used to babble here between willow bushes and reed grass, where tadpoles and dragonflies lived, and which kept babbling for a long time, soiled with oil and clay, until it died. But did it really die? In the pipe, hidden away in the dark, its water keeps babbling and gurgling—that is, it has no death [*smerti net*].[41]

The fixtures of *byt* (a square, benches, and elderly residents) are interconnected with the city's unending growth, a scene familiar from the epilogue of Trifonov's Moscow novellas. The pipe's subterranean flow is one of Trifonov's last portrayals of history as current. However, it is more optimistic than others. The trickle has not "disappeared": like the lifestream of history Tolstoy describes in *War and Peace*, it burbles beneath us, alive but unnoticed. As with Antipov's memories, the stream survives the passage of time and is the only hopeful material image in Trifonov's conception of history. The protagonist's recollections are sincere and complete, a welcome contrast to the silences, fragments, and falsity bedeviling those in his other works when they recall the personal or national past.[42]

This ability to remember comes from Antipov's success in avoiding moral compromise; he has little to hide. The protagonist passes from youth to middle age while preserving honesty and kindness. Woll observes that

94 Utopia Lost

Antipov picks ethics over expediency, as when during Stalinism he angers a publisher after refusing to denounce a scholar for plagiarism. At the novel's end, he is one of the least tainted protagonists in Trifonov's oeuvre, thanks in part to his childhood friend, Andrei. Antipov makes small missteps but forgoes the larger ones that would have brought greater success. Most of Trifonov's characters, by contrast, reflect the dual consciousness Kormer despised in the intelligentsia: the group publicly endorsed one view while believing another, thus maintaining access to state privileges and claims on moral authority.[43]

At the conclusion of *Time and Place* Antipov meets with Andrei on Tverskoi Boulevard, where they had strolled as teenagers. The novel closes with their shared impressions: "Moscow surrounded us like a forest. We had crossed through it. Everything else did not matter."[44] The two have traversed the "forest" of compromise, oppression, and the ordinary struggles of life, surviving with *iskrennost'* intact. This is a modest but rare feat in Trifonov's works, showing one can complete the journey of life without committing serious errors. Yet the novel gives no vision of the future—in fact, Antipov has already had a heart attack and is in his final years. The past determines the present within the retrospective temporality of Trifonov's last works: characters and their society lack any real sense of tomorrow.[45]

THE ABANDONED HOME:
SINCERITY AND THE POWER OF THE PAST

As with *Time and Place*, *The Abandoned Home* (*Oprokinutyi dom*, 1981) used memory to envision life as a voyage. However, its conclusion is less optimistic. Following well-established patterns of travel writing, in this collection of autobiographical stories impressions of the United States, Italy, and other locales let Trifonov examine his own ethics and those of Soviet culture. Publication and praise in state-sanctioned venues brought the status permitting the author to travel outside the USSR: in this sense, *The Abandoned Home* was the result of Trifonov's moral compromises and the privileges these secured. This autobiographical irony was not lost on the author, as I explore in the introduction when discussing "Memories of Genzano" and "Cats or Hares?"[46]

In *The Abandoned Home* the United States serves a backdrop for Trifonov's concerns over consumption. The author was intrigued by Disneyland, which he praised for preserving in adults the freshness of childhood. A different picture emerged during a later interview with a Soviet journal: he scorned Americans for loving spectacle and chasing after the phantoms of consumer culture. Trifonov further observed that those in the US sometimes seemed simpleminded, even infantile. The author was especially incensed by *The Price Is Right* and guessing the value of objects; such a program promoted television and the cult of things, twinned evils that for the author spawned greed and vacuity. His comments were more than just Cold War rhetoric against soulless capitalism. They indicated a fear of consumption without shores, where *meshchanstvo* united the two superpowers and threatened the intelligentsia.[47]

Flawed memories are another theme in this cycle. Woll notes that characters in *The Abandoned Home* manipulate recollection, whether purposely or otherwise, to assure themselves that they acted correctly. The tellingly titled story "A Short Stay in the Torture Chamber" ("Nedolgoe prebyvanie v kamere pytok") exemplifies this problem. Visiting the dungeon of a medieval Austrian castle in 1964, the narrator confronts N., whom he remembers having denounced him after the publication of *Students* and the uproar over his father's identity. Trifonov imagines N. admitting his guilt, but pleading that he and Trifonov's persecutors acted "sincerely."[48] Trifonov then envisions an impassioned response: "'If one sincerely forgets about conscience and the pain of others, then to hell with [sincerity]! You did not think through what your sincerity turns into! You could not care less about what happened to those who ran right into your sincerity [*kto natykalsia na vashu iskrennost'*], glowing with its satanic light! Did you know that on the day of that cursed meeting my mother. . . . Your sincerity is an act of evil [*zlodeist-vie*]!'"[49] Sincerity must be grounded in "conscience" and awareness of "the pain of others." Otherwise, it becomes a lie, dazzling and blinding with a "satanic light" that fools N. into committing "an act of evil." Trifonov alludes to his mother having a stroke the day he was denounced, thus making her also a victim of this false *iskrennost'*.

However, the imagined conversation breaks off when N. retorts that he actually had tried to help Trifonov. The autobiographical narrator then admits that: "Yes, I had forgotten, not remembered, gotten confused, everything disappeared in the darkness of time. . . . After being in the torture chamber fifteen years went by and they are also in darkness." The story describes three periods: the early 1950s (the "torture chamber" of Stalinism), then years later when Trifonov confronts N. in Austria during the Thaw, and finally the late 1970s, when the author wrote the story. What joins them is "the darkness of time," which should be pierced by the light of memory but instead obscures the past.[50] Even if a character sincerely tries to remember, personal history is entombed under layers of time that recall the catacombs in *The Old Man*. In a compulsive ritual that Etkind sees in Soviet culture, Trifonov's prose buries the traumas of Stalinism and then repeatedly exhumes it.[51] *The Abandoned Home* pictures how memories and loss shape Trifonov's travels; the present has no identity apart from the past. The collection of stories was published posthumously. Soon perestroika would render the Brezhnev era itself a part of history that the USSR hurried to abandon.

Disappearance: Trauma and the Roots of Consumption

Trifonov's final narrative was *Disappearance*, a novel that was unfinished when he died. Closely resembling events before and after Valentin Trifonov's arrest, it details the 1930s purges from the viewpoint of father Nikolai Grigor'evich and his son, Gorik, who live in the House on the Embankment. Gorik is later evacuated from Moscow during the Nazi invasion then returns to the city. The novel was published during the Gorbachev years, appearing alongside Anatoli Rybakov's *Children of the Arbat* in the wave of formerly banned prose about the purges.[52]

In *Disappearance* Nikolai Grigor'evich, an Old Bolshevik, uses two material images to depict past and present. Predictably, he views history as a current he can neither fathom nor stop as arrests become more frequent. Earlier he makes a more interesting comment about how time effects people, not only through weakening the flesh but also by "changes in the components of the soul." With these words Nikolai Grigor'evich suggests that he and others who won the Civil War have already forfeited their morality. Even before the purges' crescendo, the authorities had gradually contaminated the "soul" of the country's leaders. As with *The Old Man*, this novel shows how true believers created the totalitarian system that compromised their sincerity before destroying their bodies.[53]

In *Disappearance* the *telesnost'* and property of both victims and persecutors signal their owners' ethics. When NKVD officers search an apartment in the House on the Embankment, Sergey, Gorik's cousin, remarks to himself that one of the agents seems different: "Sergey looked at his plain face, with its prominent cheekbones and [thin] slit of a mouth, watched him purse his lips diligently and in a businesslike way, raising his brows while doing so and groaning slightly—not so much from tiredness as from some extraneous cares, no doubt—and Sergey thought: 'A guy like that will do anything he's told. The most terrible things. And all he'll do in the process is groan and purse his peasant lips.'"[54]

The unnamed agent has "prominent cheekbones" and "peasant lips," the physiognomy of the *narod*. Sergey believes he will obey orders and do "the most terrible things." In the next sentence the agent complains about not being able to see his wife because of work during the increased arrests in 1937. This representative of the common people elicits sympathy for a moment before the novel returns to the tragedy of the purges. Trifonov's focus on the intelligentsia elides the connections between the intelligentsia's trauma and the bodies of the *narod*.[55]

The arrest of Nikolai Grigor'evich in the novel's unwritten portion guides the plot and culminates the Hamlet allusions in Trifonov's prose. Beginning with its title, *Disappearance* foregrounds the horror of losing one's father, a motif that ironically began with the pro-Stalinist *Students*.[56] Gorik's childhood, like that of his creator, implodes after his father's death. Unlike Shakespeare's doubting Dane, however, Gorik was never fooled by the lies of his society. Trifonov's last novel thus reversed the assumptions of his first, in which Vadim cannot see that the USSR is a land of violence and falsehood. The Hamlet images in his prose comprise a cultural history of silences and hesitant admissions. As Etkind notes, ghosts took the place of corpses whose gravesites remained unknown. Hamlet haunted the dotted line and *nedoskazannost'* of Trifonov's late writing, where the terrifying truth of the past could only be presented in fragments.[57]

Disappearance also illustrates what happened to the objects of the dictator's intelligentsia victims. These former elites were about to become parts of the state machine as prisoners cutting timber in the Urals or mining for Kolyma gold. The physical world was suddenly far from inert. Trifonov wrote in his diary as a child that, after his parents' arrest, he feared the sound of elevators in the night.[58] In *Disappearance*, when Sergey's girlfriend's husband has been arrested, a similar fate befalls the man's possessions: the NKVD seizes papers, a typewriter, binoculars, and a letter opener. Together these items impart the suddenly changed status of their owner, formerly a supporter of the purges. Before his arrest they hinted at luxury. During the search they become evidence of past crimes (paper, typewriter) or preparations for future transgressions (the binoculars and letter opener can be used for reconnaissance and attack). Lotman argues that *byt* is a world of things that remain in the background until life is disrupted. Trifonov portrays how

98 Utopia Lost

during the purges household objects harbored a meaning the state could distort and employ in its search for enemies.[59]

Disappearance also uses objects to compare Nikolai Grigor'evich to Florinskii, the craven prosecutor who will eventually arrest him. As Selemeneva argues, Gorik's father assumed many of those repressed before him were guilty, thus allowing him to justify and maintain his own comfort. Both he and Florinskii live in the House on the Embankment, which itself reifies the ties between sham egalitarianism, hierarchy, and destruction. Woll notes that comparing the characters' apartments hints at the fates of their owners. Nikolai Grigor'evich, visiting Florinskii's home, sees that his dining room and antique furniture resemble a museum—he then wonders who is advancing the man's career. Florinskii moves into an apartment whose previous owner was purged; to symbolically cleanse it the authorities even change the parquet. Consumption goes hand in hand with political repression.[60] Trifonov demonstrated how the 1930s revised Marx's postulate about capitalism reducing people to things: under Stalin, both humans and objects were replaceable. Yet Nikolai Grigor'evich's apartment is also telling in this regard. As Slezkine notes, the *kabinety* of high-ranking men in the House on the Embankment were usually the largest rooms; Gorik enjoys playing in his father's study and admires its books and weapons.[61] The narrator observes that, "The study was large, full of mysterious things. In four cabinets there were books crowded together, thousands of books. . . . On the wall there, in the space between one of the cabinets and a window, hung Father's weapons: an English carbine, a small Winchester with a polished green stock, a double-barreled Belgian hunting rifle, a saber in an antique scabbard, a plaited Cossack whip, soft and flexible, with a little tail at the tip, and a broad Chinese sword with two silk ribbons, scarlet and dark green (Father had brought that sword from China. It had been used to chop off the heads of criminals, and in an album that Father had also brought from there, Gorik had seen a photograph of such an execution. . . .)."[62]

Nikolai Grigor'evich's study is a quiet room, with books and weapons from his travels around the globe. In China he fought alongside the communists and was even witness to the executions of "criminals" (or possibly political opponents) killed with the sword on the wall. These objects are luxuries coming from loyalty to the state, a precursor of the Big Deal in late Stalinism. The study resembles two other such locations: Kozel'skii's apartment in *Students* and the *kabinet* of his double, the nobler Ganchuk in *House on the Embankment*. In a material sense Nikolai Grigor'evich, Kozel'skii,

Utopia Lost

and Ganchuk resemble the despicable Florinskii. Three of the four even live in the House on the Embankment, amassing objects beyond the reach of most Muscovites, let alone the victims of collectivization and famine. In *Disappearance* the hanging sword in the study hints at the connection between possessions and death as Nikolai Grigor'evich realizes that his time on the executioner's block is near.[63]

Trifonov tries to differentiate these men. Kozel'skii is a victim of Stalinism, as *House on the Embankment* would later explore via Ganchuk's more sympathetic character. In the 1930s Nikolai Grigor'evich still believes in the revolution's goals, while Florinskii simply wants power. Ganchuk purged literary opponents after destroying political ones during the Civil War; in the late 1940s he laments not killing one of his persecutors when he earlier had the chance. Violence established his position even before Stalinism. In an interview Trifonov noted that Ganchuk was a "judge" in the 1920s and a victim twenty years later, a recognition of the character's moral malleability that he spares Nikolai Grigor'evich due to the latter's affinities with Valentin Trifonov. Their possessions, however, reveal that Nikolai Grigor'evich, Florinskii, Ganchuk, and Kozel'skii are similar in one important way. All have been seduced by the world of things. This demonstrates that greed predated Stalinism but was exacerbated by the period's duplicity, which in turn corrupted subsequent generations. The four men and their furnishings display how Old Bolsheviks (Ganchuk, Nikolai Grigor'evich) fell victim first to consumption and only then to cynical successors such as Florinskii. In Trifonov's late works objects and bodies tell a truth their owners cannot admit and that the author himself never explicitly voiced: by the end of the 1930s the USSR's founders had already lost their battle with the material world.[64]

Disappearance and the author's late prose as a whole yield new insights into Soviet culture. The Brezhnev years were marked by the intelligentsia's weary retrospection as the group retreated into the past to avoid a present dominated by lies. Trifonov's works, however, insinuated that the socialist experiment was flawed from the beginning; the body and the objects Soviet citizens coveted had always been stronger than the ideals promulgated by state or intelligentsia. Those characters who tried to understand history could only grasp at shadows hinting at a trauma too large to confront. The author's final narratives showed that past and present flowed together in a way humanity could neither comprehend nor control. *Iskrennost'* seemed impossible within a society where sincerity was coopted by consumption and the temptation to distort personal as well as national history.

Conclusion

Echoes of Trifonov and Soviet Culture

Across the river from the Kremlin looms the House on the Embankment. Next to one of its many entrances is a small plaque for the museum Trifonova curates to honor her late husband and the building's other luminaries. Trifonov's legacy is closely linked with this complex, a material and metaphorical reminder of Soviet culture's lingering presence long after 1991. The House, once a symbol of socialist elitism, now underscores the connections between power and wealth by occupying desirable real estate in the very center of Moscow. The Russian capital that Trifonov so loved is once more marred by oppression after Putin's 2022 attack on Ukraine and crackdown on dissent.[1]

Trifonov has had a profound influence on culture, particularly through shaping other authors and their ideas of everyday life. The conclusion of my study is less a postscript than an afterlife, using a chronological approach to analyze Trifonov's impact on literature and cultural conceptions of *byt* during the Brezhnev era, perestroika, the 1990s, and the twenty-first century. The author's images of the quotidian expanded the themes of morality, body, and consumption that his prose legitimated in Soviet culture. The authors whose careers he aided include figures that otherwise have little in common. Trifonov helped Aleksandr Prokhanov, who supports Putin's war in Ukraine; postmodernist Viktor Erofeev notes that Trifonov was the first to call Erofeev a "great writer." Trifonov's legacy reveals how traditional divisions of literature and politics obscure as well as illuminate—he is a figure whose influence supersedes boundaries and compels new thinking about culture.[2]

Selemeneva describes how, after Trifonov's death in 1981, critics saw him as an author of Russian twentieth-century literature (instead of merely the Brezhnev era). She labels him the major writer of the Moscow text, believing

100

Conclusion 101

he follows Anton Chekhov in picturing the city.[3] While Trifonov shares this honor with Pasternak, Bulgakov, and others, his portrayal of the capital is powerful and enduring. Others critics, however, distorted the author's legacy. Trifonov chafed at the moniker of "*byt* writer." His representation of the quotidian involves more than the ephemeral details that some detractors paired with everyday life. Trifonov's *byt* is transhistorical, encompassing the echoing trauma of the past and the specter of a future ruled by technology and consumption. His vision of daily life draws readers into a complex, troubling universe.[4]

Trifonov and the Long 1970s

Some critics maintain that Trifonov was being considered for the Nobel Prize before his death in an ordinary Moscow hospital that was even short on aspirin. This sad circumstance reiterated a central trope of the intelligentsia: the genius of a great author lives on despite material adversity.[5] During the "long seventies" that concluded in 1985 Trifonov influenced several writers. Lipovetsky and Leiderman outline how he shaped Vladimir Makanin; the author Iurii Nagibin sees traits of Trifonov in the writers of his era.[6] Iconoclast Andrei Bitov recalls reading *Students* (and later Trifonov wrote the first review of Bitov's prose). In the novel *Pushkin House* this author created one of the most imaginative pictures of *byt*, conflating the image of Leningrad/St. Petersburg, *intelligenty*, and the cult of literature.[7]

Trifonov had an especially important impact on women's prose (*zhenskaia proza*) from the 1960s to the 1990s. Baranskaia and Grekova were his contemporaries, using a realistic style to portray the Moscow intelligentsia. They adapted the focus on everyday life to portray alcoholism, abortion, and other taboo topics. Grekova's novel *The Rapids* (1981), set in a cybernetics department, depicted the difficulty of acting with sincerity.[8] Critics played a central role in establishing the ties between Trifonov, the quotidian, and women's prose; however, often their comments confused more than clarified. Stiazhkina, for example, argues Grekova's and Ulitskaia's female characters embody the materialism of Lena in *The Exchange*. This description does not fit the altruistic *intelligentki* these two writers portray. It does, however, show how critics persistently linked *byt* to a female realm of cunning and consumption. Trifonov himself once dismissed women's writing as lacking "metaphysics," a comment that reminds us that authors' statements can be far less perceptive than their fiction. His Moscow novellas portray how men as well as women suffer from a love of objects.[9]

102   Conclusion

PERESTROIKA: THE UNMAKING OF SOVIET CULTURE?

During the late 1980s bodies and objects were evidence of widespread crisis, as the film *Little Vera* made clear. This scandalous account of sex, alcoholism, and hopelessness showed perestroika was willing to unflinchingly depict the problems of everyday life. Critic Mark Amusin notes that the Gorbachev years at first appeared to realize the dreams of the liberal intelligentsia as society more honestly assessed past and present problems. However, *byt* soon devolved into a nightmare of economic and cultural collapse.[10] Consumption had a new, inescapable prominence due to shortages, increased awareness of Western prosperity, and the illegal economy. Golubev summarizes how the state and intelligentsia tried to control "the vibrant lives of Soviet things" and consumers alike—perestroika made clear that this effort had failed.[11]

In 1985 Aitmatov, Voznesenskii, and others praised Trifonov in a television program devoted to him. Biographer Semen Ekshtut cites Trifonov's comment that Solidarity was the beginning of the USSR's end. Despite this being a rare mention of politics in Trifonov's private writing, the biographer places him in the ranks of those who foresaw perestroika.[12] The writer's daughter believed his ethos was part of glasnost and its revelations of Stalin's crimes. Some critics at the time also linked Trifonov to the themes and conflicts of the late 1980s. His prose does contain some Gorbachev-era issues (the power of the material world, the past as lie, struggles of daily life). There was another similarity: both attacked the morality of the Civil War generation, undermining the foundational myth that the Soviet Union began as a just society. However, Trifonov's love of sincerity and his attempt to understand history, as opposed to simply negating the past, placed him within the literary milieu of the Brezhnev years instead of perestroika.[13]

In 1988 critic Igor' Zolotusskii compared *Disappearance* and Andrei Platonov's *Foundation Pit*. Despite the works' obviously differing structure, language, and time of writing, both were published in the USSR's final years and saw Soviet society as an edifice of oppression: for Trifonov this building was the House on the Embankment, while Platonov envisioned a mass grave for the state's victims. In the two works characters perish within a terrifying dystopia portrayed in physical terms.[14] *Disappearance* was a battleground for the warring liberal and conservative intelligentsia. Émigré scholar Mikhail Lekhmin notes that some critics dismissed Trifonov as a Soviet (viz., hack) author; conservative Iurii Bondarenko mocked Nikolai Grigor'evich as "intelligentsia trash."[15] Critic Aleksandr Kazintsev assailed Gorik for living

Conclusion   103

well in Moscow while others were eating grass to survive. This view emphasizes the protagonist's status as consumer, instead of seeing him as a boy who will soon lose his father. Kazintsev pities the unnamed NKVD officer who searches Sergey's lover's apartment, speculating that he fled hunger in his village in the early 1930s only to end up working with the secret police. Such an idea signals the longstanding allegation that the liberal intelligentsia was privileged and hypocritical; Kazintsev's reasoning also exonerates low-level agents who carried out Stalin's crimes. The critic conflates Trifonov's focus on Moscow, *intelligenty*, and the material world, condemning him as out of touch with Soviet reality (as defined by the conservative intelligentsia).[16]

The Yeltsin Years: Apotheosis of Things

Trifonov's reputation in the decades after 1991 at first followed the fate of many other *shestidesiatniki* whose prose was discarded as another vestige of the devalued Soviet past. Poverty, pirated videos, and the collapse of state subsidies radically altered the literary landscape. Despair, national humiliation, and the cult of wealth made sincerity a quaint virtue quickly forgotten. Trifonova claims that her late husband foresaw the time when former Komsomol directors would take charge of banks, shifting their rhetoric to exploit the new era. One critic, unabashedly longing for the USSR, argues that Trifonov would see the commercial market's control over literature as worse than the Soviet censor.[17] Both conservatives and former dissidents critiqued the *shestidesiatniki* for dishonesty and conformity. It was during the 1990s that Lipovetsky and Leiderman equivocated that Trifonov was not a "Soviet author" but an "author of the Soviet era." In this way they tried to distinguish him from the newly discredited communist regime.[18]

Vladimir Pirozhok maintains that Trifonov was read even in the "crazy 1990s." This passing observation hints at the worries of the intelligentsia, which feared that Russian literature and *intelligenty* themselves would not survive Yeltsin's *smuta*. Masha Gessen only slightly overdramatized the group by describing it as "dead again": after 1991 the world of things reigned supreme, robbing the intelligentsia of material and metaphorical authority. However, a host of talented new authors emerged, from Ulitskaia to mystery writer Boris Akunin (pseudonym of Grigorii Chkhartishvili) and postmodernist Ol'ga Slavnikova.[19]

Trifonov influenced Petrushevskaia, an author who in many ways defined Russian writing from the late 1980s to the early 2000s. Her prose, building on the concerns of Baranskaia and Grekova, depicts the vicissitudes of the material world. Yet, as Ivanova and Helena Goscilo point out, the misery, cramped quarters, and violence in her works reflect characters' tortured souls. As in Trifonov's writing, *telesnost'* and objects indicate deeper issues.[20] His late prose is a compendium of silences that hint at Stalinism's horror; Petrushevskaia's narrators bury the truth of broken lives beneath gossip and innuendo. Both authors rely on the reader to connect *byt* with trauma that leaves scant hope for the future.[21]

On a broader level, Trifonov helped form what Paperno labels the "privatization of history," an explosion in personal accounts of the socialist era after the end of the USSR. This obsession with what has come before stems from Thaw works such as *The Bonfire's Glow*. Its post-Soviet incarnation was a new phase of the 'taking stock' prevalent in Trifonov's late prose, where retrospection leads to reevaluating choices at the personal and national level. In an optimistic but deeply mistaken prediction, in the 1990s Trifonova's daughter asserted that the poverty and inequality of the Yeltsin years would give way to a future providing a "dignified human life."[22]

PUTIN'S RUSSIA: THE GLAMOR OF OPPRESSION

The Putin era began with a recovery from the Yeltsin era's economic free-fall. However, beginning in 2014 unstable oil prices and Western sanctions over the seizure of Crimea became a slow-moving crisis aggravated by the covid pandemic. While skyscrapers in Moscow City and the glamour prose of authors such as Oksana Robski rebranded Russia as a prosperous state, reality was bleaker for most (especially outside of large cities). Putin increasingly politicized culture. Persecution of the LGBTQ community and NGOs expanded into a hunt for 'foreign agents' and those straying from the pro-Soviet script for history. In February 2022 the war in Ukraine changed Russian society overnight. New sanctions, total restriction of the media, a full-scale military draft, and the rage of the international community rendered the country isolated, unstable, and paranoid. Trudoliubov claims the war has turned Russian culture into a "zombie," a creature without a mind or soul that destroys everything in its path. This dramatic picture encapsulates the despair of the liberal intelligentsia, many of whose members fled the country after the invasion began. The metaphor also continues Trifonov's vision of the USSR and its allies as a lifeless body that will take a long time to rot. Combining this image with that of Trudoliubov, Russian culture becomes a moving corpse with no real sense of its past or thought for the future. The zombie likewise fits Etkind's portrayal of Russia: a country that cannot come

Conclusion 105

to terms with the trauma that renders it the land of the undead and the unburied.[23]

The distant Thaw and Brezhnev years are once again relevant for readers. This is partially due to Putin's rehabilitation of the Soviet empire over the past two decades, evident in series such as *KGB Agent in a Tuxedo*. The process accelerated rapidly after February 2022. When Pirozhok argues that Trifonov's topics are still valued, he implies the continuity of sincerity and other intelligentsia ethics through the dismal 1990s and cynical Putin era. Bykov, a writer who has vocally opposed the president's hold on power and now lives in the United States, argues that Trifonov's prose militates against the mendacious careerism of some in the Kremlin. The author would be outraged at calculating technocrats crafting Putin's image of a wise ruler who gained control via two forces Trifonov despised: the security agencies and money.[24]

The twenty-first-century reception of Trifonov mixes nostalgia for the Soviet past, mourning for intelligentsia ideals, reminiscences of childhood, and worry that *nedochuvstvie* and insincerity are more powerful than ever. In recent years his works have become a profitable presence on bookshelves, attracting ordinary readers as well as *intelligenty*. Including Trifonov in *Lives of Notable People* canonized him within one of Russia's most popular series. Ekshtut first links the writer to a "naïve" time of affordable public transit and deliciously cheap ice cream, then reminds readers this was also the era of Solzhenitsyn and Andrei Sakharov. His ambivalent assessment of the Soviet years is now a dangerous exception. Putin extols the vanished socialist empire in a manner that resembles the selective memories of Trifonov's protagonists, excising guilt and ignoring trauma. The Kremlin has intensified its falsely heroic image of the USSR since the 2022 invasion: one prowar symbol features a grandmother clutching the Soviet flag. The aging body has been harnessed as a loyal servant of the communist cause, a distortion of memory that ignores the tens of millions eradicated by Soviet policies.[25]

The House on the Embankment remains a physical, contradictory reminder of the state and Trifonov's ties to it. Slezkine deems him the de facto historian of the building. If Trifonov is the chronicler of his onetime home, then his widow is the curator of Trifonov. The person most responsible for preserving his literary reputation, Trifonova published a comprehensive bibliography of Trifonov's works and criticism. She helped the tireless scholar Aleksandr Shitov, and in the 2000s published several books dealing with the author and the House on the Embankment. Trifonova has reinvented her late husband as the soul of the Soviet capital, broadening his appeal for Russians who remember the city during the USSR.[26]

Trifonov continues to influence Russian literature in the 2000s. Selemeneva points out his influence on Ulitskaia: both belonged to the intelligentsia, upheld *iskrennost'*, shaped Moscow's image in literature, were concerned by Stalinism and consumption, and combined these issues with evocative images of everyday life.[27] Ulitskaia's focus on *byt* is more connected to women's bodies, particularly how *telesnost'* reflects the trauma of Stalinism. Her works have an optimism alien to Trifonov's prose as protagonists resist the linked temptations of despair over oppression and seduction by the state. After the 2022 war began, Ulitskaia emigrated to Berlin with its large Russophone diaspora. The Jewish themes that are essentially absent from Trifonov's work are prominent in her writing. This difference highlights how Ulitskaia recognizes ethnic identity as a key to her own life and the Soviet experience.[28]

Trifonov never reconciled the contradictions of his own identity or culture. The son of a Cossack father and Jewish mother, he secured his literary reputation by justifying policies that had destroyed his family. Decades later he praised those who tried to honestly remember the past. Trifonov's oeuvre extended from Stalinism to the early 1980s but his concerns are timeless. How can we live the *iskrennost'* the intelligentsia cherishes? Can ethics and ideas survive the desire for material comfort and the lure of technology? Trifonov provides only partial and unsatisfying answers: not only does his later prose not give us solutions, it questions whether such solutions exist. Instead, the writer created a fictional realm as changing and incomplete as the universe it depicts; neither life nor the writing that describes it are finished works. The Soviet Union tried to forcibly remake the physical and ideational world only to create a reality where bodies and things shaped ideas. It was in the realm of everyday life, an arena the USSR could never control, that Trifonov offered a hint of optimism. Through *byt*'s fragmented memories and small moments of morality, his better characters give hope that sincerity can outlive lies.

NOTES

Introduction

1. On the purchase of the box, see the published excerpts from Trifonov's diaries and writer's notebooks, edited by his widow, Ol'ga Trifonova-Miroshnichenko (referred to in my study as "Trifonova"): Ol'ga Trifonova and Iurii Trifonov, "Iz dnevnikov i rabochikh tetradei," *Druzhba narodov*, no. 6 (1998), http://magazines.russ.ru/druzhba/1998/6/trifon.html.

2. Concerning the Nobel Prize, see Trifonova and Trifonov, "Iz dnevnikov i rabochikh tetradei," *Druzhba narodov*, no. 3 (1999), http://magazines.russ.ru/druzhba/1999/3/trif.html; Vladimir Pirozhok, "Pravda i krasota Iuriia Trifonova," in *Iurii Trifonov. Otblesk lichnosti*, comp. N. G. Kataeva (Moscow: Galeriia, 2015), 7. Scholars have formulated Soviet culture's conflict between ideals and the material world in various ways. Katerina Clark, for instance, defines it as the antagonism between spontaneity and consciousness. The first term is often a problem rooted in the realm of things (whether on the factory floor or at the front), while consciousness represents how Party-minded thinking will resolve this issue. See Katerina Clark, *The Soviet Novel: History as Ritual* (Chicago: University of Chicago Press, 1981).

3. Elizabeth Grosz, *Volatile Bodies: Toward a Corporeal Feminism, Theories of Representation and Difference* (Bloomington: Indiana University Press, 1994), vii. For one of the many studies on sexuality and folklore, see *Seks i erotika v traditsionnoi russkoi kul'ture*, comp. A. L. Toporkov (Moscow: Ladomir, 1996). On the erotic in Russian culture, see Igor Kon, *The Sexual Revolution in Russia: From the Age of the Czars to Today*, trans. James Riordan (New York: Free Press, 1995).

4. Paulina Bren and Mary Neuberger, "Introduction," in Paulina Bren and Mary Neuberger, *Communism Unwrapped: Consumption in Cold War Eastern Europe* (New York: Oxford University Press, 2012), 5, 4; Pierre Bourdieu, *Distinction: A Social Critique of the Judgement of Taste*, trans. Richard Nice (Cambridge, MA: Harvard University Press, 1984), 169. Bren and Neuberger distinguish consumption from consumerism—the second term "assumes a [capitalist] society that is driven and mobilized by marketing and corporate strategies that stimulate and then fulfill ever more unquenchable

108 Notes to Pages 4–6

desires" (4–5). On consumption in the USSR, see also Natalya Chernyshova, *Soviet Consumer Culture in the Brezhnev Era* (New York: Routledge, 2013); Andrew Chapman, "Queuetopia: Second-World Modernity and the Soviet Culture of Allocation" (PhD diss., University of Pittsburgh, 2013).

5. On *meshchanstvo*, see S. N. Ikonnikova and V. P. Kobliakov, *Moral' i kul'tura razvitogo sotsialisticheskogo obshchestva* (Moscow: Znanie, 1976), 18, quoted in Nataliia Lebina, "Retsept pis'ma o 'zastoe,'" *Novoe literaturnoe obozrenie*, no. 3 (2015), https://magazines.gorky.media/nlo/2015/3/reczept-pisma-o-zastoe.html. Considering *poshlost'*, see this influential study: Svetlana Boym, *Common Places: Mythologies of Everyday Life in Russia* (Cambridge, MA: Harvard University Press, 1994), 45. Boym draws on Vladimir Nabokov's analysis of *poshlost'* in fiction: Vladimir Nabokov, "Philistines and Philistinism," in *Lectures on Russian Literature*, ed. Fredson Bowers (New York: Harcourt Brace Jovanovich, 1981), 309.

6. For the state's changing attitudes toward consumerism, see Anna Paretskaya, "The Soviet Communist Party and the Other Spirit of Capitalism," *Sociological Theory*, no. 4 (2010): 390–91; Serguei Oushakine, "'Against the Cult of Things': On Soviet Productivism, Storage Economy, and Commodities with No Destination," *Russian Review*, no. 4 (2014): 200.

7. Susan Reid, "This Is Tomorrow! Becoming a Consumer in the Soviet Sixties," in *The Socialist Sixties: Crossing Borders in the Second World*, ed. Anne Gorsuch and Diane Koenker (Bloomington: Indiana University Press, 2013), 32; Sheila Fitzpatrick, *Everyday Stalinism: Ordinary Life in Extraordinary Times: Soviet Russia in the 1930s* (New York: Oxford University Press, 1999), 1.

8. See the insightful study by Alexey Golubev: *The Things of Life: Materiality in Late Soviet Russia* (Ithaca, NY: Cornell University Press, 2020), 2, 3. For discussion of rationing, see Elena Stiazhkina, "The 'Petty-Bourgeois Woman' and the 'Soulless Philistine': Gendered Aspects of the History of Soviet Everyday Life from the Mid-1960s to the Mid-1980s," trans. Liv Bliss, *Russian Studies in History*, no. 2 (2012): 68.

9. Concerning nostalgia, see Anna Ivanova, "Socialist Consumption and Brezhnev's Stagnation: A Reappraisal of Late Communist Everyday Life," *Kritika*, no. 3 (2016): 666.

10. Lionel Trilling, *Sincerity and Authenticity* (Cambridge, MA: Harvard University Press, 1973), 2; Ellen Rutten, *Sincerity after Communism: A Cultural History* (New Haven, CT: Yale University Press, 2017), viii, 36, 37. For a classic analysis of the intelligentsia, consult Isaiah Berlin, "Introduction," in *Russian Intellectual History: An Anthology*, ed. Marc Raeff (New York: Harcourt, Brace, and World, 1966).

11. Concerning sincerity as Trifonov's most important concept, see Ol'ga Trifonova, interview with Benjamin Sutcliffe, Moscow, June 18, 2015. For Trifonov's pronouncement on *iskrennost'*, see the television show *Iurii Trifonov: Stranitsy tvorchestva* (Glavnaia redaktsiia literaturno-dramaticheskikh programm TsT, 1985), 17:24. On the assumptions that pair honesty and literary talent, see, for example, Tzvetan Todorov, *The Poetics of Prose*, trans. Richard Howard (Ithaca, NY: Cornell University Press, 1977), 82. Elena Bykova links Trifonov and Turgenev in "Problemy lichnosti v tvorchestve Iuriia Trifonova" (abstract of candidate dissertation, Moscow State Pedagogical University, 1995), 9.

Notes to Pages 6–8

12. For connections between sincerity and kindness, see Anna Wierzbicka, "Russkie kul'turnye skripty i ikh otrazhenie v iazyke," *Russkii iazyk v nauchnom osveshchenii*, no. 4 (2002): 25, quoted in Rutten, *Sincerity after Communism*, 41. See also M. Gorelikov, "Predstavlenie o dukhovno-nravstvennom vospitanii v sovetskoi pedagogike," *Vestnik KRAUNTS: Gumanitarnye nauki*, no. 2 (2015): 82.

13. Andrei Voznesenskii, *Iurii Trifonov: Stranitsy tvorchestva*, 42:45. For one of the many scholars discussing the Soviet conception of time, see Simon Franklin, "Russia in Time," in *National Identity in Russian Culture: An Introduction*, ed. Simon Franklin and Emma Widdis (Cambridge: Cambridge University Press, 2004), 18.

14. Concerning Evgeniia Lur'e, see "Evgeniia Abramovna Lur'e-Trifonova, 1904–1975," Muzei "Dom na naberezhnoi, " accessed January 9, 2023, https://dnnmuseum.ru/евгения-абрамовна-лурье-трифонова-1904-1975/. On Slovatinskaia and Valentin Trifonov, see Ol'ga Trifonova, *Iurii i Ol'ga Trifonovy vspominaiut* (Moscow: Sovershenno sekretno, 2003), 10–11. Yuri Slezkine discusses Trifonov, his family, and the House on the Embankment in the mammoth study *The House of Government: A Saga of the Russian Revolution* (Princeton, NJ: Princeton University Press, 2017).

15. Evgeny Dobrenko, *Late Stalinism: The Aesthetics of Politics* (New Haven, CT: Yale University Press, 2020), 10–11. On Trifonov's activities during the war, see Trifonova and Trifonov, "Iz dnevnikov i rabochikh tetradei," *Druzhba narodov*, no. 6 (1998). David Gillespie also discusses this period in *Iurii Trifonov: Unity through Time* (Cambridge: Cambridge University Press, 1992), 3. Trifonova describes the success of *Students* in *Iurii i Ol'ga Trifonovy vspominaiut*, 3–4. As shown by her comments on Trifonov's family and *Students*, Trifonova's perspective is deeply subjective: she is an important albeit partisan source of information for my study. Concerning Trifonov's parents, see Trifonov, "Zapiski soseda: Iz vospominanii," in *Kak nashe slovo otzovetsia . . .*, comp. A. Shitov, notes by O. Trifonova and A. Shitov (Moscow: Sovetskaia Rossiia, 1985), 144. On Trifonov wanting to believe in Stalinism, see Natal'ia Ivanova, interview with Sutcliffe, Moscow, June 22, 2015.

16. Lilya Kaganovsky, *How the Soviet Man Was Unmade: Cultural Fantasy and Male Subjectivity under Stalin* (Pittsburgh: University of Pittsburgh Press, 2008). 1. Dobrenko makes a similar argument in *Late Stalinism*, 31.

17. Grosz, *Volatile Bodies*, 9; Keith Livers, *Constructing the Stalinist Body: Fictional Representations of Corporeality in the Stalinist 1930s* (Lanham, MD: Lexington Books, 2004), 2.

18. Polly Jones, *Myth, Memory, Trauma: Rethinking the Stalinist Past in the Soviet Union, 1953–70* (New Haven, CT: Yale University Press, 2013), 6; Anna Alekseyeva, *Everyday Soviet Utopias: Planning, Design and the Aesthetics of Developed Socialism* (New York: Routledge, 2019), 15.

19. For Trifonov's belief that writers should contribute to Soviet society, see his "Mysli pered nachalom," *Smena*, no. 21 (1951): 4. Concerning the Komsomol's reaction, see Trifonova, *Iurii i Ol'ga Trifonovy vspominaiut*, 3–4.

20. On Trifonov simultaneously working on the sequel to *Students* as well as *The Disappearance*, see Trifonova and Trifonov, "Iz dnevnikov i rabochikh tetradei," *Druzhba narodov*, no. 6 (1998).

110 Notes to Pages 9–11

21. Gillespie discusses the author's first marriage and trips to Turkmenia: *Iurii Trifonov*, 4–5. In her superlative study, Natal'ia Ivanova discusses Trifonov's time in Central Asia. See *Proza Iuriia Trifonova* (Moscow: Sovetskii pisatel', 1984), 50. Trifonova describes her late husband's feeling of servitude in Trifonova and Trifonov, "Iz dnevnikov i rabochikh tetradei," *Druzhba narodov*, no. 6 (1998).

22. Tadeusz Drewnowski, "Kuźnia młodych charakterów," in *Studenci* (Warsaw: Iskry, 1953), 6. This foreword appeared in March 1953, before Thaw policies had begun. L. Aleksandrov, "Vremia rabotat' vslast'," *Literaturnaia Rossiia*, October 26, 1963, 15. Ivanova and Gillespie are the two major critics who substantially addressed Trifonov's works before the mid-1960s. Ivanova's monograph, which was the first book-length study of Trifonov and appeared before perestroika, courageously critiqued how the state manipulated literature.

23. Igor' Dedkov, "Vertikali Iuriia Trifonova," *Novyi mir*, no. 8 (1985): 234; Marko Dumančić, *Men Out of Focus: The Soviet Masculinity Crisis in the Long Sixties* (Toronto: University of Toronto Press, 2021), 7, 9.

24. Denis Kozlov and Eleonory Gilburd, "The Thaw as an Event in Russian History," in *The Thaw: Soviet Society and Culture during the 1950s and 1960s*, ed. Denis Kozlov and Eleonory Gilburd (Toronto: University of Toronto Press, 2013), 45. For the kitchen debates, see Susan Reid, "Cold War in the Kitchen: Gender and the De-Stalinization of Consumer Taste in the Soviet Union under Khrushchev," *Slavic Review*, no. 2 (2002); Bren and Neuberger, "Introduction," 8.

25. Larissa Zakharova, *S'habiller à la soviétique: La mode et le Dégel en URSS* (Paris: CNRS, 2011), 369. On privatizing leisure, see Paretskaya, "The Soviet Communist Party," 392; Reid, "This Is Tomorrow!," 49. Concerning films and cartoons, see Dumančić, *Men out of Focus*, 9; L. N. Zhilina and N. T. Frolova, *Problemy potrebleniia i vospitanie lichnosti* (Leningrad: Mysl', 1969), 42.

26. Golubev, *The Things of Life*, 23; A. Metchenko, "Paradoksy NTR i sotsialisticheskii realizm," *Moskva*, no. 9 (1974): 190, 196.

27. Rutten, *Sincerity after Communism*, viii. See also Rutten, *Unattainable Bride Russia: Gendering Nation, State, and Intelligentsia in Russian Intellectual Culture* (Evanston, IL: Northwestern University Press, 2012), 4; Petr Vail' and Aleksandr Genis, *60-e. Mir sovetskogo cheloveka* (Moscow: Novoe literaturnoe obozrenie, 1996), 100.

28. Boym, *Common Places*, 40.

29. Andrew Jenks comments on Gagarin: "The Sincere Deceiver: Yuri Gagarin and the Search for a Higher Truth," in *Into the Cosmos: Space Exploration and Soviet Culture*, ed. James Andrews and Afis Siddiqi (Pittsburgh: University of Pittsburgh Press, 2011), 108.

30. Vladimir Pomerantsev, "Ob iskrennosti v literature," *Novyi mir*, no. 12 (1953): 218. On truthfulness in literature, see Iurii Trifonov, "Vozvrashchenie k 'prosus,'" in *Kak nashe slovo otzovetsia . . .* , 77.

31. Jones, *Myth, Memory, Trauma*, 15. For Dmitrii Likhachev there could be no conscience without memory: both *iskrennost'* and remembrance rely on honesty yet fall prey to distortion and selective gaps in memory (Ivanova cites Likhachev in *Proza Iuriia Trifonova*, 229). Ivanova, Gillespie, and Josephine Woll extensively discussed memory per se in the author's oeuvre; I focus on the ties between recollection and sincerity and how these are influenced by consumption and depicted via the body.

Notes to Pages 11–14

32. Andrew Wachtel, *An Obsession with History: Russian Writers Confront the Past* (Palo Alto, CA: Stanford University Press, 1994), 12. Jenne Powers explores how Trifonov employs a range of "counterdevices" to contradict Soviet manipulations of history (Jenne Powers, "Novel Histories: Repudiation of Soviet Historiography in the Works of Iurii Trifonov, Vladimir Makanin, and Liudmila Ulitskaia" [PhD diss., University of North Carolina at Chapel Hill, 2009], 61).

33. Concerning Trifonov, Solzhenitsyn, and *Novyi mir*, see Roi Medvedev, "Vospominaniia o Iurii Trifonove," in *Iurii Trifonov: Otblesk lichnosti*, 56, 51.

34. Vladimir Gusev, *V predchuvstvii novogo: O nekotorykh chertakh literatury shestidesiatykh godov* (Moscow: Sovetskii pisatel', 1974), 169. The term "Brezhnev era," like "Stalinism" and "Thaw," denotes a top-down focus on how Kremlin politics influenced culture. I use these problematic phrases because they have become so widely accepted in the field. For a discussion of the cultural stakes of such terminology, see Dina Fainberg and Artemy Kalinovsky, "Introduction," in *Reconsidering Stagnation in the Brezhnev Era: Ideology and Exchange*, ed. Dina Fainberg and Artemy Kalinovsky (Lanham, MD: Lexington Books, 2016), xi.

35. Gillespie, *Iurii Trifonov*, 159; Trifonova, *Iurii i Ol'ga Trifonovy vspominaiut*, 4.

36. Georgii Daneliia, *Osenii marafon* (Mosfil'm, 1979); Paretskaya, "The Soviet Communist Party," 390–91. On the personality's spiritual development, see Ikonnikova and Kobliakov, *Moral' i kul'tura razvitogo sotsialisticheskogo obshchestva*, 18; see also V. Rogovin, "Razvitie sotsialisticheskogo obraza zhizni i voprosy sotsial'noi politiki," *Sotsiologicheskie issledovaniia*, no. 1 (1975): 84; Oushakine, "'Against the Cult of Things,'" 205.

37. Lev Anninskii was one of the few to discuss Trifonov's concerns over technology: "Rassechenie kornia: O publitsistike Iuriia Trifonova," in *Kak nashe slovo otzovetsia . . .*, 11. On civic engagement and two faces, see Liubov' Kabo, *Neveselo byt' meshchaninom!* (Moscow: Izdatel'stvo politicheskoi literatury, 1965), 9, 12; Chernyshova, *Soviet Consumer Culture*, 64.

38. Dumančić, *Men out of Focus*, 187; Stiazhkina, "The 'Petty-Bourgeois Woman,'" 73.

39. Ekaterina Novoselova, "Evoliutsiia khudozhestvennogo voploshcheniia odnogo siuzheta: 'Pereulok zabytykh lits' i 'Vremia i mesto' Iu. V. Trifonova," *Vestnik Tomskogo gosudarstvennogo universiteta*, no. 467 (2021): 42; Pierre Nora, "Between Memory and History: Les Lieux de Mémoire," trans. Marc Roudebush, *Representations*, no. 26 (1989): 7, 9.

40. Trifonov, "Koshki ili zaitsy?," in *Iurii Trifonov: Sobranie sochinenii v chetyrekh tomakh*, ed. S. A. Baruzdin et al. (Moscow: Khudozhestvennaia literatura, 1985), vol. 4, 193–94 (in subsequent references this collection is abbreviated as *Iurii Trifonov: SS*). "Cats or Hares?" was part of the cycle *Abandoned Home* (*Oprokinutyi dom*), which depicts Trifonov's travels abroad.

41. On Rome's colors, see L. Ruzhanskaia, "'Ital'ianskii tekst' v proze Iuriia Trifonova," in *Russkaia literatura v inostrannoi auditorii: Sbornik nauchnykh statei*, comp. I. I. Tolstukhina (St. Petersburg: Izdatel'stvo RGPU imeni A. I. Gertsena, 2020), 119. On "Cats or Hares?" deliberately revising Trifonov's first impressions of Italy, see Novoselova, "Evoliutsiia khudozhestvennogo voploshcheniia," 41.

Notes to Pages 14–16

42. Novoselova connects lack of astonishment to a sense that death is near. See her article "Final kak sistemoobrazuiushchii element v tsikle Iu. V. Trifonova 'Oprokinutyi dom,'" *Ural'skii filologicheskii vestnik*, no. 5 (2013): 184. A critic at the time noted that "Cats or Hares?" represented taking stock, where the body reflects the loss of youthful sincerity: G. Rogova, "Itogi i razdum'ia," *Pod"em*, no. 11 (1982): 136; Ivanova, *Proza Iuriia Trifonova*, 287.

43. Trifonov, "Vospominaniia o Dzhentsano," in *Iurii Trifonov: Izbrannye proizvedeniia v dvukh tomakh* (Moscow: Khudozhestvennaia literatura, 1978), vol. 2, 430 (subsequent references to this collection denote it as *Iurii Trifonov: IP*); Nora, "Between Memory and History," 13.

44. Iurii Lotman, *Besedy o russkoi kul'ture: Byt i traditsii russkogo dvorianstva (XVIII–nachalo XIX veka)* (St. Petersburg: Iskusstvo-SPB, 1994), 10. On Trifonov and interpreting everyday life, see Novoselova, "Poetika povsednevnosti v khudozhestvennoi proze Iu. V. Trifonova" (candidate dissertation, Ural State University, 2017).

45. Bren and Neuberger, *Communism Unwrapped*, 6. On Andropov, see Joshua Rubinstein, "Millenarian Bolshevism?," *Kritika*, no. 4 (2018): 878.

46. Trifonov, "Vybirat', reshat'sia, zhertvovat'," in *Kak nashe slovo otzovetsia . . .*, 88; Trifonov, "Net, ne o byte—o zhizni! ," in *Kak nashe slovo otzovetsia . . .*, 103–4; Pomerantsev, "Ob iskrennosti," 240.

47. Igor' Reif, "Pisatel' na vse vremena," *Voprosy literatury*, no. 1 (2013), https:// voplit.ru/article/pisatel-na-vse-vremena/. On patterns in critics' responses to *byt*, see Novoselova, "Poetika povsednevnosti," 20. For an example of *byt* as steppingstone, see N. Tiul'pinov, "Otblesk drugoi zhizni," *Zvezda*, no. 2 (1976): 218.

48. Anninskii, "Rassechenie kornia," 8; Natal'ia Baranskaia, "Nedelia kak nedelia," *Novyi mir*, no. 11 (1969). On *byt* and *The Exchange*, see Trifonova and Trifonov, "Iz dnevnikov i rabochikh tetradei," *Druzhba narodov*, no. 11 (1998), https://magazines .gorky.media/druzhba/1998/11/iz-dnevnikov-i-rabochih-tetradej-4.html. For a discussion of *byt* in Soviet culture, see Benjamin Sutcliffe, *The Prose of Life: Russian Women Writers from Khrushchev to Putin* (Madison: University of Wisconsin Press, 2009), 3–23. Woll, Gillespie, Ivanova, and Marina Selemeneva examine Trifonov's use of everyday life but do not explore how *byt* involves bodies and consumption.

49. Dedkov, "Vertikali Iuriia Trifonova," 224; Nora, "Between Memory and History," 9. Andrei Levkin comments on the sticky sense of tiredness: "'Odna bol'shaia i obshchaia ustalost' Iuriia Trifonova," *God literatury*, August 28, 2015, https://godliter atury.ru/articles/2015/08/28/odna-bolshaya-i-obshhaya-ustalost, quoted in Ivan Bratus, Zoriana Sverdlyk, and Anna Hunka, "Osmyslennia radians'koi diisnosti v povisti Iuriia Tryfonova 'Poperedni pidsumky,'" *Molodyi vchenyi*, no. 2 (2021): 146, https://molodyiv chenyi.ua/index.php/journal/article/view/389.

50. Cathy Caruth, "Introduction," in *Trauma: Explorations in Memory*, ed. Cathy Caruth (Baltimore: Johns Hopkins University Press, 1995). 4–5.

51. Aleksandr Etkind, *Warped Mourning: Stories of the Undead in the Land of the Unburied* (Palo Alto, CA: Stanford University Press, 2013), 14–15.

52. Jay Winter, "Thinking about Silence," in *Shadows of War: A Social History of Silence in the Twentieth Century*, ed. Efrat Ben-Ze'ev, Ruth Ginio, and Jay Winter (Cambridge: Cambridge University Press, 2010), 4; Dmitrii Bykov, "Otsutstvie: O

Notes to Pages 17–20   113

proze Iuriia Trifonova," *Russkaia zhizn'*, February 1, 2008, http://rulife.ru/old/mode/article/517/. Reif cites Tvardovsky's diary in Aleksandr Tvardovskii, "Iz rabochikh tetradei," *Znamia*, no. 7 (1989): 175, https://imwerden.de/pdf/znamya_1989_07__ocr.pdf, quoted in "Pisatel' na vse vremena." On trauma as event and process, see Ushakin, "'Nam etoi bol'iu dyshat'?' O travme, pamiati i soobshchestvakh," in *Travma: punkty*, ed. Sergei Ushakin and Elena Trubina (Moscow: Novoe literaturnoe obozrenie, 2009), 7; Maksim Trudoliubov, "My zhivem v shkafu, nabytom skeletami," *Meduza*, March 24, 2022, https://meduza.io/feature/2022/03/24/my-zhivem-v-shkafu-nabitom-skeletami.

53. Yury Trifonov, *The House on the Embankment*, in *"Another Life" and "The House on the Embankment*," trans. Michael Glenny (Evanston, IL: Northwestern University Press, 1999), 189.

54. Maya Nadkarni, *Remains of Socialism: Memory and Futures of the Past in Postsocialist Hungary* (Ithaca, NY: Cornell University Press, 2020), 7.

55. For Trifonov's similarities with village prose authors, see Ivanova, *Proza Iuriia Trifonova*, 99. Trifonov discusses his respect for Valentin Shukshin, for instance, in Elena Vail', "Interv'iu s Iuriem Trifonovym," *Obozrenie*, no. 6 (1983): 33.

56. On the state's supposed interest in *iskrennost'*, see Ikonnikova and Kobliakov, *Moral' i kul'tura*, 37.

57. Alekseyeva, *Everyday Soviet Utopias*, 4–5

58. For critics' interest in Trifonov's transformation, see Thomas Seifrid, "Trifonov's *House on the Embankment* and the Fortunes of Aesopian Speech," *Slavic Review*, no. 4 (1990): 611. See also Josephine Woll's excellent study: *Invented Truth: Soviet Reality and the Literary Imagination of Iurii Trifonov* (Durham, NC: Duke University Press, 1991), 21. Several other Western monographs appeared during this time.

59. For Trifonov's focus on the intelligentsia, see, for instance, Anatolii Lanshchikov, "Geroi i vremia . . . ," *Don*, no. 11 (1973): 174, 176.

60. Trifonov, *Kak nashe slovo otzovetsia . . .* , 348n2.

61. Tat'iana Trifonova, "Vmesto predisloviia," in Aleksandr Shitov, *Iurii Trifonov: Khronika zhizni i tvorchestva, 1925–1981* (Yekaterinburg: Izdatel'stvo Ural'skogo universiteta, 1997). 9.

62. Aleksandr Solzhenitsyn, "The Smatterers," in *From under the Rubble*, trans. A. M. Brock et al. (Boston: Little, Brown, 1975), 240–41.

63. Marina Selemeneva, *Poetika gorodskoi prozy Iu. V. Trifonova* (Voronezh: Nauchnaia kniga, 2008), 125. Aleksandr Shitov stated that the author had a philosophy of humanism; like Selemeneva's assertion, this claim is correct yet obscures Trifonov's Stalinist period. Shitov was the most prolific critic writing on Trifonov. See his *Gumanizm v plenu . . . Nravstvennaia uprugost' prozy Iuriia Trifonova* (Moscow: Liubimaia Rossiia, 2010), 16.

64. Trifonov, *Kak nashe slovo otzovetsia . . .* , 350. The author first made this objection in Trifonov, "Nado verit' v khoroshikh liudei," interview with V. Lavretskaia, *Uchitel'skaia gazeta*, July 19, 1979.

65. Mark Lipovetskii and Naum Leiderman, *Ot "sovetskogo pisatelia" k pisateliu sovetskoi epokhi: Put' Iuriia Trifonova* (Yekaterinburg: Izdatel'stvo AMB, 2001), 3. One critic derided Trifonov's publication within the USSR as a state ploy to simulate openness. See Leonid Terakopian, quoted in Iurii Leving, "Vlast' i slast' ('Dom na

114   Notes to Pages 20–25

naberezhnoi' Iu. V. Trifonova)," *Novoe literaturnoe obozrenie*, no. 5 (2005), http://mag azines.russ.ru/nlo/2005/75/le24.html.

66. Alexei Yurchak, *Everything Was Forever, until It Was No More: The Last Soviet Generation* (Princeton, NJ: Princeton University Press, 2006). On Trifonov and the black market, see Boris Pankin, "Ego pravde ne nuzhna byla 'ezopovshchina,'" in *Iurii Trifonov: Otblesk lichnosti*, 61. Concerning Solzhenitsyn, see Medvedev, "Vospominaniia o Iurii Trifonove," 49. For mention of Kopelev, see Trifonova and Trifonov, "Iz dnevnikov i rabochikh tetradei," *Druzhba narodov*, no. 2 (1999), https://magazines .gorky.media/druzhba/1999/2/iz-dnevnikov-i-rabochih-tetradej-6.html.

67. Concerning Trifonov's fear of *Students*, see "Zapiski soseda," 147. His widow claims that Stalin, seeing Trifonov's name on the list of awardees for the prize, downgraded him from first category to third category due to lingering hatred for the writer's father (Trifonova and Trifonov, "Iz dnevnikov i rabochikh tetradei," *Druzhba narodov*, no 6 (1998).

68. Anne Dwyer, "Runaway Texts: The Many Life Stories of Iurii Trifonov and Christa Wolf," *Russian Review*, no. 64 (2005): 618; Ivanova, *Proza Iuriia Trifonova*, 27.

Chapter 1. A Radiant Future of Things

1. "V podmoskovnoi Kommunarke na poligone NKVD otkryli memorial zhertvam terrora," *Novye Izvestiia*, October 29, 2018, https://newizv.ru/news/2018-10-27/v -podmoskovnoy-kommunarke-na-poligone-nkvd-otkryli-memorial-zhertvam-ter rora-276791. Concerning the Stalin Prize, see Medvedev, "Vospominaniia o Iurii Trifonove," 50. In her commentary to one of the writer's notebooks, Trifonova describes discovering that Trifonov's father had been buried next to the Kommunarka communal farm (which would be later associated with yet another tragedy: Putin's botched response to the 2020 coronavirus outbreak). Trifonova and Trifonov, "Iz dnevnikov i rabochikh tetradei," *Druzhba narodov*, no. 2 (1999). For the "liquidation" of Memorial, I consulted the group's website, last updated February 28, 2022, https://www .memo.ru/ru-ru/.

2. Dobrenko, *Late Stalinism*, 3.

3. On the changing nature of late-Stalinist ideological campaigns, see Juliane Fürst, *Stalin's Last Generation: Soviet Post-War Youth and the Emergence of Mature Socialism* (New York: Oxford University Press, 2010), 73; Mikhail Chiaureli, *Padenie Berlina* (Mosfil'm, 1949). On film and masculinity, see Dumančić, *Men out of Focus*, 29.

4. Vladimir Dobrovol'skii, *Troe v serykh shineliakh* (Moscow: Molodaia gvardiia, 1950).

5. Boris Polevoi, *Povest' o nastoiashchem cheloveke* (Moscow: Izdatel'stvo khudozhestvennoi literatury, 1969). See Kaganovsky's provocative reading of Meres'ev in *How the Soviet Man Was Unmade*, 122.

6. Ivan Pyr'ev, *Kubanskie kazaki* (Mosfil'm, 1950). Vladimir Padunov first introduced me to this film. Aleksandr Pyzhikov discusses late-Stalinist attempts to better rural conditions in "Soviet Postwar Society and the Antecedents of the Khrushchev Reforms," *Russian Studies in History*, no. 3 (2012). On deaths due to starvation, see Nicholas Ganson, *The Soviet Famine of 1946–47 in Global and Historical Perspective* (New York: Palgrave Macmillan, 2009).

Notes to Pages 25–28

7. Fürst, *Stalin's Last Generation*, 3; Vera Dunham, *In Stalin's Time: Middleclass Values in Soviet Fiction* (New York: Cambridge University Press, 1976), 4. Concerning the supposed absence of shortages, see Randi Cox, "All This Can Be Yours! Soviet Commercial Advertising and the Social Construction of Space, 1928–1956," in *The Landscape of Stalinism: The Art and Ideology of Soviet Space*, ed. Evgeny Dobrenko and Eric Naiman (Seattle: University of Washington Press, 2003), 145.

8. On the perceptions of soldiers, see Pyzhikov, "Soviet Postwar Society," 28.

9. For discussion of the 1947 draft law, see Pyzhikov, "Soviet Postwar Society," 40.

10. Liudmila Ulitskaia, *Sviashchennyi musor* (Moscow: Astrel', 2012), 266. Concerning the NTR beginning in the late 1950s, see V. Ivasheva, *Na poroge XXI veka* (Moscow: Khudozhestvennaia literatura, 1979), 4. Ivasheva bases her arguments on the Russian translation of Chester Snow: Ch.-P. Snou, *Dve kul'tury* (Moscow: Progress, 1973), 129.

11. Dunham, *In Stalin's Time*, 46; Nataliia Kozlova, "Socialist Realism: Producers and Consumers," *Russian Social Science Review*, no. 5 (1998): 14, 6.

12. Kozlova, "Socialist Realism," 6.

13. Lewis Siegelbaum, "Introduction: Mapping Private Spheres in the Soviet Context," in *Borders of Socialism: Private Spheres of Soviet Russia*, ed. Lewis Siegelbaum (New York: Palgrave Macmillan, 2006), 3.

14. On academics resembling Kozel'skii, see Trifonov's comments in "Obsuzhdenie povesti Iu. Trifonova 'Studenty,'" *Novyi mir*, no. 2 (1951): 227. For discussion of *Students* and *House on the Embankment*, see Gillespie, *Iurii Trifonov*, 15; Medvedev, "Vospominaniia o Iurii Trifonove," 46. Concerning Trifonov as son of the Stalin era, see Iu. Karasev, "Povest' o studentakh," *Ogonek*, no. 12 (1951): 24. Some passages in this chapter were adapted from Benjamin Sutcliffe, "Iurii Trifonov's *Students*: Body, Place, and Life in Late Stalinism," *Toronto Slavic Quarterly*, no. 48 (2014), http://sites.utoronto.ca/tsq/48/tsq48_sutcliffe.pdf.

15. On correcting mistakes in future versions, see "Obsuzhdenie povesti Iu. Trifonova 'Studenty,'" 227. S. L'vov compares Trifonov's youth and the strength of Soviet literature in "Povest' o sovetskom studenchestve," in *Vydaiushchiesia proizvedeniia sovetskoi literatury: 1950 god. Sbornik statei*, comp. S. Babenysheva (Moscow: Sovetskii pisatel', 1952), 265. For studying as labor, see L'vov, "Povest' o sovetskom studenchestve," 267.

16. Trifonov, *Studenty*, in *Iurii Trifonov: SS*, vol. 1, 266. Gillespie comments on *Students*, Stalinism, and everything being permitted in *Iurii Trifonov*, 25. Discussion of the connections between Trifonov and Dostoevsky is modified from Benjamin Sutcliffe, "When Trifonov Read Dostoevsky: Ideology, Avarice, and Violence in Late Soviet Culture," *Dostoevsky Studies*, no. 24 (2021), https://dostoevsky-studies.dlls.univr.it/article/view/1008.

17. The work was labeled both "povest'" and "roman" by Trifonov and others; see the excellent analysis by Selemeneva: "Oppozitsiia 'razum/chuvstvo' v povesti Iu. V. Trifonova 'Studenty,'" in *Ratsional'noe i emotsional'noe v literature i fol'klore: Materialy IV Mezhdunarodnoi nauchnoi konferentsii, posviashchennoi pamiati Aleksandra Matveevicha Bulanova, Volgograd, 29 oktiabria–3 noiabria 2007 goda. 2 chasti*, ed. L. N. Savina et al. (Volgograd: Izdatel'stvo VGIPK RO, 2008), vol. 1, 337–38.

18. On feeling young, see Trifonov, "Zapiski soseda," 138.

116 Notes to Pages 28–34

19. Trifonov, *Studenty*, 28, 387, 396; B. Platonov, "Literaturnoe obozrenie: Zametki o russkoi sovetskoi proze 1950 goda. Stat'ia vtoraia," *Zvezda*, no. 2 (1951), 160–61. Kozel'skii's love of tennis, in contrast to Sergei's passion for volleyball, indicates self-promotion over self-sacrifice (Gillespie, *Iurii Trifonov*, 25).

20. Trifonov, *Studenty*, 102, 384, 382, 386.

21. Trifonov, *Studenty*, 323.

22. Oleg Kharkhordin, "Reveal and Dissimulate: A Genealogy of Private Life in Soviet Russia," in *Public and Private in Thought and Practice: Perspectives on a Grand Dichotomy*, ed. Jeff Weintraub and Krishan Kumar (Chicago: University of Chicago Press, 1997), 357.

23. Trifonov, "V kratkom—beskonechnoe: Beseda s kritikom A. Bocharovym," in *Kak nashe slovo otzovetsia . . .* , 239.

24. Trifonov, *Studenty*, 281. Russian culture has long paired women with the natural world. See, for example, Joanna Hubbs, *Mother Russia: The Feminine Myth in Russian Culture* (Bloomington: Indiana University Press, 1988).

25. Trifonov, *Studenty*, 289. On Stalinism's circumspect images of sexuality, see Fürst, *Stalin's Last Generation*, 268. As Gillespie notes, maturity, interest in the collective, and "sincerity" make Olia everything materialistic Lena is not (Gillespie, *Iurii Trifonov*, 23–24). Olia, in contrast to Lena, is not merely a woman whom Vadim loves—she is worthy of him and shares his attitudes (Selemeneva, "Oppozitsiia 'razum/chuvstvo,'" 342).

26. Yuri Trifonov, *Students*, trans. Ivy Litvinova and Margaret Wetlin (Moscow: Izdatel'stvo literatury na inostrannykh iazykakh, 1956), 497–98.

27. Trifonov, *Studenty*, 136, 137.

28. Trifonov, *Studenty*, 142. Concerning the problem of veterans, see Dunham, *In Stalin's Time*, 4. L'vov discusses partisan chaos in "Povest' o sovetskom studenchestve," 270.

29. Trifonov, *Students*, 99.

30. Trifonov, *Students*, 103–4.

31. Dobrenko, *Late Stalinism*, 11.

32. Trifonov, *Studenty*, 211.

33. Trifonov, *Studenty*, 53; Trifonov, *Students*, 49–50.

34. Trifonov, *Studenty*, 309, 318. On the problem of the elegant female wardrobe, see the important early study by Xenia Gasiorowska, *Women in Soviet Fiction, 1917–1964* (Madison: University of Wisconsin Press, 1968), 12. Fürst also notes the era's apprehensions: dressing with style was acceptable but those too interested in clothing were seen as "devoid of true emotions" (*Stalin's Last Generation*, 274). Vadim's own appearance is never emphasized; in *House on the Embankment* this lack of distinguishing features becomes sinister, signaling Glebov's absent morality.

35. Karasev, "Povest' o studentakh," 24.

36. On *poshlost'*, see L'vov, "Povest' o sovetskom studenchestve," 272.

37. Trifonov, *Studenty*, 148.

38. In later decades Trifonov mentioned his admiration for Bunin, whom he read in the late 1940s on the advice of his mentor, Konstantin Fedin (Trifonov, "I. A. Bunin," in *Kak nashe slovo otzovetsia . . .* , 26).

39. Trifonov, *Students*, 88.

40. Trifonov, *Studenty*, 221. On generational conflict and student novellas, see Dunham, *In Stalin's Time*, 205. Ivanova notes that Trifonov based much of Kozel'skii's appearance on Fedin. Trifonov admired the author, unlike the professor in *Students* (Ivanova, *Proza Iuriia Trifonova*, 20–21).

41. Trifonov, "Zimnii den' v garazhe," in *Pod solntsem: Rasskazy* (Moscow: Sovetskii pisatel', 1959), 93, 98, 101, 100. Trifonov's mother being Jewish may have made him more sympathetic to the fate of those murdered in the Holocaust.

42. Trifonov, *Studenty*, 34, 24. Many critics comment on Trifonov's shattered childhood. See Gillespie, *Iurii Trifonov*, 3. For Woll, Trifonov's works depict childhood as luminous yet short-lived, a portrayal that is rooted in Valentin Trifonov's arrest and the subsequent breakup of the family (*Invented Truth*, 21).

43. Etkind, *Warped Mourning*, 1.

44. Beth Holmgren, "Writing the Female Body Politic, 1945–1985," in *A History of Women's Writing in Russia*, ed. Adele Barker and Jehanne Gheith (Cambridge: Cambridge University Press, 2002), 228. On Trifonov lying about his father's death, see Trifonov, "Nedolgoe prebyvanie v kamere pytok," in *Iurii Trifonov: SS*, vol. 4, 207; S. Boiko, "'. . . v kamere pytok.' Chelovek na sobranii v rannei i pozdnei proze Iuriia Trifonova," *Vestnik RGGU. Seriia: Literaturovedenie. Iazykoznanie. Kul'turologiia. Filologiia. Vostokovedenie*, no. 8 (2015): 116.

45. Trifonov, *Studenty*, 24; Ivanova, *Proza Iuriia Trifonova*, 14.

46. On Hamlet in Soviet culture, see Tat'iana Snegireva and Aleksei Podchinenov, "'Syn za ottsa ne otvechaet?' Kompleks bezottsovshchiny v sovetskoi literature," in *Semeinye uzy: Modeli dlia sborki*, comp. and ed. Sergei Ushakin (Moscow: Novoe literaturnoe obozrenie, 2004), vol. 2, 87. The two critics note how Trifonov comments on Tvardovskii's loss of his own father—Tvardovskii had denounced his parent during the anti-kulak campaign (98). Ironically, Tvardovskii was instrumental in publishing *Students*, a novel by a son with a complex sense of guilt over support for the state that had destroyed Valentin Trifonov.

47. Kevin Platt, "'Dom na naberezhnoi' Iu. V. Trifonova i pozdnesovetskaia pamiat' o stalinskom politicheskom nasilii: Dezavuirovanie i sotsial'naia ditsiplina," trans. Nina Stavrogina, *Novoe literaturnoe obozrenie*, no. 1 (2019), https://www.nlobooks.ru/magazines/novoe_literaturnoe_obozrenie/155_nlo_1_2019/article/20649/. Dumančić discusses Stalinism and Hamlet in *Men out of Focus*, 138.

48. Rolf Hellebust, *Flesh to Metal: Soviet Literature and the Alchemy of Revolution* (Ithaca, NY: Cornell University Press, 2003); Trifonov, *Studenty*, 23; Trifonov, *Students*, 14, 36. Novoselova observes that *Students* uses bright, open spaces and repeated references to the future to assure readers of a better tomorrow. See her "Poetika povsednevnosti v khudozhestvennoi proze Iu. V. Trifonova," 32.

49. Stalin is never mentioned explicitly in the narrative, but his presence is everywhere, as one cunning student discerned when praising the novel: "Obsuzhdenie povesti Iu. Trifonova 'Studenty,'" 222. Vadim and his comrades happily sacrifice a free day to lay the gas pipes that literally and symbolically join these young scholars to the Soviet power grid (Trifonov, *Studenty*, 160).

50. Trifonov, "V stepi," in *Pod solntsem*, 166. For a discussion of the victims of collectivization in the Kazakh SSR, see Sarah Cameron, *The Hungry Steppe: Famine, Violence, and the Making of Soviet Kazakhstan* (Ithaca, NY: Cornell University Press,

2018). Concerning Trifonov's mother, see his sister's discussion of the camp: T. Trifonova, "Vmesto predisloviia," 8.

51. Drewnowski, "Kuźnia młodych charakterów," 6–7.

52. Trifonov, *Studenty*, 38; Trifonov, *Students*, 33.

53. Trifonov, *Studenty*, 44.

54. Trifonov, *Studenty*, 33.

55. Trifonov, *Students*, 301.

56. For the problem of outmoded *byt*, see L'vov, "Povest' o sovetskom studenchestve," 272. In the *studencheskaia povest'* an academic's bachelor status is also a warning; Kozel'skii is neither physically nor symbolically adding to the Great Family (Dunham, *In Stalin's Time*, 211). The late Karen Dawisha brought this point to my attention.

57. Trifonov, *Students*, 50.

58. Trifonov, *Studenty*, 312, 315. On Lena's mother and luxury, see "Obsuzhdenie povesti Iu. Trifonova 'Studenty,'" 222. Gasiorowska noted how authors accused privileged Stalinist mothers of spawning spoiled daughters: *Women in Soviet Fiction*, 219. For mention of Lena's father providing the power that guarantees the family's wealth, see the problematic study by Carolina de Maegd-Soëp, *Trifonov and the Drama of the Russian Intelligentsia* (Ghent: Russian Institute, 1990), 36.

CHAPTER 2. ENTHUSIASM AND AMBIVALENCE

1. For a discussion of the encounter between Trifonov and Solzhenitsyn as well as the meeting with Trifonov and Mikoyan, see Trifonova and Trifonov, "Iz dnevnikov i rabochikh tetradei," *Druzhba narodov*, no. 1 (1999), http://magazines.russ.ru/druzhba/1999/1/trif.html.

2. Stephen Bittner, *The Many Lives of Khrushchev's Thaw: Experience and Memory in Moscow's Arbat* (Ithaca, NY: Cornell University Press, 2008), 8–11.

3. Golubev, *The Things of Life*, 15.

4. Ivanova, Gillespie, and to a lesser extent Woll discuss Central Asia but only in an episodic manner. For Trifonov's ideas about "It Was Noon in Summertime," see "V kratkom—beskonechnoe," 242.

5. On the Thaw's hope for the future, see Jones, "The Personal and the Political: Opposition to the Thaw and the Politics of Literary Identity in the 1950s and 1960s," in *The Thaw*, 232.

6. Bykov, "Otsutstvie," 9, 7; Vail' and Genis, *60-e*, 278. Trifonova notes that her husband did not approve of the invasion: email to Benjamin Sutcliffe, 19 May 2022.

7. Feliks Mironer and Marlen Khutsiev, *Vesna na Zarechnoi ulitse* (Odessa Film Studio, 1956); Marlen Khutsiev, *Zastava Il'icha* (Gorky Film Studio, 1964). On patterns the Thaw inherited from Stalinism, see Aleksandr Prokhorov, *Unasledovannyi diskurs: Paradigm stalinskoi kul'tury v literature i kinematografe "ottepeli"* (St. Petersburg: Akademicheskii proekt/Izdatel'stvo DNK, 2007).

8. Aleksandr Solzhenitsyn, "Odin den' Ivana Denisovicha," *Novyi mir*, no. 11 (1962); Andrei Tarkovskii, *Ivanovo detstvo* (Mosfil'm, 1962); Lida Oukaderova, *The Cinema of the Soviet Thaw: Space, Materiality, Movement* (Bloomington: Indiana University Press, 2017), 4, 14; Josephine Woll, *Real Images: Soviet Cinema and the Thaw* (London: I.B. Tauris, 2000).

Notes to Pages 43–46

9. Caruth, "Introduction," 4–5; Grigorii Kozintsev, *Gamlet* (Lenfil'm, 1964).

10. Etkind, *Warped Mourning*, 17. Concerning Hamlet's opponents, see Dumančić, *Men out of Focus*, 16, 17.

11. Rutten, *Sincerity after Communism*, 36; Trilling, *Sincerity and Authenticity*, 3–4.

12. Grekova, "Letom v gorode," *Novyi mir*, no. 4 (1965). Concerning Thaw culture's ideas about sexuality and love, see Deborah Field, "Communist Morality and Meanings of Private Life in Post-Stalinist Russia, 1953–1964" (PhD diss., University of Michigan, 1996), 301. Gasiorowska asserted that the Thaw connected eroticism with sincerity, even if women had sex outside of marriage (*Women in Soviet Literature*, 228).

13. For the 1962 announcement about the coming of communism, see Vail' and Genis, *60-e*, 12.

14. On food riots, see Zakharova, "Soviet Fashion in the 1950s–1960s: Regimentation, Western Influences, and Consumption Strategies," in *The Thaw*, 403. Reid examines consumerism as competition in "Cold War in the Kitchen"; see also Kozlov and Gilburd, "The Thaw as an Event in Russian History," in *The Thaw*, 45; Gleb Tsipursky, *Socialist Fun: Youth, Consumption, and State-Sponsored Popular Culture in the Soviet Union, 1945–1970* (Pittsburgh: University of Pittsburgh Press, 2016), 4.

15. Vail' and Genis, *60-e*, 14; Kabo, *Neveselo byt' meshchaninom!*, 8–9. Kabo notes that *meshchanstvo* also threatened intelligentsia values (12).

16. Reid, "This is Tomorrow!," 44.

17. Grekova, "Damskii master," *Novyi mir*, no. 11 (1963). On the promises and failures of new chemicals, see Natal'ia Lebina, "Plus the *Chemicalization* of the Entire Wardrobe," *Russian Studies in History*, no. 1 (2009).

18. Susan Costanzo, "The 1959 Liriki-Fiziki Debate: Going Public with the Private?," in *Borders of Socialism*, 255. She cites Il'ia Erenburg, "Otvet na odno pis'mo," *Komsomol'skaia pravda*, September 2, 1959, 2–3.

19. Grekova, "Za prokhodnoi," *Novyi mir*, no. 11 (1962).

20. Costanzo, "The 1959 Liriki-Fiziki Debate," 255. The "culture of feelings" reappears in Brezhnev-era worries over materialism.

21. Jones discusses being on the right side of history in "The Personal and the Political," 253–54. Kozlov and Gilburd, "The Thaw as an Event," 55. In reality both Lenin and Stalin implemented absolutism and oppression. For a damning discussion of the links between these two rulers, see Vasilii Grossman, *Everything Flows*, trans. Robert Chandler and Elizabeth Chandler with Anna Aslanyan (New York: New York Review Books, 2009).

22. On the natural world, see Dumančić, *Men out of Focus*, 195.

23. Trifonov, "Prodolzhitel'nye uroki," in *Iurii Trifonov: IP*, vol. 2, 509, quoted in Ivanova, *Proza Iuriia Trifonova*, 34.

24. For background on Trifonov's mother, see "Evgeniia Abramovna Lur'e-Trifonova." On trying to make Central Asia his own, see Trifonov, "Impul's pervoi knigi," in *Kak nashe slovo otzovetsia . . .* , 132.

25. Edith Clowes argues that Russia may realize that it as a country is marginal if it cannot distinguish its more "European" center from Central Asia (Clowes, *Russia on the Edge: Imagined Geographies and Post-Soviet Identity* [Ithaca, NY: Cornell University Press, 2011, 10]).

120   Notes to Pages 46–51

26. Trifonov, "Bako," in *Pod solntsem*, 207–8.

27. Z. Finitskaia, "Pod iarkim solntsem," *Oktiabr'*, no. 12 (1960): 231; L. Iakimenko, "Lik vremeni," in Trifonov, *Utolenie zhazhdy* (Moscow: Khudozhestvennaia literatura, 1967), 4–5. For praise similar to Iakimenko's, see Eduard Babaev, "Rasskazy romanista," *Novyi mir*, no. 9 (1970): 269, 271.

28. Trifonov, "Bako," 205, 208.

29. Trifonov, "Pesochnye chasy" in *Pod solntsem*, 211–13; Gillespie, *Iurii Trifonov*, 29–30. Gillespie translates "Pesochnye chasy" as "Clock of Sand." I use the more metaphorical "Hourglass," which underscores the unease the narrator feels when contemplating the passage of time.

30. Trifonov, "Pesochnye chasy," 211.

31. Trifonov's story "The Last Hunt" ("Posledniaia okhota") more sympathetically depicts the harsh Central Asian terrain. A Stalinist Party boss illegally shoots antelopes; the narrator contrasts the "gas heart" of his lumbering truck to the doomed creatures attempting to escape. This is Trifonov's first characterization of people through how they treat animals and the natural world, a description with overtones scorning Stalinist rapaciousness (Trifonov, "Posledniaia okhota," in *Pod solntsem*, 149). On people and animals, see Gillespie, *Iurii Trifonov*, 29.

32. Trifonov, "Polet," *Pod solntsem*, 95; Trifonov, "Pod solntsem," in *Pod solntsem*, 266.

33. Ewa Nikadem-Malinowska, "Droga przez pustynię. Polski epizod w twórczoci Jurija Trifonowa," *Acta Polono-Ruthenica*, no. 5 (2000): 135.

34. On Abramov's compliment, see "Iz dnevnikov i rabochikh tetradei," *Druzhba narodov*, no. 11 (1998).

35. For Trifonov's dismissal of praise, see Vail', "Inter'viu s Iuriem Trifonovym," 32. Portions of the discussion of *Slaking the Thirst* have been modified from Benjamin Sutcliffe, "The Thin Present of Trifonov's Thaw: Time in *Slaking the Thirst*," *Australian Slavonic and East European Studies*, nos. 1–2 (2016). Gillespie identifies Koryshev as Trifonov's first doubting protagonist: see *Iurii Trifonov*, 39–40.

36. Trifonov, *Utolenie zhazhdy* in *Iurii Trifonov: SS*, vol. 1, 648, 749. Ivanova argues that these characters are mired in a moment of time that is nothing more than contemporaneity (*Proza Iuriia Trifonova*, 66). For two critics unsatisfied by the ending, see Iakimenko, "Lik vremeni," 11; Ia. Tikhonov, "Delo, kotoromu ty sluzhish'," *Oktiabr'*, no. 1 (1964): 245. In reality the Karakum Canal was not completed until 1988.

37. Trifonov, *Utolenie zhazhdy*, 561, 497; Abdulla Muradov, *Moi russkii brat* (Ashkhabad: Izdatel'stvo Turkmenistan, 1965), 97.

38. Trifonov, *Utolenie zhazhdy*, 521, 714.

39. Concerning the canal's environmental consequences, see Philip Micklin, "Desiccation of the Aral Sea: A Water Management Disaster in the Soviet Union," *Science*, no. 241 (1988).

40. Trifonov, *Utolenie zhazhdy*, 750.

41. Vs. Savateev, "Molodost' dushi: grani rabochei temy," *Nash sovremennik*, no. 7 (1973). Iakimenko praises Trifonov's biography in "Lik vremeni," 5.

42. Trifonov, *Utolenie zhazhdy*, 421–22, 735, 745. Marina fits a pattern of positive female characters in the Thaw who use work to escape personal problems (Gasiorowska, *Women in Soviet Fiction*, 234).

Notes to Pages 51–55   121

43. Trifonov, *Utolenie zhazhdy*, 411, 413, 414, 699.

44. Trifonov, *Utolenie zhazhdy*, 700. On interfering in private life, see Adrienne Edgar, "Bolshevism, Patriarchy, and the Nation: The Soviet 'Emancipation' of Muslim Women in Pan-Islamic Perspective," *Slavic Review*, no. 3 (2006), summarized in Laura Adams, "Can We Apply Postcolonial Theory to Central Eurasia?," *Central Eurasian Studies Review*, no. 1 (2008): 3. One Turkmen scholar argued that Trifonov solidified the bonds between Russian and Turkmen literature; she ignored his systemic condescension (Aidzhamal Akmuradova, "Ideino-khudozhestvennoe voploshchenie obraza stroitelia Karakumskogo kanala v proizvedeniiakh russkoi i turkmenskoi sovetskoi literatury (v plane sravnitel'no-tipologicheskogo analiza)" (abstract of candidate dissertation, Ashkhabad Institute of Language and Literature, 1982), 2–3. For more praise of Trifonov's Turkmen characters, see Muradov, *Moi russkii brat*, 94.

45. Trifonov, *Utolenie zhazhdy*, 431, 485.

46. On internalizing the legacy of Stalinism, see F. F. Svetov, "Utolenie zhazhdy," *Novyi mir*, no. 11 (1963): 236.

47. Trifonov, *Utolenie zhazhdy*, 477, 516; Ushakin, "'Nam etoi bol'iu dyshat'?," 8–9.

48. Trifonov, *Utolenie zhazhdy*, 440, 653, 434, 555,

49. Trifonov, *Utolenie zhazhdy*, 726. Concerning Kuznetsov nobly sacrificing himself, see Tikhonov, "Delo, kotoromu ty sluzhish," 214.

50. Trifonov, *Utolenie zhazhdy*, 662. The translation is modified from Gillespie, *Iurii Trifonov*, 40.

51. For two critics focusing on this conversation, see Svetov, "Utolenie zhazhdy," 236; V. Rosliakov, "Utolennaia zhazhda," *Moskva*, no. 10 (1963): 204.

52. Trifonov, *Utolenie zhazhdy*, 721. On this scene and prominent speeches in other Trifonov works, see Ivanova, *Proza Iuriia Trifonova*, 70. A liberal critic even feared that making the canal a priority could justify a new wave of arrests to ensure its construction (Svetov, "Utolenie zhazhdy," 240).

53. Trifonov, *Utolenie zhazhdy*, 604, 576. Concerning momentum, see Aleksandrov, "Vremia rabotat' vslast'," 15; Tikhonov, "Delo, kotoromu ty sluzhish," 213, 214.

54. Trifonov, *Utolenie zhazhdy*, 585. This is a modified version of Gillespie's translation in *Iurii Trifonov*, 39.

55. Trifonov, *Utolenie zhazhdy*, 634, 697. For examples of misreading the current, see Rosliakov, "Utolennaia zhazhda," 204; M. Kaminskii and Iu. Lopusov, *Rabochii kharakter: Sovremennaia sovetskaia literatura o rabochem klasse* (Moscow: Prosveshchenie, 1975), 129.

56. Trifonov, *Otblesk kostra*, in *Iurii Trifonov: SS*, 9; T. Trifonova, "Vmesto predisloviia," 8. Concerning similarities between *Slaking the Thirst* and *The Bonfire's Glow*, see Ivanova, *Proza Iuriia Trifonova*, 78.

57. Clemens Günther, "Die metahistoriographische Revolution. Problematisierungen historischer Erkenntnis in der russischen Gegenwartsliteratur" (PhD diss., Free University of Berlin, 2019), 58.

58. Trifonov, *Otblesk kostra*, 8.

59. On the trunk as invention, see Jones, "Iurii Trifonov's *Fireglow* and the 'Mnemonic Communities' of the Brezhnev Era," *Cahiers du monde russe*, nos. 1–2 (2013): 56.

Notes to Pages 56–62

60. Trifonov, *Otblesk kostra*, 9, 47.

61. Viacheslav Sukhanov, "Lichnyi dnevnik v strukture dokumental'nogo i khudozhestvennogo povestvovaniia: 'Otblesk kostra' i 'Starik' Iu. Trifonova," *Tekst. Kniga. Knigoizdanie*, no. 20 (2019): 38. On readers in the 1960s, see Jones "Fireglow," 67. For a wide-ranging discussion of documentary genres in the USSR and beyond, see the papers from the conference "Firsthand Time: Documentary Aesthetics in the Long 1960s," Berlin, January 16–19, 2020, https://www.zfl-berlin.org/event/firsthand-time-documentary-aesthetics-in-the-long-1960s.html.

62. Ivanova, *Proza Iuriia Trifonova*, 93.

63. Trifonov, *Otblesk kostra*, 48. Connecting Valentin Trifonov to 1917 echoes a statement Koryshev makes about his own father in *Slaking the Thirst* (Trifonov, *Utolenie zhazhdy*, 715).

64. Trifonov, *Otblesk kostra*, 8, 144.

65. One Thaw-era critic voiced a similar idea: Valentin Trifonov's name had been restored by the Party, whose fire would illuminate future generations (P. Lavrov, "Iurii Trifonov: Otblesk kostra," *Don*, no. 7 [1965]: 168). Concerning the Leninist course, see Gillespie, *Iurii Trifonov*, 141. Gillespie and Woll translate the novel's title as "campfire," emphasizing the comforting and manageable image at the work's close as opposed to the roaring pyre that opens it. On the translation as "campfire," see Gillespie, *Iurii Trifonov*, 140; Woll, *Invented Truth*, 22.

66. Dobrenko, *Late Stalinism*, 5; Dedkov, "Vertikali Iuriia Trifonova," 222. Jones points out that *The Bonfire's Glow* appeared at the same time as works connecting the 1937 purges to the tragedies of the Great Patriotic War, where Stalin's previous elimination of talented military commanders caused enormous losses ("Fireglow," 216).

67. On Valentin Trifonov finding the location for the Lubyanka prison, see Trifonova and Trifonov, "Iz dnevnikov i rabochikh tetradei," *Druzhba narodov*, no. 1 (1999). Concerning the illusions of the *shestidesiatniki*, see Bykov, *Obrechennye pobediteli: Shestidesiatniki* (Moscow: Molodaia gvardiia, 2019), 5–6. *The Bonfire's Glow* was the author's only work to ignore private life; perhaps the son did not wish to uncover what caused Valentin Trifonov to marry the daughter of his first wife.

68. Trifonov, "Byl letnii polden'," in *Iurii Trifonov: IP*, vol. 1, 167, 165, 171.

69. Trifonov, "Byl letnii polden'," 174.

70. Dedkov, "Vertikali Iuriia Trifonova," 224. Gusev also notes the story's similarities to *The Bonfire's Glow*: both attempt to recover the past after decades of silence stemming from political repression (Gusev, *V predchuvstvii novogo*, 167).

71. Trifonov, "Byl letnii polden'," 174. Ivanova, *Proza Iuriia Trifonova*, 97.

72. On the intelligentsia becoming hostages, see Vail' and Genis, *60-e*, 283.

CHAPTER 3. EMPIRE OF OBJECTS

1. Trifonov, "Iadro pravdy," in *Iadro pravdy: Stat'i, interv'iu, esse* (Moscow: Izdatel'stvo Pravda, 1987), 12.

2. Trifonov, "Iadro pravdy," 12.

3. On the term "stagnation," see Fainberg and Kalinovsky, "Introduction," vii; Yurchak, *Everything Was Forever*.

Notes to Pages 62–64

4. The best analyses of history in Trifonov's later works come from Ivanova, Woll, and Selemeneva. Anninskii for his part cogently argues that Trifonov's turn to the past is essential to the author's final stage of writing ("Rassechenie kornia," 17).

5. Platt, "'Dom na naberezhnoi' Iu. V. Trifonova.'"

6. Trifonov discussed past and present flowing together in: "Voobrazit' beskonechnost': Beseda s korrespondentom 'Literaturnogo obozreniia,'" in *Kak nashe slovo otzovetsia . . .* , 288.

7. Vladimir Men'shov, *Moskva slezam ne verit* (Mosfil'm, 1979). Concerning happiness and the bodies of Trifonov's characters, see Bratus, Sverdlyk, and Hunka, "Osmyslennia radians'koi diisnosti," 146. On population growth, see Michele Rivkin-Fish, "From 'Demographic Crisis' to 'Dying Nation': The Politics of Language and Reproduction in Russia," in *Gender and National Identity in Twentieth-Century Russian Culture*, ed. Helena Goscilo and Andrea Lanoux (Dekalb: Northern Illinois University Press, 2006).

8. Ol'ga Klimova, "Soviet Youth Films under Brezhnev: Watching between the Lines" (PhD diss., University of Pittsburgh, 2013), iv; Rudol'f Noibert, *Novaia kniga o supruzhestve*, ed. V. N. Kolbanovskii (Moscow: Progress, 1969), quoted in Kon, *The Sexual Revolution in Russia*, 96–97.

9. Valentin Rasputin, *Poslednii srok, Proshchanie s Materoi: Povesti i rasskazy* (Moscow: Sovetskii pisatel', 1985); Grekova, *Vdovii parokhod, Porogi. Roman, povesti* (Moscow: Sovetskii pisatel', 1986). Reif and Selemeneva note the similarities between Trifonov and Grekova (Reif, "Pisatel' na vse vremena"; Selemeneva, "Khudozhestvennyi mir Iu. V. Trifonova v kontekste gorodskoi prozy vtoroi poloviny XX veka," abstract of doctoral dissertation [Moscow State Humanities University, 2009], 4, 33).

10. James Millar, "The Little Deal: Brezhnev's Contribution to Acquisitive Socialism," *Slavic Review*, no. 4 (1985): 695–98. This was part of an effort to convince citizens that society was working for the individual as opposed to the individual working for society (see Paretskaya, "The Soviet Communist Party," 390).

11. Alekseyeva, *Everyday Soviet Utopias*, 187; Oushakine, "'Against the Cult of Things,'" 222. For a discussion of *veshch'* (thing) as term, see also Yulia Karpova, *Comradely Objects: Design and Material Culture in Soviet Russia, 1960s–80s* (Manchester: Manchester University Press, 2020), 7. Rogovin used "healthy" Soviet consumption to distinguish the USSR from China, differentiating "Marxist" ideas about a reasonable standard of living from the asceticism and poverty of Maoism ("Razvitie sotsialisticheskogo obraza zhizni," 82).

12. For connections between significance and objects, see Chernyshova, *Soviet Consumer Culture in the Brezhnev Era*, 12. On objects' cachet overshadowing their utility, see Alekseyeva, *Everyday Soviet Utopia*, 179. For one example of intelligentsia worries, see A. Bocharov, *Beskonechnost' poiska: Khudozhestvennye poiski sovremennoi sovetskoi prozy* (Moscow: Sovetskii pisatel', 1982), 102. Katerina Clark outlines how the state and intelligentsia both feared materialism: see "The King Is Dead, Long Live the King: Intelligentsia Ideology in Transition," paper presented at the conference "Russia at the End of the Twentieth Century: Culture and Its Horizons in Politics and Society," Stanford University, October 1998, http://www.stanford.edu/group/Russia20/volumepdf/clark_fin99.pdf.

124 Notes to Pages 64–68

13. Viktoriia Tokareva, "Iaponskii zontik," in *Banketnyi zal* (Moscow: AST, 2001), 139.

14. Kabo, *Ne veselo byt' meshchaninom!*, 13; Ikonnikova denotes this as a "culture of feelings," a phrase suggesting Thaw conceptions of ethics and behavior. See her *Moral' i kul'tura razvitogo sotsialisticheskogo obshchestva*, 47.

15. Stiazhkina, "The 'Petty-Bourgeois Woman,'" 64. On gender roles, see Dumančić, *Men out of Focus*, 18. The 1850–1860s concern over the "superfluous man," for instance, feared men in the nobility were incapable of managing their own lives, let alone contributing to the nation.

16. A. Metchenko, "Paradoksy NTR i sotsialisticheskii realizm," *Moskva*, no. 9 (1974): 191; Leonid Gaidai, *Ivan Vasil'evich meniaet professiiu* (Mosfil'm, 1973). Chapman analyzes the film in "Queuetopia," 142. On the NTR satisfying consumer demands, see Rogovin, "Razvitie sotsialisticheskogo obraza zhizni," 75. O. S. Bliakhman and O. I. Shkaratan discuss the sphere of moral consumption in *NTR, rabochii klass, intelligentsiia* (Moscow: Politizdat, 1973), 260.

17. Golubev, *The Things of Life*, 147; Trifonov, "V pervye chasy tvoreniia: Zametki o sportivnom televidenii," in *Kak nashe slovo otzovetsia . . .*, 209, 210. On television ownership, see Reid, "This Is Tomorrow!," 32. See also the readable, well-researched work by Christine Varga-Harris, *Stories of House and Home: Soviet Apartment Life during the Khrushchev Years* (Ithaca, NY: Cornell University Press, 2015), 44.

18. Trifonov, "Iadro pravdy," 13. Concerning books fitting décor, see T. Simonova, "Kopit' znaniia, a ne izdaniia," *V mire knig*, no. 9 (1985): 56, quoted in Golubev, *The Things of Life*, 151.

19. Anninskii, "Rassechenie kornia," 19. Concerning Carlos the Jackal, the Baader-Meinhof Group, and terrorists as film stars, see Trifonov, "Nechaev, Verkhovenskii i drugie . . . ," in *Kak nashe slovo otzovetsia . . .*, 48, 50. For worries over terrorism and atomic weapons, see Trifonova and Trifonov, "Iz dnevnikov i rabochikh tetradei," *Druzhba narodov*, no. 3 (1999).

20. Vail' and Genis, *60-e*, 282; Rutten, *Sincerity after Communism*, viii.

21. Trifonov, "Vybirat', reshat'sia, zhertvovat'," 85. Selemeneva discusses Kormer's allegation in *Poetika gorodskoi prozy Iu. V. Trifonova*, 135. See also O. Altaev, "The Dual Consciousness of the Intelligentsia and Pseudo-Culture," in *The Political, Social and Religious Thought of Russian "Samizdat": An Anthology*, trans. Nickolas Lupinin, ed. Michael Meerson-Aksenov and Boris Shragin (Belmont, MA: Nordland, 1977), 145.

22. Ivanova, *Proza Iuriia Trifonova*, 188; Sukhanov, "Fenomen zhizne-smerti v povestiakh Iu. Trifonova," in *Russkaia povest' kak forma vremeni: Sbornik statei* (Tomsk: Tomsk State University, 2002), 306.

23. On morality and comfort, see Sarra Shtut, "Rassuzhdeniia i opisaniia," *Voprosy literatury*, no. 10 (1975): 68.

24. Yury Trifonov, *The Exchange*, in *"The Exchange" and Other Stories*, trans. Ellendea Proffer (Ann Arbor, MI: Ardis, 1991), 20–21.

25. Trifonov, *The Exchange*, 22.

26. For eager readers in the library, see N. Avtonomova, "Kogo vybiraet vremia? Po stranitsam 'gorodskikh povestei' Iu. V. Trifonova," *Sem'ia i shkola*, no. 7 (1988): 48;

Notes to Pages 68–72

M. Sinel'nikov, "Ispytanie povsednevnost'iu: Nekotorye itogi," *Voprosy literatury*, no. 2 (1972): 60. Note the title of this article, which equates daily life with testing morality.

27. Sinel'nikov, "Ispytanie povsednevnost'iu," 49; Trifonov, *Obmen*, in *Iurii Trifonov: IP*, vol. 2, 37; Selemeneva, "Problema tipologii personazhei 'gorodskoi' prozy Iu. V. Trifonova (k voprosu o dominantnykh/periferiinykh modeliakh zhenstvennosti v literature XX v.)," *Voprosy filologii*, no. 2 (2007): 82. 85.

28. Trifonov, *Predvaritel'nye itogi*, in *Iurii Trifonov: IP*, vol. 2, 69. Part of the discussion of *Taking Stock* is adapted from Benjamin Sutcliffe, "Trifonov's Turkmenia: Optimism, Despair, and the Intelligentsia," in *Borders and Beyond: Orient-Occident Crossings in Literature*, ed. Adam Bednarczyk, Magdalena Kubarek, and Maciej Szatkowski (Wilmington, DE: Vernon Press, 2018).

29. Trifonov, *Predvaritel'nye itogi*, 77, 78.

30. Trifonov, *Taking Stock*, in *The Long Goodbye: Three Novellas*, trans. Helen Burlingame (New York: Harper and Row, 1978), 108–9.

31. Ivanova, *Proza Iuriia Trifonova*, 135. Trifonov commented in an interview that a "fever" for things was especially dangerous for teenagers (Trifonov, "Shestnadtsatiletnim: Otvety na anketu 'Alogo parusa' gazety 'Komsomol'skaia pravda,'" in *Kak nashe slovo otzovetsia . . .* , 268).

32. Concerning water, see Ivanova, *Proza Iuriia Trifonova*, 109.

33. Trifonov, *Taking Stock*, 200.

34. Trifonov, *Taking Stock*, 123.

35. Trifonov, *Predvaritel'nye itogi*, 90; Lipovetskii and Leiderman, *Ot "sovetskogo pisatelia" k pisateliu sovetskoi epokhi*, 17. Ivanova notes that Gennadii Sergeevich has betrayed others so completely that he has betrayed himself (Ivanova, *Proza Iuriia Trifonova*, 130).

36. Woll, *Invented Truth*, 26.

37. Trifonov, "Taking Stock," 200. On husbands in bad health, see Irina Velembovskaia, "Simpatii i antipatii Iuriia Trifonova," *Novyi mir*, no. 9 (1980): 257.

38. Ivanova, *Proza Iuriia Trifonova*, 132. Concerning the morally dead intelligentsia, see Selemeneva, *Poetika gorodskoi prozy Iu. V. Trifonova*, 137.

39. Ivanova, *Proza Iuriia Trifonova*, 152.

40. Trifonov, *Dolgoe proshchanie*, in *Iurii Trifonov: IP*, vol. 2, 177–78.

41. Gillespie, *Iurii Trifonov*, 82.

42. Trifonov, *Drugaia zhizn'*, in *Iurii Trifonov: IP*, vol. 2, 294. Anninskii maintained that Ol'ga Vasil'evna is not an *obyvatel'* but an altruist who happens to be successful ("Ochishchenie proshlym," 157). This distinction tries to avoid tarring the character with any hint of *meshchanstvo*.

43. Trifonov, *Drugaia zhizn'*, 345–46. Trifonov watched *One Flew Over the Cuckoo's Nest* in Frankfurt but did not connect the film to the ongoing imprisonment of dissidents in psychiatric hospitals, despite *The Bonfire's Glow* depicting an Old Bolshevik tormented this way during Stalinism. Concerning *One Flew over the Cuckoo's Nest*, see Trifonov, "Iadro pravdy," 14; Trifonova and Trifonov, "Iz dnevnikov i rabochikh tetradei," *Druzhba narodov*, no. 3 (1999); Trifonov, *Otblesk kostra*, 24.

44. Trifonov, *Drugaia zhizn'*, 296, 255; S. Eremina and V. Piskunov, "Vremia i mesto prozy Iu. Trifonova," *Voprosy literatury*, no. 5 (1982): 49. Their article is one of the most insightful accounts of Trifonov to appear before perestroika.

126 Notes to Pages 72–79

45. Trifonov, *Another Life*, in *"Another Life" and "House on the Embankment,"* trans. Michael Glenny (Evanston, IL: Northwestern University Press, 1999), 102.

46. Trifonov, "Tolstoi, Lev Nikolaevich," in *Kak nashe slovo otzovetsia . . .* , 34.

47. Trifonov, "Tolstoi," 34; Boym, *Common Places*, 147.

48. Trifonov, *Drugaia zhizn'*, 243, 356.

49. Dwyer, "Runaway Texts."

50. Yury Trifonov, *The House on the Embankment*, in *"Another Life" and "The House on the Embankment,"* 196–97. Parts of the discussion of *House on the Embankment* are modified from Benjamin Sutcliffe, "Cake, Cabbage, and the Morality of Consumption in Iurii Trifonov's *House on the Embankment*," in *Seasoned Socialism: Gender and Food in Late Soviet Everyday Life*, ed. Angela Brintlinger, Anastasia Lakhtikova, and Irina Glushchenko (Bloomington: Indiana University Press, 2019).

51. Nora, "Between Memory and History," 13. On fashion and the overweight male body, see Brandon Miller, "Between Creation and Crisis: Soviet Masculinities, Consumption, and Bodies after Stalin" (PhD diss., Michigan State University, 2013), 158.

52. Trifonov, *Dom na naberezhnoi*, in *Iurii Trifonov: SS*, vol. 2, 411, 422; Selemeneva, *Poetika gorodskoi prozy Iu. V. Trifonova*, 99; Ivanova, *Proza Iuriia Trifonova*, 220.

53. Trifonov, *Dom na naberezhnoi*, 453–54; Trifonov, *The House on the Embankment*, 299–300. I have modified the translation.

54. Trifonov, *Dom na naberezhnoi*, 454.

55. Trifonov, *The House on the Embankment*, 211.

56. On cake and architecture, see Leving, "Vlast' i slast'."

57. Trifonov, *House on the Embankment*, 211. I have modified the translation.

58. Trifonov, *Dom na naberezhnoi*, 382. Il'ia Utekhin discusses the closed space of the communal apartment in *Ocherki kommunal'nogo byta* (Moscow: OGI, 2001, 28).

59. Trifonov, *The House on the Embankment*, 231–32.

60. Irina Paperno, "Personal Accounts of the Soviet Experience," *Kritika*, no. 4 (2002): 596.

61. Nadkarni, *The Remains of Socialism*, 10. Viktor Erofeev was impressed by the detail of the napoleon, singling it out in his praise of *House on the Embankment* (Erofeev, "Tsena svobody," in *Iurii Trifonov: Otblesk lichnosti*, 168).

62. Trifonov, *The House on the Embankment*, 338–39. The italics are in the original but I have modified the translation.

63. Platt, "'Dom na naberezhnoi' Iu. V. Trifonova.'"

64. Trifonov, *Dom na naberezhnoi*, 416–17, 414, 456. Concerning Spinoza, see Marat Grinberg, "Who is Grifanov? David Shrayer-Petrov's Dialogue with Yury Trifonov," in *The Parallel Universes of David Shrayer-Petrov*, ed. Roman Katsman, Maxim Shrayer, and Klavdia Smola (Boston, MA: Academic Studies Press, 2021), 299. Platt notes that Ganchuk's comfortable home implies he has benefited from the power that comes from political violence (Platt, "'Dom na naberezhnoi' Iu. V. Trifonova.'").

65. Fyodor Dostoevsky, *The Demons*, trans. Richard Pevear and Larissa Volokhonsky (New York: Vintage Classics, 1994). On the author's struggle with Dostoevsky, see Trifonova and Iurii Trifonov, "Iz dnevnikov i rabochikh tetradei," *Druzhba narodov*, no. 2 (1999).

66. Trifonov, *Dom na naberezhnoi*, 452.

67. Trifonov, "V kratkom—beskonechnoe," 244.

Notes to Pages 80–85

68. Trifonov, *Dom na naberezhnoi*, 396–97, 473; Seifrid, "Trifonov's *House on the Embankment*," 611.

69. Platt, "'Dom na naberezhnoi' Iu. V. Trifonova." On the incompleteness of life, see Mikhail Bakhtin, "Epic and Novel," in *The Dialogic Imagination: Four Essays by M. M. Bakhtin*, ed. Michael Holquist, trans. Caryl Emerson and Michael Holquist (Austin: University of Texas Press, 1981), 31.

Chapter 4. Utopia Lost

1. Trifonova and Trifonov, "Iz dnevnikov i rabochikh tetradei," *Druzhba narodov*, no. 3 (1999).

2. Selemeneva, *Poetika gorodskoi prozy Iu. V. Trifonova*, 254; Vladimir Amlinskii, "O dniakh edinstvennykh," *Literatunoe obozrenie*, no. 1 (1982): 17; Ol'ga Tangian, "Nemetskie aksenty Iuriia Trifonova," *Znamia*, no. 12 (2015), https://znamlit.ru/publi cation.php? id=6130.

3. Ol'ga Gurova, "Ideology of Consumption in the Soviet Union," in *Communism and Consumerism: The Soviet Alternative to the Affluent Society*, ed. Timo Vihavainen and Elena Bogdanova (Leiden: Brill, 2016), 80; El'dar Riazanov, *Garazh* (Mosfil'm, 1979); Chingiz Aitmatov, "I dol'she veka dlitsia den'," *Novyi mir*, no. 11 (1980). Trifonov, Rasputin, and Aitmatov all equate losing memory with death (whether of the community or individual). On this point, see Eremina and Piskunov, "Vremia i mesto prozy Iu. Trifonova," 52.

4. Reid, "This Is Tomorrow!" 44. For the potential of television, radio, and books, see Zhilina and Frolova, *Problemy potrebleniia*, 57. Concerning *Clockwork Orange*, see Metchenko, "Paradoksy NTR," 192.

5. Trifonov, "Travnichek i khokkei," in *Iurii Trifonov: IP*, vol. 2, 445–46. On Kansas and cars, see Trifonova and Trifonov, "Iz dnevnikov i rabochikh tetradei," *Druzhba narodov*, no. 3 (1999).

6. Sergei Dovlatov, *Kompromiss* (New York: Serebrianyi vek, 1981); Boris Shragin, *The Challenge of the Spirit*, trans. P. S. Falla (New York: Knopf, 1978), 12.

7. Grekova, *Malen'kii Garusov, Kafedra. Povesti* (Moscow: Sovetskii pisatel', 1980).

8. Trifonov, *Neterpenie*, in *Iurii Trifonov: SS*, vol. 3, 8.

9. Trifonov, *Neterpenie*, 381, 384, 391, 394; Vladimir Novokhatko, "Belye vorony Politizdata (zapiski zavreda)," in *Iurii Trifonov: Otblesk lichnosti*, 80. Pavel Khazanov makes a similar argument: see "The Most Important Thing is to Remain a Human Being: Decembrist Protest, Soviet *Lichnost'*, and the Post-1968 Mass-Market Histories of Natan Eidelman and Bulat Okudzhava," *Slavic and East European Journal*, no. 3 (2021): 490. Gillespie comments on how Zheliabov refuses to take responsibility for the terror unleashed by the People's Will, instead blaming the state (*Iurii Trifonov*, 133).

10. Trifonov, *Neterpenie*, 384.

11. Trifonova discusses *Impatience* (and admits the publishing house paid well) in Trifonova and Trifonov, "Iz dnevnikov i rabochikh tetradei," *Druzhba narodov*, no. 1 (1999). On interest in the People's Will, see Ivanova, *Proza Iuriia Trifonova*, 166. Ivanova advanced the claims about subversive material that Trifonova would later make (181).

128 Notes to Pages 85–88

12. Polly Jones, "The Fire Burns On? The 'Fiery Revolutionaries' Biographical Series and the Rethinking of Propaganda in the Brezhnev Era," *Slavic Review*, no. 1 (2015): 36–37; Khazanov, "The Most Important Thing," 478. Concerning fear of apathy and the role of Pastukhova, see Polly Jones, *Revolution Rekindled: The Writers and Readers of Late Soviet Biography* (New York: Oxford University Press, 2019), 14, 151. On distracting readers, see Novokhatko, "Belye vorony Politizdata," 72. For mention of the *kormushka*, see David Lowe, *Russian Writing since 1953: A Critical Survey* (New York: Ungar, 1987), 49, quoted in Jones, *Revolution Rekindled*, 23.

13. Trifonov, *Neterpenie*, 18, 59, 182.

14. A. Lezina-Kurochkina, "Ideal geroicheskoi lichnosti v romane 'Andrei Kozhukhov' S. M. Stepniaka-Kravchinskogo i 'Neterpenie' Iu. Trifonova," ed. M. Ia. Ermakova et al., in *Traditsii i novatorstvo v khudozhestvennoi literature* (Gorky: Gor'kovskii gosudarstvennyi pedagogicheskii institut, 1983), 104; Slezkine, *The House of Government*, 974.

15. Trifonov, "Impul's pervoi knigi," 135. Trifonov's comment about the danger of art as prosecutor was in defense of Rasputin's prose.

16. Trifonov, *Neterpenie*, 3, 386; V. Oskotskii, "Nravstvennye uroki 'Narodnoi voli,'" *Literaturnoe obozrenie*, no. 11 (1973), 58; Natal'ia Il'ina, "Iz rodoslovnoi russkoi revoliutsii: O romane Iuriia Trifonova 'Neterpenie,'" *Neman*, no. 12 (1976): 172. Novokhatko believes that he and Trifonov were cowards for cutting a paragraph on truth and history from the manuscript ("Belye vorony Politizdata," 79–80).

17. Trifonov, "Nechaev, Verkhovenskii, i drugie," in *Kak nashe slovo otzovetsia . . .*, 49. On Zheliabov's similarity to Nechaev, see Aleksandr Zaitsev, "Povest' Iu. V. Trifonova "Neterpenie" v kontekste obshchestvenno-politicheskoi pozitsii I. A. Dedkova," *Neofilologiia*, no. 7 (2021): 713. On the Tsar's possible support for the constitution, see Trifonov, *Neterpenie*, 377. For the mention of "bomb-throwers," see R. Shreder, "Roman s istoriei," *Voprosy literatury*, no. 5 (1982): 69.

18. Concerning the Grand Inquisitor and assassination of Alexander II, see Ol'ga Sukhikh, "Ot velikogo inkvizatura k 'narodnoi vole' (pereosmyslenie filosofskoi problematiki proizvedenii F. M. Dostoevskogo v romane Iu. V. Trifonova 'Neterpenie')," *Vestnik Nizhegorodskogo universiteta*, no. 3 (2011): 315.

19. Trifonov, *Neterpenie*, 332.

20. Ivanova, *Proza Iuriia Trifonova*, 185; Trifonov, *Neterpenie*, 8.

21. Trifonov, *Starik*, in *Iurii Trifonov: SS*, vol. 3, 606; Ushakin, "'Nam etoi bol'iu dyshat'?,'" 9. For a discussion of *The Old Man* and taking stock, see N. Paleeva, "Sviaz' vremeni," *Molodaia gvardiia*, no. 9 (1979): 286.

22. Trifonov, *Starik*, 494, 495, 499, 500, 588; Ivanova, *Proza Iuriia Trifonova*, 241, 243; Dedkov, "Vertikali Iuriia Trifonova," 220. The "flesh of life" is a repeating image in her discussion, showing how she connects *byt* and physicality. Concerning Kandaurov as anomaly, see also Vladimir Voronov, *Khudozhestvennaia kontseptsiia: Iz opyta sovetskoi prozy 60–80-kh godov* (Moscow: Sovetskii pisatel', 1984), 168.

23. Yuri Trifonov, *The Old Man*, trans. Jacqueline Edwards and Mitchell Schneider (New York: Simon and Schuster, 1984), 16.

24. Trifonov, *Starik*, 429, 565.

25. Trifonov, *Starik*, 606.

Notes to Pages 88–94

26. Trifonov, *Starik*, 546. Boris Kagarlitsky discusses valorization of the Civil War in "1960s East and West: The Nature of the *Shestidesiatniki* and the New Left," trans. William Nickell, *boundary 2*, no. 1 (2009): 98.

27. Trifonov, *Starik*, 473; Gillespie, *Iurii Trifonov*, 156; Selemeneva, *Poetika gorodskoi prozy Iu. V. Trifonova*, 221. One critic disingenuously claimed that the image of lava comes from the protagonist and not his creator (Voronov, *Khudozhestvennaia kontseptsiia*, 152).

28. Ivanova, *Proza Iuriia Trifonova*, 168.

29. Dedkov observes that digging is an essential image for Trifonov's late prose. See his "Vertikali Iuriia Trifonova," 234. Igor' Sukhikh connects hardened lava to catacombs in "Pytka pamiat'iu," *Zvezda*, no. 6 (2002), http://magazines.russ.ru/zvezda/2002/6/su.html.

30. Trifonov, *The Old Man*, 17. The italics are in the translation, which I have modified.

31. Lipovetskii and Leiderman, *Ot "sovetskogo" pisatelia k pisateliu sovetskoi epokhi*, 32. Concerning Kandaurov, Pavel Evgrafovich, and *nedochuvstvie*, see Sinel'nikov, "Ispytanie povsednevnost'iu," 41, 43. On realizing *nedochuvstvie* after the fact, see Anna Afanas'eva, "Refleksiia 'nedochuvstviia' v proze Iuriia Trifonova kontsa 60–70-kh godakh XX veka," *Slavica Wratislaviensia*, no. 158 (2014): 270.

32. Lipovetskii and Leiderman, *Ot "sovetskogo pisatelia" k pisateliu sovetskoi epokhi*, 35.

33. Trifonov, *Starik*, 480. Herman Ermolaev addresses brutality and Soviet history in "The Theme of Terror in 'Starik,'" in *Aspects of Modern Russian and Czech Literature. Selected Papers of the Third World Congress for Soviet and East European Studies*, ed. Arnold McMillin (Columbus, OH: Slavica, 1985), 96.

34. For a discussion of art and digging out the truth, see Trifonov, "Uroki mastera," in *Kak nashe slovo otzovetsia . . .* , 179.

35. Iurii Trifonov, *Vremia i mesto*, in *Iurii Trifonov: SS*, vol. 4, 253, 260.

36. On the *shestidesitaniki*, see Selemeneva, *Poetika gorodskoi prozy Iu. V. Trifonova*, 209; Ushakin, "'Nam etoi bol'iu dyshat'?,'" 8–9.

37. Trifonov, *Vremia i mesto*, 274–5.

38. On the dotted line versus the solid line, see Shreder, "Roman s istoriei," 76. Sukhikh makes a similar claim about *The Old Man* in "Pytka pamiat'iu." Concerning the *punktir* and the reader providing missing information, see Sergei Task, "Otkrovennyi razgovor," *Literaturnaia Rossiia*, April 17, 1981, 11. This was the last interview Trifonov gave before his death.

39. Trifonov, *Vremia i mesto*, 468.

40. On the stream as image, see Sigrid McLaughlin, "Antipov's Nikiforov Syndrome and the Embedded Novel in Trifonov's *Time and Place*," *Slavic and East European Journal*, no. 2 (1988): 242.

41. McLaughlin, "Antipov's Nikiforov Syndrome," 242.

42. The stream has paschal overtones anomalous for Trifonov: it continues to live and "has no death." This formulation recalls the Eastern Orthodoxy liturgy, where Christ ensures the immortality of the soul.

43. Woll, *Invented Truth*, 95; Trifonov, *Vremia i mesto*, 410.

44. Trifonov, *Vremia i mesto*, 518.

130 Notes to Pages 94–99

45. Trifonov, *Vremia i mesto*, 507. Trifonov explicitly likens Moscow to a forest in "Kak nashe slovo otzovetsia," in *Kak nashe slovo otzovetsia . . .* , 311. Selemeneva discusses the forest in *Poetika gorodskoi prozy Iu. V. Trifonova*, 238. The conclusion of *Time and Place* recalls Ol'ga Robertovna crossing the courtyard in "It Was Noon in Summertime," Trifonov's first fictional narrative controlled by the past.

46. Ivanova discusses how foreign locales refer to the USSR in *Proza Iuriia Trifonova*, 285–86.

47. On praise of Disneyland, see Vail', "Interv'iu s Iuriem Trifonovym," 28. The negative comments about the US, simplicity, and consumerism appear in Trifonov, "Interv'iu o kontaktakh," interview with Elena Stoianovskaia, *Inostrannaia literatura*, no. 6 (1978): 247.

48. Woll, *Invented Truth*, 123.

49. Trifonov, "Nedolgoe prebyvanie v kamere pytok," 210.

50. Trifonov, "Nedolgoe prebyvanie," 210–11. For discussion of memory and darkness in this story, see Novoselova, "Final kak sistemoobrazuiushchii element," 182.

51. Etkind, *Warped Mourning*, 14–15.

52. Anatolii Rybakov, *Deti Arbata* (Moscow: Sovetskii pisatel', 1990). On *Disappearance* and *Children of the Arbat*, see Aleksei Varlamov, "Sud'ba tvorcheskogo cheloveka v nesvobodnoi strane," *Slavica Gandensia*, no. 27 (2000): 297.

53. Trifonov, *Ischeznovenie*, in *Otblesk kostra: Dokumental'naia povest'. Ischeznovenie: Roman* (Moscow: Sovetskii pisatel', 1988), 291, 283. Bykov similarly blends the physiological and historical when he asks whether *Disappearance* saw Stalinism as an aberration or the USSR as itself a malignant tumor (Bykov, "Otsustvie," 5).

54. Yury Trifonov, *Disappearance*, trans. David Lowe (Ann Arbor, MI: Ardis, 1992), 150. I have modified the translation.

55. Trifonov, *Ischeznovenie*, 277.

56. On the loss of the father, see Tat'iana Patera, "Roman *Ischeznovenie*: 'Oprokinutyi dom' na naberezhnoi, ili dolgoe proshchanie Iuriia Trifonova s detstvom," *Russian Language Journal*, nos. 156–58 (1993): 108.

57. Etkind, *Warped Mourning*, 17, 18.

58. Trifonova and Trifonov, "Iz dnevnikov i rabochikh tetradei," *Druzhba narodov*, no. 5 (1998), https://magazines.gorky.media/druzhba/1998/5/iz-dnevnikov-i-rabochih-tetradej.html.

59. Trifonov, *Ischeznovenie*, 276.

60. Selemeneva, *Poetika gorodskoi prozy Iu. V. Trifonova*, 224; Woll, *Invented Truth*, 111; Trifonov, *Ischeznovenie*, 198, 201. One critic dismisses this object-oriented characterization of Florinskii as a cliché: see E. Shklovskii, "Razrushenie doma," *Literaturnoe obozrenie*, no. 7 (1987): 48. For a trove of photographs and reminiscences about Trifonov and others in the House on the Embankment, see Ol'ga Trifonova, *Dom na naberezhnoi i ego obyvateli* (Moscow: Galeriia, 2015).

61. Karl Marx, *Capital: A Critique of Political Economy*, trans. Ben Fowkes, vol. 1 (New York: Vintage, 1977), 209; Slezkine, *The House of Government*, 487.

62. Trifonov, *Disappearance*, 16–17.

63. For a discussion of the hanging sword, see Patera, "Roman *Ischeznovenie*," 115–16.

Notes to Pages 99–102

64. Trifonov, *Dom na naberezhnoi*, 460, 489. On Ganchuk as first judge and then victim, see Trifonov, "Kazhdyi chelovek—sud'ba: Beseda s korrespondentom gazety 'Sovetskaia kul'tura,'" in *Kak nashe slovo otzovetsia* . . . , 294. One critic mistakenly assumes it was only Florinskii's generation that liked cognac and framed pictures (Igor' Zolotusskii, "'Vozvyshaiushchee slovo.' Proza-87. Stat'ia pervaia," *Literaturnoe obozrenie*, no. 6 [1988]: 29).

Conclusion

1. Leving bitterly notes that in the 1990s anyone with enough money could purchase an apartment in the House on the Embankment ("Vlast' i slast'"). His comment ignores how the complex had always been the provenance of the elite; after 1991 the nature of that privilege was monetized and the USSR's false egalitarianism was abandoned.

2. Erofeev, "Tsena svobody," 167. On Prokhanov, see Iurii Arakcheev, "Byt' sovetskim pisatelem," in *Iurii Trifonov: Otblesk lichnosti*, 85. For an unconvincing attempt to tie Trifonov to postmodernism, see Raoul Eshelman, "Wege der postmodernen Wahrheitsfindung bei Jurij Trifonov," *Zeitschrift für Slawistik*, no. 3 (1995): 304.

3. Selemeneva, "Khudozhestvennyi mir Iu. V. Trifonova," 2, 15.

4. On Trifonov resenting the designation of *byt* writer, see "Net, ne o byte—o zhizni!," 103. For critics connecting *byt* to petty details, see for instance V. Luk'ianin, "Praktichnye liudi," *Ural*, no. 7 (1972): 137.

5. On the Nobel Prize and the conditions in the hospital, see Semen Ekshtut, *Iurii Trifonov: Zhizn' zamechatel'nykh liudei*, Malaia seriia (Moscow: Molodaia gvardiia, 2014), 7–9. Ekshtut cites Trifonova and Trifonov, "Iz dnevnikov i rabochikh tetradei," *Druzhba narodov*, no. 5 (1998).

6. Lipovetskii and Leiderman, *Ot "sovetskogo pisatelia" k pisateliu sovetskoi epokhi*, 41. Andrei Bitov also discusses Trifonov and Makanin in "Peresechenie parallelei," in *Iurii Trifonov: Otblesk lichnosti*, 155. Reif references Nagibin's comment in "Pisatel' na vse vremena."

7. Bitov, "Peresechenie parallelei," 151, 152; Bitov, *Pushkin House*, trans. Susan Brownsberger (New York: Farrar, Straus and Giroux, 1987).

8. Grekova, *Porogi: Roman, Povesti* (Moscow: Sovetskii pisatel', 1986). For ways in which Trifonov's writing intersected with women's prose, see Sutcliffe, *The Prose of Life*, 29, 32, 37. The historian Thomas Lahusen notes that *Taking Stock* and Baranskaia's *A Week Like Any Other* emphasize how life tests the morality of the intelligentsia: "Du 'dialogisme' et de la 'polyphonie' dans deux ouvrages russes des années soixantes: *Une semaine comme une autre* de Natal'ja Baranskaja et *Bilan préalable* de Jurij Trifonov," *Revue des études slaves*, no. 4 (1986).

9. Stiazhkina, "The 'Petty-Bourgeois Woman,'" 63–64. On women's prose lacking metaphysics, see Trifonova and Trifonov, "Iz dnevnikov i rabochikh tetradei," *Druzhba narodov*, no. 2 (1999).

10. Vasilii Pichul, *Malen'kaia Vera* (Gor'kii Film Studio, 1988); Mark Amusin, "Intelligentsiia: Konets puti?," *Neva*, no. 6 (2016): 158, https://magazines.gorky.media/wp-content/uploads/2016/07/10_AMUSIN.pdf. The film was set in Mariupol, a city that now emblematizes Russia's assault on Ukraine as Putin attempts to restore much of the Soviet ideological and political order.

132   Notes to Pages 102–105

11. Golubev, *The Things of Life*, 164. On goods in the West and the Soviet shadow economy, see Stiazhkina, "The 'Petty-Bourgeois Woman,'" 173, 69.

12. Aitmatov, *Iurii Trifonov: Stranitsy tvorchestva*, 4:00; Ekshtut, *Iurii Trifonov*, 355. Medvedev observes that Trifonov was not widely read during the Gorbachev years, an era of shock and scandal that ignored his staid approach (Medvedev, "Vospominaniia o Iurii Trifonove," 59).

13. T. Trifonova, "Vmesto predisloviia," 11–12. Leonid Bakhnov argued during perestroika that Trifonov wrote for all who think for themselves: "Semidesiatnik," *Oktiabr'*, no. 9 (1988): 175.

14. Zolotusskii, "'Vozvyshaiushchee slovo,'" 23.

15. Mikhail Lekhmin, "Zheliabov, Nechaev, Karlos i drugoe . . . ," *Kontinent*, no. 49 (1986): 359; Vladimir Bondarenko, "Utverzhdenie real'nogo," *Literaturnaia gazeta*, 20 May 1987, 3. Bondarenko's invective stems from Nikolai Grigor'evich's supposed scorn for the common people.

16. Aleksandr Kazintsev, "Litsom k istorii: prodolzhateli ili potrebiteli: Polemicheskie zametki o tekushchem literaturnom protsesse," *Nash sovremennik*, no. 11 (1987): 174–75.

17. Trifonova and Trifonov, "Iz dnevnikov i rabochikh tetradei," *Druzhba narodov*, no. 11 (1998). On the market and censorship, see Arakcheev, "Byt' sovetskim pisatelem," 86.

18. Lipovetskii and Leiderman, *Ot "sovetskogo pisatelia" k pisateliu sovetskoi epokhi*, 4. Concerning criticism of the *shestidesiatniki*, see Kozlov and Gilburd, "The Thaw as an Event in Russian History," 57.

19. Pirozhok, "Pravda i krasota," 8; Masha Gessen, *Dead Again: The Russian Intelligentsia after Communism* (London: Verso, 1997).

20. Natal'ia Ivanova, "Bakhtin's Concept of the Grotesque and the Art of Petrushevskaia and Tolstaia," trans. Helena Goscilo, in *Fruits of Her Plume: Essays on Contemporary Russian Women's Culture*, ed. Helena Goscilo (Armonk, NY: M. E. Sharpe, 1993), 23–24; Helena Goscilo, "Coming a Long Way, Baby: A Quarter-Century of Russian Women's Fiction," *Harriman Institute Forum*, no. 1 (1992): 12. On Trifonov and Petrushevskaia, see Lipovetskii and Leiderman, *Ot "sovetskogo pisatelia" k pisateliu sovetskoi epokhi*, 41. For discussion of Petrushevskaia, Baranskaia, and Grekova, see Sutcliffe, *The Prose of Life*, 52, 59.

21. On Petrushevskaia's narrators, see Sutcliffe, *The Prose of Life*, 66–69. Tat'iana Tolstaia, another author who rose to prominence in the 1990s, endows her depictions of *byt* with a luminescence far brighter than the grim tones of Petrushevskaia (or Trifonov). See Goscilo, *The Explosive World of Tatyana N. Tolstaya's Fiction* (Armonk, NY: M. E. Sharpe, 1996).

22. Paperno, "Personal Accounts of the Soviet Experience," 584, 598; T. Trifonova, "Vmesto predisloviia," 12.

23. Trudoliubov, "My zhivem v shkafu." Etkind, *Warped Mourning*. For a discussion of Putin and glamour culture, see Helena Goscilo and Vlad Strukov, eds., *Celebrity and Glamour in Contemporary Russia: Shocking Chic* (London: Routledge, 2011). On the differences between Trifonov and Robski, see Reif, "Pisatel' na vse vremena." For an overview of embattled LGBTQ rights, see "The Facts on LGBTQ Rights in Russia,"

Notes to Pages 105–106

Council on Global Equality, accessed January 9, 2023, http://www.globalequality.org/component/content/article/1-in-the-news/186-the-facts-on-lgbt-rights-in-russia.

24. Oleg Fomin, *KGB v smokinge* (REN TV, 2006); Bykov, "Otsustvie," 3. For interest in the Thaw and Brezhnev years, see Pirozhok, "Pravda i krasota," 8. On Putin's rise to power, see Karen Dawisha, *Putin's Kleptocracy: Who Owns Russia?* (New York: Simon and Schuster, 2014).

25. Ekshtut, *Iurii Trifonov*, 5. For a discussion of the "Soviet grandmother," see "'Babushka s sovetskim flagom'—novyi simvol rossiiskoi propagandy. 9 maia ee skul'ptury ustanoviat v mnogikh rossiiskikh gorodakh," *Meduza*, May 5, 2022, https://meduza.io/feature/2022/05/05/babushka-s-sovetskim-flagom-novyy-simvol-rossiys koy-propagandy-9-maya-ee-skulpturu-ustanovyat-vo-mnogih-rossiyskih-gorodah.

26. Slezkine, *The House of Government*, 961. Trifonova's publications about her husband include *Dom na naberezhnoi i ego obytateli*, *Iurii i Ol'ga Trifonovy vspominaiut*, and *Moskva Iuriia Trifonova* (Moscow: Artkom, 2013). Goscilo comments on the trope of authors' widows devoting their lives to commemorating deceased husbands ("Vdovstvo kak zhanr i professiia à la Russe," *Preobrazhenie*, no. 3 [1995]). Trifonova, however, has had her own literary career, publishing novels and short stories.

27. Selemeneva, "Khudozhestvennyi mir Iu. V. Trifonova," 31. See also Elizabeth Skomp and Benjamin Sutcliffe, *Ludmila Ulitskaya and the Art of Tolerance* (Madison: University of Wisconsin Press, 2015), 17–18, 74, 107–8, 204n21.

28. On Jewish identity, see the strong study by Margarita Levantovskaya, "The Russian-Speaking Jewish Diaspora: Liudmila Ulitskaia's *Daniel Stein, Translator*," *Slavic Review*, no. 1 (2012). For Uitskaia's critique of the 2022 war, see Sil'viia Noinraiter, "Esli voinu ostanoviat, to eto budet zasluga zhenshchin," interview with Liudmila Ulitskaia, *Deutsche Welle*, April 1, 2022, https://www.dw.com/ru/ljudmila-ulizkaya-esli-vojna-budet-ostanovlena-eto-budet-zasluga-zhenchin/a-61326679.

BIBLIOGRAPHY

For edited volumes containing more than one work cited in the book, individual works are listed under the edited volume.

Prose, Interviews, and Articles by Iurii Trifonov and Ol'ga Trifonova-Miroshnichenko

Iurii Trifonov: Stranitsy tvorchestva. Glavnaia redaktsiia literaturno-dramaticheskikh programm, TsT, 1985.

Trifonov, Iurii. *"Another Life" and "The House on the Embankment."* Translated by Michael Glenny. Evanston, IL: Northwestern University Press, 1999.

——. *The Disappearance.* Translated by David Lowe. Ann Arbor, MI: Ardis, 1992.

——. *"The Exchange" and Other Stories.* Translated by Ellendea Proffer. Ann Arbor, MI: Ardis, 1991.

——. *Iadro pravdy: Stat'i, interv'iu, esse.* Moscow: Izdatel'stvo Pravda, 1987.

——. "Interv'iu o kontaktakh." Interview with Elena Stoianovskaia. *Inostrannaia literatura,* no. 6 (1978): 243–51.

——. "Interv'iu s Iuriem Trifonovym." Interview with Elena Vail'. *Obozrenie,* no. 6 (1983): 28–34.

——. *Iurii Trifonov: Izbrannye proizvedeniia v dvukh tomakh.* Moscow: Khudozhestvennaia literatura, 1978.

——. *Iurii Trifonov: Sobranie sochinenii v chetyrekh tomakh.* Edited by S. A. Baruzdin et al. Moscow: Khudozhestvennaia literatura, 1985.

——. *Kak nashe slovo otzovetsia . . . .* Compiled by A. Shitov, notes by O. Trifonova and A. Shitov. Moscow: Sovetskaia Rossiia, 1985.

——. *The Long Goodbye: Three Novellas.* Translated by Helen Burlingame and Ellendea Proffer. New York: Ardis and Harper and Row, 1978.

——. "Mysli pered nachalom." *Smena,* no. 563 (1950): 4. https://smena-online.ru/stories/k-soveshchaniyu-molodykh-pisatelei.

——. "Nado verit' v khoroshikh liudei." Interview with V. Lavretskaia. *Uchitel'skaia gazeta,* July 19, 1979.

136   Bibliography

———. *The Old Man.* Translated by Jacqueline Edwards and Mitchell Schneider. New York: Simon and Schuster, 1984.

———. *Otblesk kostra: Dokumental'naia povest'. Ischeznovenie: Roman.* Moscow: Sovetskii pisatel', 1988.

———. *Pod solntsem: Rasskazy.* Moscow: Sovetskii pisatel', 1959.

———. *Students.* Translated by Ivy Litvinova and Margaret Wetlin. Moscow: Izdatel'stvo literatury na inostrannykh iazykakh, 1956.

Trifonova, Ol'ga. *Dom na naberezhnoi i ego obytateli.* Moscow: Galeriia, 2015.

———. Email to Benjamin Sutcliffe. May 19, 2022.

———. Interview with Benjamin Sutcliffe. Moscow, June 18, 2015.

———. *Iurii i Ol'ga Trifonovy vspominaiut.* Moscow: Sovershenno sekretno, 2003.

———. *Moskva Iuriia Trifonova.* Moscow: Artkom, 2013.

Trifonova, Ol'ga, and Iurii Trifonov. "Iz dnevnikov i rabochikh tetradei." *Druzhba narodov,* no. 5 (1998). https://magazines.gorky.media/druzhba/1998/5/iz-dnevnikov-i-rabochih-tetradej.html.

———. "Iz dnevnikov i rabochikh tetradei." *Druzhba narodov,* no. 6 (1998). http://magazines.russ.ru/druzhba/1998/6/trifon.html.

———. "Iz dnevnikov i rabochikh tetradei." *Druzhba narodov,* no. 11 (1998). https://magazines.gorky.media/druzhba/1998/11/iz-dnevnikov-i-rabochih-tetradej-4.html.

———. "Iz dnevnikov i rabochikh tetradei." *Druzhba narodov,* no. 1 (1999). http://magazines.russ.ru/druzhba/1999/1/trif.html.

———. "Iz dnevnikov i rabochikh tetradei." *Druzhba narodov,* no. 2 (1999). https://magazines.gorky.media/druzhba/1999/2/iz-dnevnikov-i-rabochih-tetradej-6.html.

———. "Iz dnevnikov i rabochikh tetradei." *Druzhba narodov,* no. 3 (1999). http://magazines.russ.ru/druzhba/1999/3/trif.html.

OTHER WORKS

Adams, Laura. "Can We Apply Postcolonial Theory to Central Eurasia?" *Central Eurasian Studies Review,* no. 1 (2008): 2–7.

Afanas'eva, Anna. "Refleksiia 'nedochustviia' v proze Iuriia Trifonova kontsa 60–70-kh godakh XX veka." *Slavica Wratislaviensia,* no. 158 (2014): 269–77.

Aitmatov, Chingiz. "I dol'she veka dlitsia den'." *Novyi mir,* no. 11 (1980): 3–185.

Akmuradova, Aidzhamal. "Ideino-khudozhestvennoe voploshchenie obraza stroitelia Karakumskogo kanala v proizvedeniiakh russkoi i turkmenskoi sovetskoi literatury (v plane sravnitel'no-tipologicheskogo analiza)." Abstract of candidate dissertation, Ashkhabad Institute of Language and Literature, 1982.

Aleksandrov, L. "Vremia rabotat' vslast'." *Literaturnaia Rossiia,* October 26, 1963, 14–15.

Alekseyeva, Anna. *Everyday Soviet Utopias: Planning, Design and the Aesthetics of Developed Socialism.* New York: Routledge, 2019.

Altaev, Oleg [Vladimir Kormer]. "The Dual Consciousness of the Intelligentsia and Pseudo-Culture." In *The Political, Social and Religious Thought of Russian "Samizdat": An Anthology,* translated by Nickolas Lupinin, edited by Michael Meerson-Aksenov and Boris Shragin, 116–47. Belmont, MA: Nordland, 1977.

Bibliography

Amlinskii, Vladimir. "O dniakh edinstvennykh." *Literaturnoe obozrenie*, no. 1 (1982): 42–45.

Amusin, Mark. "Intelligentsiia: konets puti?" *Neva*, no. 6 (2016): 150–60. https://magazines.gorky.media/wp-content/uploads/2016/07/10_AMUSIN.pdf.

Anninskii, Lev. "Ochishchenie proshlym." *Don*, no. 2 (1977): 157–60.

———. *Tridtsatye-semidesiatye*. Moscow: Sovetskii pisatel', 1977.

Avtonomova, N. "Kogo vybiraet vremia? Po stranitsam 'gorodskikh povestei' Iu. V. Trifonova." *Sem'ia i shkola*, no. 7 (1988): 48–50.

Babaev, Eduard. "Rasskazy romanista." *Novyi mir*, no. 9 (1970): 268–72.

"'Babushka s sovetskim flagom'—novyi simvol rossiiskoi propagandy. 9 maia ee skul'pturu ustanoviat v mnogikh rossiiskikh gorodakh." *Meduza*, May 5, 2022. https://meduza.io/feature/2022/05/05/babushka-s-sovetskim-flagom-novyy-simvol -rossiyskoy-propagandy-9-maya-ee-skulpturu-ustanovyat-vo-mnogih-rossiyskih -gorodah.

Bakhnov, Leonid. "Semidesiatnik." *Oktiabr'*, no. 9 (1988): 169–75.

Bakhtin, Mikhail. "Epic and Novel." In *The Dialogic Imagination: Four Essays by M. M. Bakhtin*, edited by Michael Holquist, translated by Caryl Emerson and Michael Holquist, 3–40. Austin: University of Texas Press, 1981.

Baranskaia, Natal'ia. "Nedelia kak nedelia." *Novyi mir*, no. 11 (1969): 23–55.

Berlin, Isaiah. Introduction to *Russian Intellectual History: An Anthology*, edited by Marc Raeff, 3–11. New York: Harcourt, Brace, and World, 1966.

Bittner, Stephen. *The Many Lives of Khrushchev's Thaw: Experience and Memory in Moscow's Arbat*. Ithaca, NY: Cornell University Press, 2008.

Bliakhman, O. S., and O. I. Shkaratan. *NTR, rabochii klass, intelligentsiia*. Moscow: Politizdat, 1973.

Bocharov, A. *Beskonechnost' poiska: Khudozhestvennye poiski sovremennoi sovetskoi prozy*. Moscow: Sovetskii pisatel', 1982.

Boiko, S. "'. . . v kamere pytok'. Chelovek na sobranii v rannei i pozdnei proze Iuriia Trifonova." *Vestnik RGGU. Seriia: Literaturovedenie. Iazykoznanie. Kul'turologiia. Filologiia. Vostokovedenie*, no. 8 (2015): 110–19.

Bondarenko, Vladimir. "Utverzhdenie real'nogo." *Literaturnaia gazeta*, May 20, 1987, 3.

Borders of Socialism: Private Spheres of Soviet Russia. Edited by Lewis Siegelbaum. New York: Palgrave Macmillan, 2006.

Bourdieu, Pierre. *Distinction: A Social Critique of the Judgement of Taste*. Translated by Richard Nice. Cambridge, MA: Harvard University Press, 1984.

Boym, Svetlana. *Common Places: Mythologies of Everyday Life in Russia*. Cambridge, MA: Harvard University Press, 1994.

Bratus, Ivan, Zoriana Sverdlyk, and Anna Hunka, "Osmyslennia radians'koi diisnosti v povisti Iuriia Tryfonova 'Poperedni pidsumky.'" *Molodyi vchenyi*, no. 2 (2021): 145–50. https://molodyivchenyi.ua/index.php/journal/article/view/389.

Bren, Paulina, and Mary Neuberger. Introduction to *Communism Unwrapped: Consumption in Cold War Eastern Europe*, edited by Paulina Bren and Mary Neuberger, 3–20. New York: Oxford University Press, 2012.

Bykov, Dmitrii. *Obrechennye pobediteli: Shestidesiatniki*. Moscow: Molodaia gvardiia, 2019.

Bibliography

———. "Otsutstvie: O proze Iuriia Trifonova." *Russkaia zhizn'*, February 1, 2008. http://rulife.ru/old/mode/article/517/.

Bykova, Elena. "Problemy lichnosti v tvorchestve Iuriia Trifonova." Abstract of candidate dissertation, Moscow State Pedagogical University, 1995.

Cameron, Sarah. *The Hungry Steppe: Famine, Violence, and the Making of Soviet Kazakhstan.* Ithaca, NY: Cornell University Press, 2018.

Caruth, Cathy. Introduction to *Trauma: Explorations in Memory*, edited by Cathy Caruth, 3–12. Baltimore: Johns Hopkins University Press, 1995.

Chapman, Andrew. "Queuetopia: Second-World Modernity and the Soviet Culture of Allocation." PhD diss., University of Pittsburgh, 2013.

Chernyshova, Natalya. *Soviet Consumer Culture in the Brezhnev Era.* New York: Routledge, 2013.

Chiaureli, Mikhail. *Padenie Berlina.* Moscow: Mosfil'm, 1949.

Clark, Katerina. "The King Is Dead, Long Live the King: Intelligentsia Ideology in Transition." Paper presented at the conference "Russia at the End of the Twentieth Century: Culture and Its Horizons in Politics and Society." Stanford University, October 1998. http://www.stanford.edu/group/Russia20/volumepdf/clark_fin99.pdf.

———. *The Soviet Novel: History as Ritual.* Chicago: University of Chicago Press, 1981.

Clowes, Edith. *Russia on the Edge: Imagined Geographies and Post-Soviet Identity.* Ithaca, NY: Cornell University Press, 2011.

Cox, Randi. "All This Can be Yours! Soviet Commercial Advertising and the Social Construction of Space, 1928–1956." In *The Landscape of Stalinism: The Art and Ideology of Soviet Space*, edited by Evgeny Dobrenko and Eric Naiman, 125–62. Seattle: University of Washington Press, 2003.

Daneliia, Georgii. *Osenii marafon.* Mosfil'm, 1979.

Dawisha, Karen. *Putin's Kleptocracy: Who Owns Russia?* New York: Simon and Schuster, 2014.

Dedkov, Igor'. "Vertikali Iuriia Trifonova." *Novyi mir*, no. 8 (1985): 220–35.

Dobrenko, Evgeny. *Late Stalinism: The Aesthetics of Politics.* New Haven, CT: Yale University Press, 2020.

Dobrovol'skii, Vladimir. *Troe v serykh shineliakh.* Moscow: Molodaia gvardiia, 1950.

Dostoevsky, Fyodor. *The Demons.* Translated by Richard Pevear and Larissa Volokhonsky. New York: Vintage Classics, 1994.

Dovlatov, Sergei. *Kompromiss.* New York: Serebrianyi vek, 1981.

Drewnowski, Tadeusz. "Kuźnia młodych charakterów." In Jurij Trifonow, *Studenci*, 5–11. Warsaw: Iskry, 1953.

Dumančić, Marko. *Men Out of Focus: The Soviet Masculinity Crisis in the Long Sixties.* Toronto: University of Toronto Press, 2021.

Dunham, Vera. *In Stalin's Time: Middleclass Values in Soviet Fiction.* New York: Cambridge University Press, 1976.

Dwyer, Anne. "Runaway Texts: The Many Life Stories of Iurii Trifonov and Christa Wolf." *Russian Review*, no. 64 (2005): 605–27.

Edgar, Adrienne. "Bolshevism, Patriarchy, and the Nation: The Soviet 'Emancipation' of Muslim Women in Pan-Islamic Perspective." *Slavic Review*, no. 3 (2006): 252–72.

Bibliography

Ehrenburg, Il'ia. "Otvet na odno pis'mo." *Komsomol'skaia pravda*, September 2, 1959, 2–3.

Ekshtut, Semen. *Iurii Trifonov: Zhizn' zamechatel'nykh liudei*. Malaia seriia. Moscow: Molodaia gvardiia, 2014.

Eremina, S., and V. Piskunov. "Vremia i mesto prozy Iu. Trifonova." *Voprosy literatury*, no. 5 (1982): 34–65.

Ermolaev, Herman. "The Theme of Terror in 'Starik.'" In *Aspects of Modern Russian and Czech Literature: Selected Papers of the Third World Congress for Soviet and East European Studies*, edited by Arnold McMillin, 96–109. Columbus, OH: Slavica, 1985.

Eshelman, Raoul. "Wege der postmodernen Wahrheitsfindung bei Jurij Trifonov." *Zeitschrift für Slawistik*, no. 3 (1995): 281–304.

Etkind, Aleksandr. *Warped Mourning: Stories of the Undead in the Land of the Unburied*. Palo Alto, CA: Stanford University Press, 2013.

"Evgeniia Abramovna Lur'e-Trifonova, 1904–1975." Muzei "Dom na naberezhnoi." Accessed January 9, 2023. https://dnnmuseum.ru/евгения-абрамовна-лурье-трифонова-1904-1975/.

"The Facts on LGBTQ Rights in Russia." Council on Global Equality. Accessed January 9, 2023. http://www.globalequality.org/component/content/article/1-in-the-news/186-the-facts-on-lgbt-rights-in-russia.

Fainberg, Dina, and Artemy Kalinovsky. Introduction to *Reconsidering Stagnation in the Brezhnev Era: Ideology and Exchange*, edited by Dina Fainberg and Artmey Kalinovsky, vii–xxii. Lanham, MD: Lexington Books, 2016.

Field, Deborah. "Communist Morality and Meanings of Private Life in Post-Stalinist Russia, 1953–1964." PhD diss., University of Michigan, 1996.

Finitskaia, Z. "Pod iarkim solntsem." *Oktiabr'*, no. 12 (1960): 212–13.

"Firsthand Time: Documentary Aesthetics in the Long 1960s." January 16–19, 2020. Berlin. https://www.zfl-berlin.org/event/firsthand-time-documentary-aesthetics-in-the-long-1960s.html.

Fitzpatrick, Sheila. *Everyday Stalinism. Ordinary Life in Extraordinary Times: Soviet Russia in the 1930s*. New York: Oxford University Press, 1999.

Fomin, Oleg. *KGB v smokinge*. REN TV, 2006.

Franklin, Simon. "Russia in Time." In *National Identity in Russian Culture: An Introduction*, edited by Simon Franklin and Emma Widdis, 11–29. Cambridge: Cambridge University Press, 2004.

Fürst, Juliane. *Stalin's Last Generation: Soviet Post-War Youth and the Emergence of Mature Socialism*. New York: Oxford University Press, 2010.

Gaidai, Leonid. *Ivan Vasil'evich meniaet professiiu*. Mosfil'm, 1973.

Ganson, Nicholas. *The Soviet Famine of 1946–47 in Global and Historical Perspective*. New York: Palgrave Macmillan, 2009.

Gasiorowska, Xenia. *Women in Soviet Fiction, 1917–1964*. Madison: University of Wisconsin Press, 1968.

Geidenko, V. "Liudi na rabote." *Zvezda*, no. 12 (1964): 195–203.

Gessen, Masha. *Dead Again: The Russian Intelligentsia after Communism*. London: Verso, 1997.

Gillespie, David. *Iurii Trifonov: Unity through Time*. Cambridge: Cambridge University Press, 1992.

Golubev, Alexey. *The Things of Life: Materiality in Late Soviet Russia*. Ithaca, NY: Cornell University Press, 2020.

Gorelikov, M. "Predstavlenie o dukhovno-nravstvennom vospitanii v sovetskoi pedagogike." *Vestnik KRAUNTS. Gumanitarnye nauki*, no. 2 (2015): 79–85.

Goscilo, Helena. "Coming a Long Way, Baby: A Quarter-Century of Russian Women's Fiction." *Harriman Institute Forum*, no. 1 (1992): 1–17.

———. *The Explosive World of Tatyana N. Tolstaya's Fiction*. Armonk, NY: M. E. Sharpe, 1996.

———. "Vdovstvo kak zhanr i professiia à la Russe." *Preobrazhenie*, no. 3 (1995): 28–32.

Goscilo, Helena, and Vlad Strukov, eds. *Celebrity and Glamour in Contemporary Russia: Shocking Chic*. London: Routledge, 2011.

Grekova, I. "Damskii master." *Novyi mir*, no. 11 (1963): 89–120.

———. "Letom v gorode." *Novyi mir*, no. 4 (1965): 84–101.

———. *Malen'kii Garusov, Kafedra. Povesti*. Moscow: Sovetskii pisatel', 1980.

———. *Porogi. Roman, povesti*. Moscow: Sovetskii pisatel', 1986.

———. "Za prokhodnoi." *Novyi mir*, no. 11 (1962): 110–31.

Grinberg, Marat. "Who is Grifanov? David Shrayer-Petrov's Dialogue with Yury Trifonov." In *The Parallel Universes of David Shrayer-Petrov*, edited by Roman Katsman, Maxim Shrayer, Klavdia Smola, 285–304. Boston, MA: Academic Studies Press, 2021.

Grossman, Vasilii. *Everything Flows*. Translated by Robert Chandler and Elizabeth Chandler with Anna Aslanyan. New York: New York Review Books, 2009.

Grosz, Elizabeth. *Volatile Bodies: Toward a Corporeal Feminism*. Bloomington: Indiana University Press, 1994.

Günther, Clemens. "Die metahistoriographische Revolution. Problematisierungen historischer Erkenntnis in der russischen Gegenwartsliteratur." PhD diss., Free University of Berlin, 2019.

Gurova, Ol'ga. "Ideology of Consumption in the Soviet Union." In *Communism and Consumerism: The Soviet Alternative to the Affluent Society*, edited by Timo Vihavainen and Elena Bogdanova, 68–84. Leiden: Brill, 2016.

Gusev, Vladimir. *V predchuvstvii novogo: O nekotorykh chertakh literatury shestidesiatykh godov*. Moscow: Sovetskii pisatel', 1974.

Hellebust, Rolf. *Flesh to Metal: Soviet Literature and the Alchemy of Revolution*. Ithaca, NY: Cornell University Press, 2003.

Holmgren, Beth. "Writing the Female Body Politic, 1945–1985." In *A History of Women's Writing in Russia*, edited by Adele Barker and Jehanne Gheith, 225–42. Cambridge: Cambridge University Press, 2002.

Hubbs, Joanna. *Mother Russia: The Feminine Myth in Russian Culture*. Bloomington: Indiana University Press, 1988.

Iakimenko, L. "Lik vremeni." In Iurii Trifonov, *Utolenie zhazhdy*, 3–11. Moscow: Khudozhestvennaia literatura, 1967.

Ikonnikova, S. N., and V. P. Kobliakov. *Moral' i kul'tura razvitogo sotsialisticheskogo obshchestva*. Moscow: Znanie, 1976.

Bibliography

Il'ina, Natal'ia. "Iz rodoslovnoi russkoi revoliutsii. O romane Iuriia Trifonova 'Neterpenie.'" *Neman*, no. 12 (1976): 170–75.

Iurii Trifonov: Otblesk lichnosti. Compiled by N. G. Kataeva. Moscow: Galeriia, 2015.

Ivanova, Anna. "Socialist Consumption and Brezhnev's Stagnation: A Reappraisal of Late Communist Everyday Life." *Kritika*, no. 3 (2016): 665–78.

Ivanova, Natal'ia. "Bakhtin's Concept of the Grotesque and the Art of Petrushevskaia and Tolstaia." Translated by Helena Goscilo. In *Fruits of Her Plume: Essays on Contemporary Russian Women's Culture*, edited by Helena Goscilo, 21–31. Armonk, NY: M. E. Sharpe, 1993.

———. Interview with Benjamin Sutcliffe. Moscow, June 22, 2015.

———. *Proza Iuriia Trifonova.* Moscow: Sovetskii pisatel', 1984.

Ivasheva, V. *Na poroge XXI veka.* Moscow: Khudozhestvennaia literatura, 1979.

Jenks, Andrew. "The Sincere Deceiver: Yuri Gagarin and the Search for a Higher Truth." In *Into the Cosmos: Space Exploration and Soviet Culture*, edited by James Andrews and Asif Siddiqi, 107–32. Pittsburgh: University of Pittsburgh Press, 2011.

Jones, Polly. "The Fire Burns On? The 'Fiery Revolutionaries' Biographical Series and the Rethinking of Propaganda in the Brezhnev Era." *Slavic Review*, no. 1 (2015): 32–56.

———. "Iurii Trifonov's *Fireglow* and the 'Mnemonic Communities' of the Brezhnev Era." *Cahiers du monde russe*, nos. 1–2 (2013): 47–72.

———. *Myth, Memory, Trauma: Rethinking the Stalinist Past in the Soviet Union, 1953–70.* New Haven, CT: Yale University Press, 2013.

———. *Revolution Rekindled: The Writers and Readers of Late Soviet Biography.* New York: Oxford University Press, 2019.

Kabo, Liubov'. *Neveselo byt' meshchaninom!* Moscow: Izdatel'stvo politicheskoi literatury, 1965.

Kaganovsky, Lilya. *How the Soviet Man Was Unmade: Cultural Fantasy and Male Subjectivity under Stalin.* Pittsburgh: University of Pittsburgh Press, 2008.

Kagarlitsky, Boris. "1960s East and West: The Nature of the *Shestidesiatniki* and the New Left." Translated by William Nickell. *boundary 2*, no. 1 (2009): 95–104.

Kaminskii, M., and Iu. Lopusov. *Rabochii kharakter: Sovremennaia sovetskaia literatura o rabochem klasse.* Moscow: Prosveshchenie, 1975.

Karasev, Iu. "Povest' o studentakh." *Ogonek*, no. 12 (1951): 24.

Karpova, Yulia. *Comradely Objects: Design and Material Culture in Soviet Russia, 1960s–80s.* Manchester: Manchester University Press, 2020.

Kazintsev, Aleksandr. "Litsom k istorii: prodolzhateli ili potrebiteli. Polemicheskie zametki o tekushchem literaturnom protsesse." *Nash sovremennik*, no. 11 (1987): 166–75.

Kharkhordin, Oleg. "Reveal and Dissimulate: A Genealogy of Private Life in Soviet Russia." In *Public and Private in Thought and Practice: Perspectives on a Grand Dichotomy*, edited by Jeff Weintraub and Krishan Kumar, 333–63. Chicago: University of Chicago Press, 1997.

Khazanov, Pavel. "The Most Important Thing is to Remain a Human Being: Decembrist Protest, Soviet *Lichnost'*, and the Post-1968 Mass-Market Histories of Natan

Eidelman and Bulat Okudzhava." *Slavic and East European Journal*, no. 3 (2021): 478–98.

Khutsiev, Marlen. *Zastava Il'icha*. Gorky Film Studio, 1964.

Klimova, Ol'ga. "Soviet Youth Films under Brezhnev: Watching Between the Lines." PhD diss., University of Pittsburgh, 2013.

Kon, Igor. *The Sexual Revolution in Russia: From the Age of the Czars to Today*. Translated by James Riordan. New York: Free Press, 1995.

Kozintsev, Grigorii. *Gamlet*. Lenfil'm, 1964.

Kozlov, Denis, and Eleonory Gilburd, eds. *The Thaw: Soviet Society and Culture during the 1950s and 1960s*. Toronto: University of Toronto Press, 2013.

Kozlova, Nataliia. "Socialist Realism: Producers and Consumers." *Russian Social Science Review*, no. 5 (1998): 4–19.

Lahusen, Thomas. "Du 'dialogisme' et de la 'polyphonie' dans deux ouvrages russes des années soixantes: *Une semaine comme une autre* de Natal'ja Baranskaja et *Bilan préalable* de Jurij Trifonov." *Revue des études slaves*, no. 4 (1986): 563–85.

Lanshchikov, Anatolii. "Geroi i vremia. . . ." *Don*, no. 11 (1973): 149–78.

Lavrov, P. "Iurii Trifonov. Otblesk kostra." *Don*, no. 7 (1965): 167–68.

Lazarev, L. "Bez ekzotiki." *Druzhba narodov*, no. 5 (1959): 227–29.

Lebina, Natal'ia. "Plus the *Chemicalization* of the Entire Wardrobe." *Russian Studies in History*, no. 1 (2009): 33–45.

——. "Retsept pis'ma o 'zastoe.'" *Novoe literaturnoe obozrenie*, no. 3 (2015). https://magazines.gorky.media/nlo/2015/3/reczept-pisma-o-zastoe.html.

Lekhmin, Mikhail. "Zheliabov, Nechaev, Karlos i drugoe. . . ." *Kontinent*, no. 49 (1986): 359–69.

Levantovskaya, Margarita. "The Russian-Speaking Jewish Diaspora: Liudmila Ulitskaia's *Daniel Stein, Translator*." *Slavic Review*, no. 1 (2012): 91–107.

Leving, Iurii. "Vlast' i slast' ('Dom na naberezhnoi' Iu. V. Trifonova)." *Novoe literaturnoe obozrenie*, no. 5 (2005). http://magazines.russ.ru/nlo/2005/75/le24.html.

Levkin, Andrei. "'Odna bol'shaia i obshchaia ustalost'" Iuriia Trifonova." *God literatury*, August 28, 2015. https://godliteratury.ru/articles/2015/08/28/odna-bolshaya-i-obshhaya-ustalost.

Lezina-Kurochkina, A. "Ideal geroicheskoi lichnosti v romane 'Andrei Kozhukhov' S. M. Stepniaka-Kravchinskogo i 'Neterpenie' Iu. Trifonova." In *Traditsii i novatorstvo v khudozhestvennoi literature*, edited by M. Ia. Ermakova et al., 100–106. Gorky: Gor'kovskii gosudarstvennyi pedagogicheskii institut, 1983.

Lipovetskii, Mark, and Naum Leiderman. *Ot "sovetskogo pisatelia" k pisateliu sovetskoi epokhi. Put' Iuriia Trifonova*. Yekaterinburg: Izdatel'stvo AMB, 2001.

Livers, Keith. *Constructing the Stalinist Body: Fictional Representations of Corporeality in the Stalinist 1930s*. Lanham, MD: Lexington Books, 2004.

Lotman, Iurii. *Besedy o russkoi kul'ture: Byt i traditsii russkogo dvorianstva (XVIII–nachalo XIX veka)*. St. Petersburg: Iskusstvo-SPB, 1994.

Lowe, David. *Russian Writing since 1953: A Critical Survey*. New York: Ungar, 1987.

Luk'ianin, V. "Praktichnye liudi." *Ural*, no. 7 (1972): 134–39.

L'vov, S. "Povest' o sovetskom studenchestve." In *Vydaiushchiesia proizvedeniia sovetskoi literatury: 1950 god. Sbornik statei*, compiled by S. Babenysheva, 266–77. Moscow: Sovetskii pisatel', 1952.

Bibliography

de Maegd-Soëp, Carolina. *Trifonov and the Drama of the Russian Intelligentsia*. Ghent: Russian Institute, 1990.

Marx, Karl. *Capital: A Critique of Political Economy*. Translated by Ben Fowkes. 3 vols. New York: Vintage, 1977.

McLaughlin, Sigrid. "Antipov's Nikiforov Syndrome and the Embedded Novel in Trifonov's *Time and Place.*" *Slavic and East European Journal*, no. 2 (1988): 237–50.

Memorial. Last updated February 28, 2022. https://www.memo.ru/ru-ru/.

Men'shov, Vladimir. *Moskva slezam ne verit*. Mosfil'm, 1979.

Metchenko, A. "Paradoksy NTR i sotsialisticheskii realizm." *Moskva*, no. 9 (1974): 189–98.

Micklin, Philip. "Desiccation of the Aral Sea: A Water Management Disaster in the Soviet Union." *Science*, no. 241 (1988): 1170–76.

Millar, James. "The Little Deal: Brezhnev's Contribution to Acquisitive Socialism." *Slavic Review*, no. 4 (1985): 694–706.

Miller, Brandon. "Between Creation and Crisis: Soviet Masculinities, Consumption, and Bodies after Stalin." PhD diss., Michigan State University, 2013.

Mironer, Feliks, and Marlen Khutsiev. *Vesna na Zarechnoi ulitse*. Odessa Film Studio, 1956.

Muradov, Abdulla. *Moi russkii brat*. Ashkhabad: Izdatel'stvo Turkmenistan, 1965.

Nabokov, Vladimir. "Philistines and Philistinism." In *Lectures on Russian Literature*, edited by Fredson Bowers, 309–14. New York: Harcourt Brace Jovanovich, 1981.

Nadkarni, Maya. *Remains of Socialism: Memory and Futures of the Past in Postsocialist Hungary*. Ithaca, NY: Cornell University Press, 2020.

Nikadem-Malinowska, Ewa. "Droga przez pustynię. Polski epizod w twórczoci Jurija Trifonowa." *Acta Polono-Ruthenica*, no. 5 (2000): 131–36.

Noibert, Rudol'f. *Novaia kniga o supruzhestve*. Edited by V. N. Kolbanovskii. Moscow: Progress, 1969.

Noinraiter, Sil'viia. "Esli voinu ostanoviat, to eto budet zasluga zhenshchin." Interview with Liudmila Ulitskaia. *Deutsche Welle*, April 1, 2022. https://www.dw.com/ru/ljudmila-ulizkaya-esli-vojna-budet-ostanovlena-eto-budet-zasluga-zhenchin/a-61326679.

Nora, Pierre. "Between Memory and History: *Les Lieux de Mémoire.*" Translated by Marc Roudebush. *Representations*, no. 26 (1989): 7–24.

Novoselova, Ekaterina. "Evoliutsiia khudozhestvennogo voploshcheniia odnogo siuzheta: 'Pereulok zabytykh lits' i 'Vremia i mesto' Iu. V. Trifonova." *Vestnik Tomskogo gosudarstvennogo universiteta*, no. 467 (2021): 41–46.

———. "Final kak sistemoobrazuiushchii element v tsikle Iu. V. Trifonova 'Oprokinutyi dom.'" *Ural'skii filologicheskii vestnik*, no. 5 (2013): 182–92.

———. "Poetika povsednevnosti v khudozhestvennoi proze Iu. V. Trifonova." Candidate diss., Ural State University, 2017.

"Obsuzhdenie povesti Iu. Trifonova 'Studenty.'" *Novyi mir*, no. 2 (1951): 221–28.

Oskotskii, V. "Nravstvennye uroki 'Narodnoi voli.'" *Literaturnoe obozrenie*, no. 11 (1973): 55–61.

Oukaderova, Lida. *The Cinema of the Soviet Thaw: Space, Materiality, Movement*. Bloomington: Indiana University Press, 2017.

144   Bibliography

Oushakine, Serguei. "'Against the Cult of Things': On Soviet Productivism, Storage Economy, and Commodities with No Destination." *Russian Review*, no. 4 (2014): 198–236.

———. "'Nam etoi bol'iu dyshat'?' O travme, pamiati i soobshchestvakh." In *Travma: punkty*, edited by Sergei Ushakin and Elena Trubina, 5–41. Moscow: Novoe literaturnoe obozrenie, 2009.

Paleeva, N. "Sviaz' vremeni." *Molodaia gvardiia*, no. 9 (1979): 285–88.

Paretskaya, Anna. "The Soviet Communist Party and the Other Spirit of Capitalism." *Sociological Theory*, no. 4 (2010): 377–401.

Patera, Tat'iana. "Roman *Ischeznovenie*: 'Oprokinutyi dom' na naberezhnoi, ili dolgoe proshchanie Iuriia Trifonova s detstvom." *Russian Language Journal*, nos. 156–58 (1993): 107–22.

Platonov, B. "Literaturnoe obozrenie: Zametki o russkoi sovetskoi proze 1950 goda. Stat'ia vtoraia." *Zvezda*, no. 2 (1951): 148–62.

Platt, Kevin. "'Dom na naberezhnoi' Iu. V. Trifonova i pozdnesovetskaia pamiat' o stalinskom politicheskom nasilii: dezavuirovanie i sotsial'naia ditsiplina." Translated by Nina Stavrogina. *Novoe literaturnoe obozrenie*, no. 1 (2019). https://www.nlobooks .ru/magazines/novoe_literaturnoe_obozrenie/155_nlo_1_2019/article/20649/.

Polevoi, Boris. *Povest' o nastoiashchem cheloveke*. Moscow: Izdatel'stvo khudozhestvennoi literatury, 1969.

Pomerantsev, Vladimir. "Ob iskrennosti v literature." *Novyi mir*, no. 12 (1953): 218–45.

Powers, Jenne. "Novel Histories: Repudiation of Soviet Historiography in the Works of Iurii Trifonov, Vladimir Makanin, and Liudmila Ulitskaia." PhD diss., University of North Carolina at Chapel Hill, 2009.

Prokhorov, Aleksandr. *Unasledovannyi diskurs: Paradigm stalinskoi kul'tury v literature i kinematografe "ottepeli."* St. Petersburg: Akademicheskii proekt/Izdatel'stvo DNK, 2007.

Pyr'ev, Ivan. *Kubanskie kazaki.* Mosfil'm, 1950.

Pyzhikov, Aleksandr. "Soviet Postwar Society and the Antecedents of the Khrushchev Reforms." *Russian Studies in History*, no. 3 (2012): 28–43.

Rasputin, Valentin. *Poslednii srok, Proshchanie s Materoi: Povesti i rasskazy.* Moscow: Sovetskii pisatel', 1985.

Reid, Susan. "Cold War in the Kitchen: Gender and the De-Stalinization of Consumer Taste in the Soviet Union under Khrushchev." *Slavic Review*, no. 2 (2002): 211–52.

———. "This Is Tomorrow! Becoming a Consumer in the Soviet Sixties." In *The Socialist Sixties: Crossing Borders in the Second World*, edited by Anne Gorsuch and Diane Koenker, 25–65. Bloomington: Indiana University Press, 2013.

Reif, Igor'. "Pisatel' na vse vremena." *Voprosy literatury*, no. 1 (2013). https://voplit.ru/ article/pisatel-na-vse-vremena/.

Riazanov, El'dar. *Garazh.* Mosfil'm, 1979.

Rivkin-Fish, Michele. "From 'Demographic Crisis' to 'Dying Nation': The Politics of Language and Reproduction in Russia." In *Gender and National Identity in Twentieth-Century Russian Culture*, edited by Helena Goscilo and Andrea Lanoux, 151–73. Dekalb: Northern Illinois University Press, 2006.

Rogova, G. "Itogi i razdum'ia." *Pod"em*, no. 11 (1982): 135–38.

Bibliography

Rogovin, V. "Razvitie sotsialisticheskogo obraza zhizni i voprosy sotsial'noi politiki." *Sotsiologicheskie issledovaniia*, no. 1 (1975): 75–86.

Rosliakov, V. "Utolennaia zhazhda." *Moskva*, no. 10 (1963): 204–6.

Rubinstein, Joshua. "Millenarian Bolshevism?" *Kritika*, no. 4 (2018): 877–90.

Rutten, Ellen. *Sincerity after Communism: A Cultural History.* New Haven, CT: Yale University Press, 2017.

———. *Unattainable Bride Russia: Gendering Nation, State, and Intelligentsia in Russian Intellectual Culture.* Evanston, IL: Northwestern University Press, 2012.

Ruzhanskaia, L. "'Ital'ianskii tekst' v proze Iuriia Trifonova." In *Russkaia literatura v inostrannoi auditorii. Sbornik nauchnykh statei*, compiled by I. I. Tolstukhina, 117–23. St. Petersburg: Izdatel'stvo RGPU imeni A. I. Gertsena, 2020.

Rybakov, Anatolii. *Deti Arbata.* Moscow: Sovetskii pisatel', 1990.

Savateev, Vs. "Molodost' dushi: grani rabochei temy." *Nash sovremennik*, no. 7 (1973): 167–73.

Seifrid, Thomas. "Trifonov's *House on the Embankment* and the Fortunes of Aesopian Speech." *Slavic Review*, no. 4 (1990): 611–24.

Seks i erotika v traditsionnoi russkoi kul'ture. Compiled by A. L. Toporkov. Moscow: Ladomir, 1996.

Selemeneva, Marina. "Khudozhestvennyi mir Iu. V. Trifonova v kontekste gorodskoi prozy vtoroi poloviny XX veka." Abstract of doctoral diss., Moscow State Humanities University, 2009.

———. "Oppozitsiia 'razum/chuvstvo' v povesti Iu. V. Trifonova 'Studenty.'" In *Ratsional'noe i emotsional'noe v literature i fol'klore: Materialy IV Mezhdunarodnoi nauchnoi konferentsii, posviashchennoi pamiati Aleksandra Matveevicha Bulanova, Volgograd, 29 oktiabria—3 noiabria 2007 goda. 2 chasti*, edited by L. N. Savina et al., 1:336–49. Volgograd: Izdatel'stvo VGIPK RO, 2008.

———. *Poetika gorodskoi prozy Iu. V. Trifonova.* Voronezh: Nauchnaia kniga, 2008.

———. "Problema tipologii personazhei 'gorodskoi' prozy Iu. V. Trifonova (k voprosu o dominantnykh/periferiinykh modeliakh zhenstvennosti v literature XX v.)." *Voprosy filologii*, no. 2 (2007): 82–88.

Shitov, Aleksandr. *Gumanizm v plenu . . . Nravstvennaia uprugost' prozy Iuriia Trifonova.* Moscow: Liubimaia Rossiia, 2010.

Shklovskii, E. "Razrushenie doma." *Literaturnoe obozrenie*, no. 7 (1987): 46–48.

Shragin, Boris. *The Challenge of the Spirit.* Translated by P. S. Falla. New York: Knopf, 1978.

Shreder, R. "Roman s istoriei." *Voprosy literatury*, no. 5 (1982): 66–77.

Shtut, Sarra. "Rassuzhdeniia i opisaniia." *Voprosy literatury*, no. 10 (1975): 38–72.

Simonova, T. "Kopit' znaniia, a ne izdania." *V mire knig*, no. 9 (1985): 56.

Sinel'nikov, M. "Ispytanie povsednevnost'iu: Nekotorye itogi." *Voprosy literatury*, no. 2 (1972): 46–62.

Skomp, Elizabeth, and Benjamin Sutcliffe. *Ludmila Ulitskaya and the Art of Tolerance.* Madison: University of Wisconsin Press, 2015.

Slezkine, Yuri. *The House of Government: A Saga of the Russian Revolution.* Princeton, NJ: Princeton University Press, 2017.

Bibliography

Snegireva, Tat'iana, and Aleksei Podchinenov. "'Syn za ottsa ne otvechaet?' Kompleks bezottsovshchiny v sovetskoi literature." In *Semeinye uzy: Modeli dlia sborki*, compiled and edited by Sergei Ushakin, 2:83–102. Moscow: Novoe literaturnoe obozrenie, 2004.

Snou, Ch.-P. *Dve kul'tury*. Moscow: Progress, 1973.

Solzhenitsyn, Aleksandr. "Odin den' Ivana Denisovicha." *Novyi mir*, no. 11 (1962): 8–74.

———. "The Smatterers." In *From under the Rubble*, translated by A. M. Brock et al., 229–78. Boston: Little, Brown, 1975.

Stiazhkina, Elena. "The 'Petty-Bourgeois Woman' and the 'Soulless Philistine': Gendered Aspects of the History of Soviet Everyday Life from the Mid-1960s to the Mid-1980s." Translated by Liv Bliss. *Russian Studies in History*, no. 2 (2012): 63–97.

Sukhanov, Viacheslav. "Fenomen zhizne-smerti v povestiakh Iu. Trifonova." In *Russkaia povest' kak forma vremeni: Sbornik statei*, 301–9. Tomsk: Tomsk State University, 2002.

———. "Lichnyi dnevnik v strukture dokumental'nogo i khudozhestvennogo povestvovaniia: 'Otblesk kostra' i 'Starik' Iu. Trifonova." *Tekst. Kniga. Knigoizdanie*, no. 20 (2019): 35–54.

Sukhikh, Igor'. Pytka pamiat'iu." *Zvezda*, no. 6 (2002). http://magazines.russ.ru/zvezda/2002/6/su.html.

Sukhikh, Ol'ga. "Ot velikogo inkvizatura k 'narodnoi vole' (pereosmyslenie filosofskoi problematiki proizvedenii F. M. Dostoevskogo v romane Iu. V. Trifonova 'Neterpenie')." *Vestnik Nizhegorodskogo universiteta*, no. 3 (2011): 314–20.

Sutcliffe, Benjamin. "Cake, Cabbage, and the Morality of Consumption in Iurii Trifonov's *House on the Embankment*." In *Seasoned Socialism: Gender and Food in Late Soviet Everyday Life*, edited by Angela Brintlinger, Anastasia Lakhtikova, and Irina Glushchenko, 113–31. Bloomington: Indiana University Press, 2019.

———. "Iurii Trifonov's *Students*: Body, Place, and Life in Late Stalinism." *Toronto Slavic Quarterly*, no. 48 (2014): 207–29. http://sites.utoronto.ca/tsq/48/tsq48_sutcliffe.pdf.

———. *The Prose of Life: Russian Women Writers from Khrushchev to Putin*. Madison: University of Wisconsin Press, 2009.

———. "The Thin Present of Trifonov's Thaw: Time in *Slaking the Thirst*." *Australian Slavonic and East European Studies*, nos. 1–2 (2016): 1–21.

———. "Trifonov's Turkmenia: Optimism, Despair, and the Intelligentsia." In *Borders and Beyond: Orient-Occident Crossings in Literature*, edited by Adam Bednarczyk, Magdalena Kubarek, and Maciej Szatkowski, 125–38. Wilmington, DE: Vernon Press, 2018.

———. "When Trifonov Read Dostoevsky: Ideology, Avarice, and Violence in Late Soviet Culture." *Dostoevsky Studies*, no. 24 (2021): 79–100. https://dostoevsky-studies.dlls.univr.it/article/view/1008.

Svetov, F. F. "Utolenie zhazhdy." *Novyi mir*, no. 11 (1963): 235–40.

Tangian, Ol'ga. "Nemetskie aksenty Iuriia Trifonova." *Znamia*, no. 12 (2015): 180–92. https://znamlit.ru/publication.php?id=6130.

Tarkovskii, Andrei. *Ivanovo detstvo*. Mosfil'm, 1962.

Bibliography

Task, Sergei. "Otkrovennyi razgovor." *Literaturnaia Rossiia*, April 17, 1981, 11.

Tikhonov, Ia. "Delo, kotoromu ty sluzhish." *Oktiabr'*, no. 1 (1964): 212–15.

Tiul'pinov, N. "Otblesk drugoi zhizni." *Zvezda*, no. 2 (1976): 216–19.

Todorov, Tzvetan. *The Poetics of Prose*. Translated by Richard Howard. Ithaca, NY: Cornell University Press, 1977.

Tokareva, Viktoriia. *Banketnyi zal*. Moscow: AST, 2001.

Trilling, Lionel. *Sincerity and Authenticity*. Cambridge, MA: Harvard University Press, 1973.

Trifonova, Tat'iana. "Vmesto predisloviia." In Aleksandr Shitov, *Iurii Trifonov: khronika zhizni i tvorchestva, 1925–1981*, 6–12. Yekaterinburg: Izdatel'stvo Ural'skogo universiteta, 1997.

Trudoliubov, Maksim. "My zhivem v shkafu, nabytom skeletami." *Meduza*, March 24, 2022. https://meduza.io/feature/2022/03/24/my-zhivem-v-shkafu-nabitom-skeletami.

Tsipursky, Gleb. *Socialist Fun: Youth, Consumption, and State-Sponsored Popular Culture in the Soviet Union, 1945–1970*. Pittsburgh: University of Pittsburgh Press, 2016.

Tvardovskii, Aleksandr. "Iz rabochikh tetradei." *Znamia*, no. 7 (1989): 124–92. https://imwerden.de/pdf/znamya_1989_07__ocr.pdf.

Ulitskaia, Liudmila. *Sviashchennyi musor*. Moscow: Astrel', 2012.

Utekhin, Il'ia. *Ocherki kommunal'nogo byta*. Moscow: OGI, 2001.

Vail', Petr, and Aleksandr Genis. *60-e. Mir sovetskogo cheloveka*. Moscow: Novoe literaturnoe obozrenie, 1996.

Varga-Harris, Christine. *Stories of House and Home: Soviet Apartment Life during the Khrushchev Years*. Ithaca, NY: Cornell University Press, 2015.

Varlamov, Aleksei. "Sud'ba tvorcheskogo cheloveka v nesvobodnoi strane." *Slavica Gandensia*, no. 27 (2000): 297–301.

Velembovskaia, Irina. "Simpatii i antipatii Iuriia Trifonova." *Novyi mir*, no. 9 (1980): 255–58.

Voronov, Vladimir. *Khudozhestvennaia kontseptsiia: Iz opyta sovetskoi prozy 60–80-kh godov*. Moscow: Sovetskii pisatel', 1984.

"V podmoskovnoi Kommunarke na poligone NKVD otkryli memorial zhertvam terrora." *Novye Izvestiia*, October 27, 2018. https://newizv.ru/news/2018-10-27/v-pod moskovnoy-kommunarke-na-poligone-nkvd-otkryli-memorial-zhertvam-terrora -276791.

Wachtel, Andrew. *An Obsession with History: Russian Writers Confront the Past*. Palo Alto, CA: Stanford University Press, 1994.

Wierzbicka, Anna. "Russkie kul'turnye skripty i ikh otrazhenie v iazyke." *Russkii iazyk v nauchnom osveshchenii*, no. 4 (2002): 6–34.

Winter, Jay. "Thinking about Silence." In *Shadows of War: A Social History of Silence in the Twentieth Century*, edited by Efrat Ben-Ze'ev, Ruth Ginio, and Jay Winter, 3–31. Cambridge: Cambridge University Press, 2010.

Woll, Josephine. *Invented Truth: Soviet Reality and the Literary Imagination of Iurii Trifonov*. Durham, NC: Duke University Press, 1991.

———. *Real Images: Soviet Cinema and the Thaw*. London: I. B. Tauris, 2000.

Yurchak, Alexei. *Everything was Forever, until It Was No More: The Last Soviet Generation*. Princeton, NJ: Princeton University Press, 2006.

Zaitsev, Aleksandr. "Povest' Iu. V. Trifonova "Neterpenie" v kontekste obshchestvenno-politicheskoi pozitsii I. A. Dedkova." *Neofilologiia*, no. 7 (2021): 711–17.

Zakharova, Larissa. *S'habiller à la soviétique: La mode et le Dégel en URSS*. Paris: CNRS, 2011.

Zhilina, L. N., and N. T. Frolova. *Problemy potrebleniia i vospitanie lichnosti*. Moscow: Mysl', 1969.

Zolotusskii, Igor'. "'Vozvyshaiushchee slovo.' Proza-87. Stat'ia pervaia." *Literaturnoe obozrenie*, no. 6 (1988): 23–32.

INDEX

The Abandoned Home (*Oprokinutyi dom*, 1981), 22, 82, 94–96
abortion, 44, 47, 101
Abramov, Fedor, 49
Aesopian language, 80. See also *nedo-skazannost'* (incompletion in writing); silence
aging, 4, 62–63, 67, 69, 82, 85, 92–93, 105
Aitmatov, Chingiz, 82, 102
Aksenov, Vasilii, 84
Akunin, Boris (Grigorii Chkhartishvili), 103
Aleksandrov, L., 9
Alekseyeva, Anna, 8, 18, 64
Alexander II, 81, 84–85
Altaev, Oleg (Vladimir Kormer), 66, 83, 94
Amlinskii, Vladimir, 81
Amusin, Mark, 102
Andropov, Yuri, on Trifonov, 15
Anninskii, Lev, 15, 66
Another Life (*Drugaia zhizn'*, 1975), 71–73
apartments, 3, 5, 25, 26, 46–47, 91; *The Disappearance*, 98–99; *The Exchange*, 12, 67–68; *House on the Embankment*, 72–73, 75–78; *Students*, 37–39
atonement, 20
autobiographical and biographical references in Trifonov's works, 6, 13–14, 35, 91; *The Abandoned Home*, 22, 82, 94–96; *The Bonfire's Glow*, 42, 54–58; *The Disappearance*, 8, 96; *Slaking the Thirst*, 52; *Under the Sun*, 47–48
Autumn Marathon (film), 12
Azef, Evno, 12

Baader-Meinhof Group, 65
Bakhtin, Mikhail, 80
"Bako" (1959), 46–47
Baltics, as setting, 58–60
Baranskaia, Natal'ia, 15, 63, 101, 103
Berzer, Anna, 15
"Beyond the Checkpoint" (Grekova), 45
"Big Deal," the intelligentsia and, 25, 98–99
Bitov, Andrei, 101
Bittner, Stephen, 41
Bocharov, Anatolii, 29
bodies: aging, and the passage of time, 13–14, 62–64, 67, 71, 74, 91–92, 96, 105; ailing, and illness, 70, 74, 81, 88; healthy, 24–25, 28–29, 43, 50; male, and masculinity, 9, 28, 39, 74, 96–97; non-Russian, 30–32, 69; as a place of memory, 14, 75; traumatized, 7, 13, 24–25, 35–36, 43, 59, 71, 91–92; women's, 29, 32–33, 50–51, 67, 69, 71, 106; youth and, 42, 50, 91–92

Index

Bondarenko, Iurii, 102

The Bonfire's Glow (Otblesk kostra, 1965), 11, 20–21, 41–42, 54–58, 88–89, 104

Bourdieu, Pierre, 4

Boym, Svetlana, 10, 73

Bren, Paulina, 4, 9, 14

Brezhnev era, 11–18, 53, 61–66, 87, 90, 105, 111n34

Brzezinskii, Zbigniew, 65

Bulgakov, Mikhail, 26, 101

Bunin, Ivan, 33–34

Bykov, Dmitrii, 16, 42, 105

byt (everyday life), 3, 5, 14–16, 44, 63–66, 73, 83, 97, 101, 106; consumption and, 5, 64, 67–68, 74–77; in *The Exchange,* 15–16, 67–68; in *House on the Embankment,* 17, 21, 74–77, 91, 98; and memory, 16, 59, 63, 66–67, 77–78, 88, 91–92; of Stalinism, 75–78, 97–99; in *Students,* 7–8, 21, 33, 37–38, 98; technology and, 44, 46–47, 65; *telesnost'* of, 14, 74; in *Time and Place,* 91–93; trauma and, 16–17, 47, 83, 97–98, 104, 106; in *Under the Sun,* 46–47. *See also* material world

bytie (meaningful existence), compared to *byt,* 15, 47, 80

Carlos the Jackal, 65–66, 85

Caruth, Cathy, 16, 43

"Cats or Hares?" ("Koshki ili zaitsy?," 1981), 13–14, 92, 94

censorship, 11, 15, 20, 57, 80, 84, 92, 103

Central Asia, 12, 37, 63, 82, 120n31; in *Slaking the Thirst,* 50–51; and *Students,* 31–32; in *Taking Stock,* 12, 20, 68–70; in *Under the Sun,* 21, 45–48

Chekhov, Anton, 101

Chernyshova, Natalya, 13

childhood, 17, 38, 77, 91–92, 97, 105, 117n42

Children of the Arbat (Rybakov), 96

cinema. *See* films

Civil War, 41, 58, 79, 102; *The Bonfire's Glow,* 11, 54–57; *The Disappearance* and, 96, 99; in *The Old Man,* 82, 84, 87–90

Clark, Katerina, 26

A Clockwork Orange (film), 82

clothes and fashion, 9, 16–17, 19, 26, 33–34, 64, 69, 74, 79, 91–92

Cold War, 49, 82; consumption and, 9, 25, 44, 61, 65, 95

Compromise (Dovlatov), 83

consumer goods, 4, 9–10, 12–14, 19, 42, 44–45, 64, 82

consumption, 8–10, 12–13, 25–26, 50, 102, 107n4; in *Another Life,* 72–73; in *The Disappearance,* 97–98; in *The Exchange,* 12, 67–68, 70; in *House on the Embankment,* 21, 74–79, 89; intelligentsia and, 25, 38–40, 62, 64–65, 73, 78, 83; and *meshchanstvo,* 4–5, 9, 13, 33, 64–66, 78, 95; sincerity and the morality of, 18–19, 25, 33–34, 38–39, 44, 61–62, 64–68, 73–75, 77; in *The Old Man,* 87–89; in *Students,* 8, 33–34, 38–40, 44; technology and, 26, 36–37, 44, 50, 73; Trifonov on, 12–13, 61, 65–66, 82–83, 95; women and, 13, 33, 39, 65, 67–68, 71. *See also byt*; material world

corporeality. *See telesnost'* (corporeality)

Cossacks of the Kuban (film), 25

Costanzo, Susan, 45

cynicism, 53, 74, 83, 85, 89, 105. *See also* hypocrisy

Dawisha, Karen, 118n56

The Day Lasts Longer than a Hundred Years (Aitmatov), 82

Dedkov, Igor', 9, 16, 57, 59, 88

denunciation and betrayal, 17, 27, 29, 37, 53, 73–74, 77–80, 94–95, 117n46

The Demons (Dostoevsky), 79, 87

The Department (Grekova), 83

desert, 21, 46–50

de-Stalinization, 41–42, 49. *See also* Thaw era

The Disappearance (Ischeznovenie, 1987), 8, 22, 82, 96–99, 102

Disneyland, Trifonov on, 94–95

Dobrenko, Evgeny, 7, 24, 31, 57

Index

151

Dobrovol'skii, Vladimir, 24
Doctor Goldfoot and the Bikini Machine (film), 83
Dostoevsky, Fyodor, 5, 27, 79, 86
Dovlatov, Sergei, 83
Drewnowski, Tadeusz, 9, 37
Dumančić, Marko, 9, 13
Dunham, Vera, 25–26
Dwyer, Anne, 20, 73
Dzherzhinsky, Felix, 85

Ehrenburg, Ilya, 45
Ekshtut, Semen, 102, 105
emotion and feeling, 12, 44–45, 56, 64, 116n34
Eremina, S., 72
Erofeev, Viktor, 100
Etkind, Alexander, 16, 35, 43, 72, 96–97, 104
everyday life. See *byt* (everyday life)
Evtushenko, Evgenii, 43
The Exchange (*Obmen*, 1969), 12, 15–16, 66–68, 70, 101

Fall of Berlin (film), 24, 43
famine, 25, 27, 37, 99, 102–3
Farewell to Matyora (Rasputin), 63
Fashion. See clothes and fashion
father(s), 39–40, 51, 68–70, 73, 79; father-son relationships, 68–69, 98; loss of, 9, 35–38, 49–50, 52, 56, 87, 91, 96–97, 103, 117n46; Trifonov and his, 3, 7–8, 11, 14, 20, 23, 46, 54–58, 95
Fedin, Konstantin, 46, 117n40
feelings and emotion, 12, 44–45, 56, 64, 116n34
female characters, 29, 32–33, 47, 50–51, 67–69, 72, 101. See *also* women
Fiery Revolutionaries (series), 84–85
films, Soviet, 10, 43, 63, 65, 82–83, 102; *telesnost'* of, 12, 24–25
Finitskaia, Z., 47
fire, imagery of, 57–58, 88–89, 122n65, 129n27
Fitzpatrick, Sheila, 5

food, 16, 74–78
The Foundation Pit (Platonov), 102
friendship, 17, 28, 30, 70, 73, 94
"friendship of peoples" (Soviet concept), 32, 47
Frolova, N. T., 10
furniture, 37–39, 64, 67, 72–73, 79, 98–99
Fürst, Juliane, 25
future: anxieties about, 4, 41, 101; optimism for the, 8–9, 20–21, 25, 29, 38, 47–49, 54, 73; threatened by history and the past, 6, 11, 49–50, 54, 59–60, 62–63, 70, 80, 81, 94

Gagarin, Yuri, 10, 44
Garage (film), 82
Gasiorowska, Xenia, 39
gender, concerns over, 13, 15, 65, 68. See *also* female characters; masculinity; women
Genis, Alexander, 10, 43, 44, 66
Gilburd, Eleonory, 9, 45
Gillespie, David, 12, 18, 47, 71, 88, 110n31
Golubev, Alexey, 5, 10, 42, 65, 102
Gorky Literary Institute, 7, 46
Goscilo, Helena, 104
greed and desire, 5, 33–34, 39–40, 64, 95, 106; effects of, 61–62, 75–80, 82, 88–89; Stalinism associated with, 13, 22, 44, 99. See *also* consumption
Grekova, I. (Elena Venttsel'), 22, 44–45, 63, 65, 83, 101, 103
Grosz, Elizabeth, 4, 7
gulag, survivors of, 3, 24–25, 35–36, 43, 59, 71, 91–92
Günther, Clemens, 55
Gurova, Ol'ga, 82
Gusev, Vladimir, 11, 20, 59, 66, 122n70

Hamlet, 20, 36, 43–44, 52, 56, 58, 97
"The Heirs of Stalin" (Evtushenko), 43
Hellebust, Rolf, 36
history, 5–6, 11, 62–64, 81, 102, 104; in *The Bonfire's Glow*, 11, 21, 42, 55–58, 89; *byt* and, 16, 55, 59, 62, 77, 97; in *The*

152 Index

history (*continued*)
    Disappearance, 96–99; elemental
    metaphors for, 54, 57, 63, 86, 88–90, 93,
    96; in *House on the Embankment*, 17,
    21, 77–80, 86, 88, 91; *Impatience* and
    representations of, 84–87, 90; in "It
    Was Noon in Summertime," 58–60;
    Marxist-Leninist interpretations of, 6,
    11, 50, 72, 86–87, 92–93; and memory,
    6, 11, 16–18, 54–56, 91; in *The Old Man*,
    87–90; in *Students*, 30–32; representa-
    tions of in *Time and Place*, 90–93; and
    trauma, 6, 16, 57, 72, 79, 87, 99; in
    Under the Sun, 47–48, 57
Holmgren, Beth, 35
"Hourglass" ("Pesochnye chasy," 1959),
    47–48
House on the Embankment, building, 6,
    8, 35, 76–77, 85, 96, 98–100, 102, 105,
    131n1
House on the Embankment (*Dom na
    naberezhnoi*, 1976), 14, 17, 20–22,
    73–80, 116n34; compared to later
    works, 86–89, 91–92, 98–99; and
    Students, 14, 20, 27, 73, 79
hypocrisy, 40, 69, 103. *See also* cynicism

Iakimenko, L., 47
Ikonnikova, S., 12, 64
Il'ina, Natal'ia, 86
illness, 4, 70, 75, 84, 88, 90
Impatience (*Neterpenie*, 1973), 12, 21–22,
    81–87, 90
"In the Steppe" ("V stepi," 1948), 37
insincerity, 12–13, 22, 27, 66, 70, 71, 74, 82,
    90, 94, 105
intelligentsia: on consumption and the
    material world, 5, 10, 12–13, 15, 25,
    33–34, 38–40, 64–65, 67–68, 78, 83;
    corruption and moral poverty of, 25,
    61–62, 64, 70, 73–74, 78, 83, 94, 102–4;
    and history, 58, 60, 62, 91, 99; sincerity
    and, 10–11, 18–19, 53, 66–68, 73, 83; and
    Stalinism, 8, 27, 43–44, 62, 72, 78,
    97–99; and technology, 45, 83

iskrennost' (sincerity), 5–6, 45, 62, 88, 95,
    101, 105–6; in *Another Life*, 71–73; con-
    sumption and, 18–19, 25, 33–34, 38–39,
    44, 61–62, 64–68, 73–75, 77, 82, 88, 99;
    distortion of, in *Impatience*, 12, 21–22,
    83–87; in *Slaking the Thirst*, 52–53; and
    Students, 8, 21, 26–30, 33–34, 37–40,
    84–85, 90; in *Taking Stock*, 68–70; in
    House on the Embankment, 74, 78, 89;
    insincerity and loss of, 12–13, 22, 27, 66,
    70–71, 74, 82, 90, 94, 105; intelligentsia
    and, 10–11, 18–19, 53, 66–68, 73, 83;
    kindness and, 6, 19, 68, 70, 73–74, 83,
    93–94; memory, history, and, 53–55, 88,
    93–95, 99; and memory in *The Bonfire's
    Glow*, 11, 21, 55–58, 60; *telesnost'* of,
    28–30, 32, 34–35, 50, 70, 80, 87–88; in
    Time and Place, 90–94
"It Was Noon in Summertime" ("Byl
    letnii polden'," 1966), 42, 58–60
Italy, 13–14, 94
Ivan's Childhood (film), 43
Ivan Vasil'evich Changes His Profession
    (film), 65
Ivanova, Natal'ia, 36, 59, 67, 69, 70, 71, 86,
    88–89, 104, 110n22, 110n31; on *The
    Bonfire's Glow*, 42, 56; on *House on the
    Embankment*, 14, 20, 75

"A Japanese Umbrella" (Tokareva), 64
Jews, 6, 23; in Trifonov's prose, 35, 46, 79,
    106, 117n41
Jones, Polly, 7, 11, 85
justice, 11, 52–53, 60, 85

Kabo, Liubov', 13, 44, 64
Kaganovsky, Lilya, 7, 24
Karakum Canal, 9, 46, 48–52, 54
Karasev, Iurii, 33
Kazakhstan, 37, 46
Kazintsev, Aleksandr, 102–3
KGB Agent in a Tuxedo (series), 105
kindness, sincerity and, 6, 19, 68, 70, 73,
    83, 93–94
Kharkhordin, Oleg, 28–29

Index

Khazanov, Pavel, 85
Khrushchev, Nikita, 9, 25, 41, 45–46, 63. *See also* Thaw era
Klimova, Ol'ga, 63
Kobliakov, V., 12
Komsomol, 8, 30, 51, 103
Kopelev, Lev, 20
Kormer, Vladimir (Oleg Altaev), 66, 83, 94
Kozintsev, Grigorii, 43
Kozlov, Denis, 9, 45
Kozlova, Nataliia, 26, 29

"Ladies' Hairdresser" (Grekova), 44–45
"The Last Hunt" ("Posledniaia okhota," 1959), 120n31
Leiderman, Naum, 19, 70, 90, 101, 103
Lekhmin, Mikhail, 102
Lenin's Guard (film), 43
liberals/liberalism, and Trifonov, 19, 22, 41–44, 102–3
lies and falsehoods, 21, 36, 53, 82, 87–88, 97, 102; sincerity as antidote to, 5, 18, 23, 29. *See also* insincerity
Lipovetsky, Mark, 19, 70, 90, 101, 103
"Little Deal," intelligentsia and, 64
Little Vera (film), 102
Livers, Keith, 7
Lives of Notable People, 105
The Long Goodbye (*Dolgoe proshchanie*, 1971), 71, 73
Lopatin, German, 12
Lotman, Iurii, 14, 16, 97
Lur'e, Abram (grandfather), 6
Lur'e, Evgeniia (mother), 6–7, 37, 46, 81
L'vov, S., 27

Makanin, Vladimir, 15, 101
masculinity, and Soviet man, 9–10, 13, 24, 28–32, 42, 65, 74, 85, 101
material goods. *See* consumer goods
material world, 5, 9, 23, 45, 57, 62, 107n2; intelligentsia and, 15–16, 18, 26, 38, 71, 73; and memory, 17, 42, 56, 67; inability to control, 66–67, 78–79, 89, 99, 102–4.

See also byt (everyday life); consumption; objects
Mayakovsky, Vladimir, 5
Medvedev, Roi, 11, 27
"Memories of Genzano" ("Vospominaniia o Dzhentsano," 1960), 13–14, 94
memory, 6, 11, 13–14, 16–18; body as a place of, 14, 75; and *byt*, 37–38, 59, 62–63, 66–67, 77–78, 88, 91–93; and history, 54–56, 62, 79, 83, 91; objects of, 55–56, 77, 87, 91, 97–99; recollection and forgetting, 77–78, 88–90, 95–96, 105; and sincerity, 55–58, 60, 70, 77–78, 88, 93–95, 99, 110n31; and trauma, 43–44, 57, 60, 71–73, 79, 87, 91, 95, 99
meshchanstvo (love of objects): anxiety about, 4–5, 9, 13, 33, 44, 64–66, 95; and insincerity, 13, 27, 66; Trifonov's characters and, 34, 68–69, 77–79. *See also* consumption; *poshlost'* (philistinism); *veshchizm* (love of things)
Metchenko, A., 65
Mikoyan, Anastas, 41
Millar, James, 64
morality, 5, 10, 12–13, 15, 18, 53, 81, 96, 102; consumption and, 39, 61–62, 64–69, 75, 94; *telesnost'* of, 32, 68, 70, 80, 87–88, 92. See also *iskrennost'* (sincerity)
Moscow, 5, 36, 46, 64, 100–101, 104, 105–6; depictions of, 7, 16, 31–33, 43, 93–94, 101; intelligentsia, 41–42, 64, 71–73, 101
Moscow Does Not Believe in Tears (film), 63, 65
Moscow novellas, 21, 62, 93, 101; *Another Life*, 71–73; *The Exchange*, 66–67; *House on the Embankment*, 73–80; *The Long Goodbye*, 71; *Taking Stock*, 67–70, 73
mourning and grieving, 9, 16, 35, 52, 72. *See also* trauma

Nadkarni, Maya, 17, 78
Nagibin, Iurii, 101
natural world: NTR and, 46, 48–50, 55, 60; *telesnost'* and, 29

Index

Nechaev, Sergei, 86
nedochuvstvie (insufficient feeling), 61, 64, 90, 105
nedoskazannost' (incompletion in writing), 79–80, 82, 92–93, 97. *See also* silence
Nekrasov, Nikolai, 34
Nelina, Nina (first wife), 8, 11
Neuberger, Mary, 4, 9, 14
Nikadem-Malinowska, Ewa, 48
Nora, Pierre, 13–14, 16, 75
Novokhatko, Vladimir, 84–85
Novoselova, Ekaterina, 13
Novyi mir, 7, 11, 15, 41
NTR (scientific-technical revolution), 10, 22, 45, 25, 72–73; and consumption, 42, 44–45, 65–66, 82; optimism of, 36–37, 40, 49, 60; intelligentsia and, 18, 65–66; *Slaking the Thirst* and, 21, 46, 49–51, 54; *Under the Sun* and, 46–48

objects, 5, 12, 16–17; of memory and history, 37–38, 55–56, 66, 77, 83, 87, 91, 97–99; as signals, 37–39, 64, 76, 79, 83, 96–98; sincerity and morality and, 25, 34, 73; of trauma, 16–17, 47, 83, 97–98, 104, 106. See also *byt* (everyday life); consumption; material world; *meshchanstvo* (love of objects)
Old Bolsheviks, 8, 59, 67, 87–90, 96, 99. *See also* revolutionaries
The Old Man (*Starik*, 1978), 20–21, 57–58, 81–84, 87–90, 96
"On Sincerity" ("Ob iskrennosti"), 10, 45
One Day in the Life of Ivan Denisovich (Solzhenitsyn), 43
One Flew Over the Cuckoo's Nest (film), 125n43
Oskotskii, V., 86
Oukaderova, Lida, 43
Oushakine, Serguei, 5, 12, 52, 64, 87, 91

Paperno, Irina, 77, 104
Paretskaya, Anna, 12

past: in *The Bonfire's Glow*, 11, 20–21, 42, 54–58, 89; escaping the, 30, 42, 62, 68–70; impact on the present and future, 79–80, 86–88, 96, 99; impact of, in *Taking Stock*, 66, 68–70; material world and understanding the, 16, 55–56, 77, 83, 88–89, 97–99; *telesnost'* and understanding the, 59, 62; *See also* history; memory
Pasternak, Boris, 26, 101
Pastukhova, Alla (second wife), 11, 42, 85
People's Will, 12, 81, 83–86
Petrushevskaia, Liudmila, 22, 103–4
Pirozhok, Vladimir, 103, 105
Piskunov, V., 72
Platonov, Andrei, 102
Platonov, B., 28
Platt, Kevin, 36, 62, 78, 80
Polevoi, Boris, 24
Pomerantsev, Vladimir, 10–11, 15, 18, 45
poshlost' (philistinism), 4, 33, 65, 68. See also *meshchantsvo* (love of objects); *veshchizm* (love of things)
possessions, as signifiers, 5, 25, 32, 34, 72, 79, 97, 99. *See also* consumption
Prague Spring, 18, 43, 58, 66, 80, 84
The Price Is Right, Trifonov on, 95
Prokhanov, Aleksandr, 100
prosperity, 8, 14, 17, 27, 29, 37–39, 44, 64
purges. *See* Stalinism, trauma of
Pushkin, Aleksandr, 32
Pushkin House (Bitov), 101
Putin, Vladimir, 7, 16, 22, 100, 104–5
Pyr'ev, Ivan, 25

The Rapids (Grekova), 101
Rasputin, Valentin, 63
readers, Soviet: and descriptions of *byt*, 7, 26, 39, 68, 101, 105; and *telesnost'*, 29, 32, 70; inferences by, 47, 59, 79, 90, 92–93, 104; and historical truth, 55–56, 85
Reid, Susan, 5, 10, 44, 82
Reif, Igor', 15

Index

revolution/revolutionaries, 57, 59, 85–87, 89; corruption of and loss of sincerity, 22, 90, 99. *See also* Old Bolsheviks
Robski, Oksana, 104
Rutten, Ellen, 5, 10, 44, 66
Rybakov, Anatoli, 96

Sakharov, Andrei, 105
scientific-technical revolution. *See* NTR (scientific-technical revolution)
Seifrid, Thomas, 80
Selemeneva, Marina, 19, 68, 70, 75, 81, 88, 98, 100–101, 106
sex and sexuality, 4, 44, 51, 63, 67, 69; lust and ambition, 75, 88–89; in *Students*, 29–30, 32–33, 39. *See also* bodies
shestidesiatniki (people of the sixties), 15, 45, 58, 91, 103
The Ship of Widows (Grekova), 63
Shitov, Aleksandr, 105
"A Short Stay in the Torture Chamber" ("Nedolgoe prebyvanie v kamere pytok," 1981), 95
shortages, 5, 25, 44, 82, 102
Shragin, Boris, 83
Siegelbaum, Lewis, 26
silence, 16, 36, 80, 92, 102. See also *nedoskazannost'* (incompletion in writing)
sincerity. See *iskrennost'* (sincerity)
Sinel'nikov, M., 68
Slaking the Thirst (*Utolenie zhazhdy*, 1962), 8–9, 11, 20–21, 42, 46, 49–55, 57, 84
Slavnikova, Ol'ga, 103
Slezkine, Yuri, 85, 98, 105
Slovatinskaia, Tat'iana (grandmother), 6–7
socialist realism, 24–26, 32, 34, 36, 49–51
Solidarity, Trifonov on, 81, 102
Solzhenitsyn, Aleksandr, 11, 18, 19, 20, 41, 83, 105
sports, 26, 28, 38, 63, 65. *See also* bodies
Spring on Zarechnaia Street (film), 43
Stagnation. *See* Brezhnev era

Stalin Prize, for *Students*, 3, 7, 8, 20, 23, 36, 114n67
Stalinism, 7–9, 20, 23–24, 31–33, 106, 111n34; *byt* and, 26, 75–78, 97–99; and consumption, 9–10, 26, 36, 40, 42, 44, 64, 98–99; as disease, 51, 61, 76; and *House on the Embankment*, 17, 20, 75–78, 99; silence and avoidance of, 16, 36, 43, 62, 104; sincerity and, 10–11, 18, 21, 23–25, 28–29, 40–42, 94; in *Slaking the Thirst*, 9, 20–21, 49, 50–55, 57; *Students* and, 7, 14, 21, 27, 29, 36–37, 44, 52–53; *telesnost'* of, 16–17, 24–25, 28–29, 35–36, 47, 58–61, 91–92, 96–97, 98–99, 106; trauma of, 4–5, 7, 35, 49, 52–54, 57–58, 79, 95–96, 104; Trifonov and, 13, 44, 50, 76
standard of living, 8–9, 25, 37, 44, 47, 82, 123n11; of intelligentsia, 62, 64, 73, 102–3
Stiazhkina, Elena, 13, 65, 101
Story of a Real Man (Polevoi), 24, 43
student novellas (*studencheskie povesti*), 28, 34, 118n56
Students (*Studenty*, 1949), 11, 14, 19–21, 26–40, 56, 71, 72, 95, 101, 117n46; and *House on the Embankment*, 73–74, 75, 76, 79, 98; non-Russians in, 30–32, 46; reception to and style of, 7–9, 20, 26, 46, 59, 84; Trifonov on, 20, 29
style, writing, 59, 66, 79–80, 82, 84. See also *nedoskazannost'* (incompletion in writing)
Sukhanov, Viacheslav, 56, 67
Sukhikh, Ol'ga, 86
"Summer in the City" (Grekova), 44
Surprise Attack (painting, Vereshchagin), 21

"taking stock" (as concept), 12, 63, 82, 104, 112n42
Taking Stock (*Predvaritel'nye itogi*, 1970), 12, 20, 68–70, 73
Tarkovskii, Andrei, 43
technology: in *Another Life*, 72; and consumption, 10, 26, 42, 44–45, 65–66, 82;

156   Index

technology (*continued*)
   Slaking the Thirst and, 21, 46, 49–51, 54;
   in *Students*, 36–37; Trifonov and, 4, 13,
   22, 61, 65, 82–83; *Under the Sun* and,
   46–48. *See also* consumption; NTR
telesnost' (corporeality), 4, 9, 12, 42–43,
   62, 81, 104; consumption and, 33–34,
   67–68, 74–75; in *Disappearance*, 96–97;
   and *The Exchange*, 67–68; in *House on
   the Embankment*, 21, 74–75, 92, 116n34;
   Impatience and, 85; in "It Was Noon in
   Summertime," 59; *The Long Goodbye*
   and, 71–72; in *The Old Man*, 87–89;
   and sincerity, 24, 28–30, 32, 34–35, 39,
   50, 67–68, 70, 75, 80, 87–88; in *Slaking
   the Thirst*, 50–52, 54; and Stalinism,
   24–25, 28–29, 35–36, 59, 96–97; *Students* and, 7, 27–36, 71, 90; in *Taking
   Stock*, 63, 69–70; and *Time and Place*,
   91–92; trauma and, 59, 71, 91–92, 106
television, 9, 38, 61, 64–66, 88, 95
terror. *See* Stalinism
terrorism and terrorists: and *Impatience*,
   83–87; Trifonov on technology and,
   65–66
time, 6, 14, 17; as current, 57, 86, 91, 93;
   experiences of, 48, 51–52, 54, 95;
   fragmentation of, 62
Time and Place (*Vremia i mesto*, 1981), 82,
   90–94
Thaw era, 8–10, 28, 41–45, 62, 80, 105,
   111n34; *The Bonfire's Glow* and, 55–58;
   in *Slaking the Thirst*, 49–54; in *Under
   the Sun*, 46–48. *See also* Khrushchev,
   Nikita
Three Men in Gray Overcoats
   (Dobrovol'skii), 24
Tokareva, Viktoriia, 64
Tolstoy, Lev, 4, 6, 32, 72–73, 93
"Travnicek and Hockey" ("Travnichek i
   khokkei," 1967), 82
trauma: *byt* and objects of, 16–17, 47, 83,
   97–98, 104, 106; of fatherlessness, 9, 20,
   35–37, 49–50, 56–57; history, memory,
   and, 6, 16, 43–44, 57, 60, 71–73, 79, 87,

91, 95, 99, 105; *Impatience* as prelude to,
   84–85; and *The Old Man*, 87–90; and
   the past in *The Bonfire's Glow*, 42,
   55–58, 89, 104; silences around, 16,
   24–25, 35–36, 57–58, 62, 72, 92, 97, 102,
   105; sublimation of, in *Students*, 27,
   35–36, 52, 56, 95; *telesnost'* of, 13, 35–36,
   51–52, 58–59, 71–72, 91–92, 106. *See also*
   mourning and grieving; Stalinism
Trifonov, Evgenii (uncle), 6, 59
Trifonov, Iurii Valentinovich, 3, 6–8,
   11–13, 20, 42, 52, 101, 106; on *byt* and
   bytie, 15, 63, 101; on consumption,
   12–13, 61, 65–66, 82–83, 95; on his own
   writing, 20, 29, 49, 79, 86; influence
   on Russian culture, 22, 100–106; on
   iskrennost', 6, 18, 29, 45; on the Soviet
   project, 81, 99; and Stalinism, 13, 44,
   50, 76
Trifonov, Valentin (father), 6, 20, 50, 85,
   114n1; allusions to, 14, 35, 58–59, 96, 99;
   and *The Bonfire's Glow*, 11, 20, 42,
   54–58
Trifonova, Ol'ga (widow), 5, 7, 11–12, 46,
   57, 84, 100, 103–5, 114n67, 114n1
Trifonova, Tat'iana (sister), 19, 55
Trilling, Lionel, 5, 44
Trudoliubov, Maksim, 16, 104
truth, 52–53, 55–56, 89–90, 99. *See also*
   iskrennost' (sincerity)
Tsipursky, Gleb, 44
Turgenev, Ivan, 6, 29
Turkmenia, 8, 42, 45; in *Slaking the Thirst*,
   49–54; in *Taking Stock*, 12, 20, 68–70;
   Under the Sun and, 46–48
Tvardovskii, Aleksandr, 7, 16, 41, 42,
   117n46

Ukraine, Putin's war against, 7, 16, 23, 100,
   104, 131n10
Ukrainians, in Trifonov's prose, 30, 32
Ulitskaia, Liudmila, 22, 25–26, 101, 103,
   106
Under the Sun (*Pod solntsem*, 1959) (collection of stories), 8, 21, 46–48, 57

Index

"Under the Sun" ("Pod solntsem," 1959) (story), 48

Uzbeks, in Trifonov's prose, 30–32, 37, 46

Vail, Pyotr, 10, 43, 44, 66

Venttsel', Elena. *See* Grekova, I.

Vereshchagin, Vasilii, 31

veshchizm (love of things), 34, 64, 68, 74, 78, 99, 101. See also *meshchantsvo* (love of objects)

village prose writers (*derevenshchiki*), 18, 49, 63, 82

violence, and misplaced sincerity, 84–85, 89

Voinovich, Vladimir, 84

Voznesenskii, Andrei, 6, 102

Wachtel, Andrew, 11

Walser, Martin, 61, 66, 67

water, 17, 52–53, 69, 86, 88, 93

A Week Like Any Other (Baranskaia), 16, 63

Winter, Jay, 16

"Winter Afternoon in the Garage" ("Zimnii den' v garazhe," 1946), 35

Woll, Josephine, 18, 42, 43, 70, 93–94, 95, 98, 110n31, 117n42

women, as consumers, 13, 33, 39–40, 65, 67–68. *See also* bodies; female characters; gender

youth: depictions of, 27–30, 43, 50; loss of, 17, 52, 63, 71, 74, 91–92

Yurchak, Alexei, 20, 62

Zakharova, Larissa, 9

Zhilina, L. N., 10

Zolotusskii, Igor', 102